Futures of Organizations

Issues in Organization and Management Series
Arthur P. Brief and Benjamin Schneider, *Editors*

Employee Ownership in America: The Equity Solution
Corey Rosen, Katherine J. Klein, and Karen M. Young

Generalizing from Laboratory to Field Settings
Research Findings from Industrial-Organizational Psychology,
Organizational Behavior, and Human Resource Management
Edwin A. Locke, editor

Working Together to Get Things Done
Managing for Organizational Productivity
Dean Tjosvold

Self-Esteem at Work
Research, Theory, and Practice
Joel Brockner

Implementing Routine and Radical Innovations
A Comparative Study
Walter Nord and Sharon Tucker

The Outsiders
Jews and Corporate America
Abraham Korman

Organizational Citizenship Behavior
The Good Soldier Syndrome
Dennis W. Organ

Facilitating Work Effectiveness
F. David Schoorman and Benjamin Schneider, editors

Futures of Organizations
Innovating to Adapt Strategy and Human Resources to Rapid
Technological Change
Jerald Hage, editor

The Lessons of Experience
How Successful Executives Develop on the Job
Morgan W. McCall, Jr., Michael A. Lombardo, and Ann M. Morrison

Futures of Organizations

Innovating to Adapt Strategy and Human Resources to Rapid Technological Change

Edited by

Jerald Hage
Center for Innovation
University of Maryland

With contributions by

Stephen J. Carroll
André L. Delbecq
Jay R. Galbraith
Rosalie J. Hall
Robert K. Kazanjian
Katherine J. Klein
Gary P. Latham
Joseph J. Lengermann

Daniel J. Power
Joan Rentsch
Denise M. Rousseau
Benjamin Schneider
Kenneth G. Smith
Thomas C. Tuttle
Joseph Weiss

Lexington Books
D.C. Heath and Company/Lexington, Massachusetts/Toronto

ROBERT MANNING
STROZIER LIBRARY

SEP 22 1988

Tallahassee, Florida

Library of Congress Cataloging-in-Publication Data

Futures of organizations.

Includes index.
1. Organizational effectiveness. 2. Organizational change. I. Hage, Jerald, 1932–
HD58.9.F88 1988   658.4'06   86-45752
ISBN 0-669-14250-6 (alk. paper)

Copyright © 1988 by Lexington Books
with the exception of chapter 9 © by Thomas C. Tuttle

All rights reserved. No part of this publication may be reproduced or transmitted in any
form or by any means, electronic or mechanical, including photocopy, recording, or any
information storage or retrieval system, without permission in writing from the publisher.

Published simultaneously in Canada
Printed in the United States of America
International Standard Book Number: 0-669-14250-6
Library of Congress Catalog Card Number: 86-45752

The paper used in this publication meets the minimum requirements of American National
Standard for Information Sciences—Permanence of Paper for Printed Library Materials,
ANSI Z39.48-1984. ∞™

88 89 90 91 92 8 7 6 5 4 3 2 1

Contents

Figures

Tables

Foreword

Benjamin Schneider
Arthur P. Brief

*F*utures of Organizations is a book about what behavioral and social sciences suggest human organizations will look like in the future. Books offering such suggestions are not rare; however, it is unusual to find a single volume offering varying disciplinary perspectives by a collection of accomplished scholars.

Jerry Hage, himself a predictor of the future, has assembled here a diverse group of talent and turned them loose to prognosticate the future. In the book we have views of organization theorists from both sociological and management perspectives, work motivation experts from both psychological and sociological foci, and perspectives on leadership and organizational culture from management and psychology.

The totality of these commentaries is richer than their simple sum. A reading of the book reveals the many layers and levels of phenomena that simultaneously cause and produce change for the organization of the future. Thus, while the larger environment presses in on organizations—for example, in the way of international competitiveness—innovation in organizations yields a counterforce on the environment. Or, as the nature of the work force changes in terms of expectations, decision makers in organizations respond with approaches that require workers to identify their own values and to learn to control their own futures. Finally, as technology changes the nature of work and work relationships, the organizations for which new technology and innovation are their products change the environment in which other organizations must behave.

In short, *Futures* is a book that yields insight at many levels. It can be read as a series of separate chapters because those chapters are each individually informative. Or, it can be read as a complex message regarding the interplay of person, organization, and larger environment involved in a spiral of mutual futures. Because of this duality of message, we are delighted to have this book in our series.

Preface

R ecently many books have appeared to suggest to American business people one best model on how to compete. Peters and Waterman's *In Search of Excellence* (1982) and Naisbitt and Aburdene's *Reinventing the Corporation* (1985) became instant successes, suggesting how much interest there is in the topic of the futures of organizations.

The trouble with these books is that they provide single prescriptions. Worse yet, Peters (1987) has just retreated from his magic formula of one kind of organizational structure with a move toward sudden recognition that the world is much more complex. Another difficulty with these books is that frequently they make projections on the basis of trends rather than on informed judgment. Finally, they usually look at only a few parts of what is a complex problem.

Recognizing these difficulties, the Center for Innovation decided to call together a group of experts in organizations, including individuals who do a great deal of consulting and are therefore not just academics who lack experience as consultants.

The conference, which was held in the spring of 1986, was organized around four fundamental themes that reflected the diverse interests of the Center, which is itself a multidisciplinary unit (industrial psychology, management, and organizational sociology): (1) strategy and structure, (2) managerial roles, (3) nonmanagerial roles, and (4) the problem of motivation. The choice of nonmanagerial roles as a theme was designed to correct an omission since many of these kinds of works give little attention to the nonmanager. Clearly, these topics can also reflect the different levels of analysis associated with the three disciplines whose representatives participated in the conference.

To provide some integration of the many disparate interests of the members of the Center for Innovation, we agreed not only that we would make the overall focus the futures of organizations, but also that in particular we would examine the effects of new knowledges and technologies, broadly defined in these different arenas of interest.

With these themes in mind, participants prepared short papers, and some distinguished scholars, most notably André Delbecq, Jay Galbraith, Lymon

Porter, and Denise Rousseau, were invited to participate. The papers were kept short to allow for maximum dialogue. The outside participants were asked to critique the ideas of the members of the Center for Innovation rather than to prepare papers themselves. The outside participants were chosen not only because of their contributions to the conference's area of interest, but also because each of them had extensive consulting experience. The members of the Center for Innovation thought that this would ground our speculations in some reality and keep the enterprise from becoming too academic.

The conference went well and there appeared to be much more agreement than we had thought possible, so a collective decision was made to assemble a series of chapters or essays on the themes that had been the focus of the conference and that had emerged during the discussion. The outside participants were invited to prepare papers as well. Everyone except Lymon Porter was able to participate, and papers were prepared, with the advantage of everyone's having had the earlier free discussion. Only Gary Latham, who was asked to write a paper on motivation, did not have this advantage.

To provide integration and a framework, I wrote an introductory essay on the new rules of competition. I also made suggestions about ways in which the different chapters might be connected. Finally, I wrote introductions to each of the parts, as well as the concluding chapter.

As a result, these contributions are probably more fully integrated than is typical for a book based on a conference and especially one that involves three different disciplines. Usually, each chapter begins with some assumptions about changes that are occurring in the environment and then moves on to discuss the nature of the responses of the organization or of its members to these responses. However, *the contributions do vary in the degree of emphasis on what will happen and in the amount of stress on what to do in response.* For example, Rousseau describes how human resources should be managed, while Schneider and Rentsch suggest how culture and climate can be controlled. In contrast, the contributions by Hage, Power, and Carroll are more concerned with what will happen. Many of the other contributions are mixtures of these approaches.

Likewise, the chapters vary in how much they discuss the past, the present, and the future. In some cases, the present is considered as a wave of the future, as it is in the material presented by Galbraith and Kazanjian; in other cases, the present is considered unlikely to be replicated in the future, as is suggested by Delbecq and Weiss in their report on Silicon Valley. Power perhaps goes the furthest in the direction of the future, attempting to anticipate what might happen in the twenty-first century. Latham reviews earlier approaches to the problem of motivation. Some of these differences in temporal focus result from whether the authors believe that the future will be different from the past. Latham has doubts that motivation problems will be different, whereas others perceive considerable changes, usually in structures. Lengermann thinks that the problems of control will continue to repeat themselves and that it is naive to believe that the future will be free of these classic issues. Klein and Hall observe that many of the traditional elements of industrial psychology—job enlargement, training, pay systems, and the like—can address a wide variety of economic, demographic, and technological changes. Similarly, Schneider and Rentsch observe that classic methods of dealing with the problem of climate can be applied with great success to the issue of culture. Thus, some authors perceive changes but believe that they can be handled with tools and techniques similar to those of the past.

The past in some instances becomes the necessary foundation for establishing the future directions of evolution or change. For example, Hage in chapter 3 and Carroll in chapter 5 build their speculations about the future in this way. A number of the contributors perceive the continuation of various trends that have already been reported in the literature. Galbraith and Kazanjian, Carroll, Klein and Hall, and Tuttle emphasize this way of anticipating the future. But Delbecq and Weiss observe that extrapolation from the Silicon Valley trend may be dangerous. Others perceive considerable discontinuities, such as Power, Smith, and to some extent Hage.

Generally, contributors to the first half of the book, those concerned with strategy and structure and with the effect on managerial roles, tend to see much greater change occurring. Contributors to the third section vary in the amount of change they consider likely, while those in the last section perceive much more continuity, including continuation of classic problems of employee control and participation in the firm. Interestingly, the level of analysis, whether micro or macro, tends to be associated with the perceived differences in continuity or change. Then too one might argue that the problem of motivation is a constant, whereas structure is anything but a constant.

Finally, the source of materials for the chapters varies as well, again reflecting different attitudes about the likelihood of major changes. Some contributors emphasize current research and current experiments by specific organizations, whether observed by the author or reported in the press. The book is enriched by these different angles that reflect the group's deep concern that speculation be informed speculation, deriving either from the scholarly literature or from consultation in organizations that are experimenting and attempting to construct the new strategies and structures needed. About half of the contributions have been written by people with consulting experiences, whose efforts are grounded in the "real world." The other half are based on scholarly research and extrapolation from it. These starting points reflect concerns of the members of the Center for Innovation about attempting to anchor our work both in known research and in real world experience. The more rapid the rate of change, however, in the phenomenon, the more that the contributor had to rely upon less academic sources of data.

Another way of thinking about the themes in the book aside from the basic groupings is to ask what the major changes occurring in the environment are, which society is most typically affected, and what responses organizations can make to these changes. Environmental change has four manifestations, as the contributors see it. The first and perhaps the most important is the development of much more competition and the creation of a global economy (see chapters 1, 2, 3, 4, 6, and 10). Correspondingly, a number of market changes associated with this development have occurred, the most common changes being the much greater diversity and the smaller size of the new markets, which create some major problems for managers, especially in large organizations.

Demographic changes appear in different contexts: the aging of the population, the increased importance of women, the greater racial integration of society, and the greater differentiation across the life cycle (see chapters 1, 6, 8, and 10).

Probably the most common theme, however—but it was a deliberate focus of the conference—is the effect of new knowledges and technologies, ranging all the way from automation to new information processing systems. On the one hand, this means that people have to learn more and that the knowledge bases of the workers and managers will continue to grow. On the other hand, this also means that many new ways of handling this information now exist. Nor does the impetus for new technologies come only from new knowledge; it also emerges because of other changes occurring in the environment (see chapters 1, 2, 3, 4, 5, 6, 8, 9, 10, and the epilogue).

Finally, political and economic instabilities figure in several of the contributions. These instabilities manifest themselves in many ways, from deregulation to political upheavals. Certainly as the world becomes smaller during the process of becoming a global economy (if it has not become one already) then political effects are felt everywhere, contributing to the general sense of uncertainty (see chapters 5, 6, and 11).

Organizations can respond to these changes in many ways. Given the interests of the participants in the conference and also the current preoccupations of the various disciplines, the responses are conveniently classified as strategies, structures, networks or interdependences, and cultures. Discussion of strategies can be found in chapters 1, 2, 3, 5, 8, 10, and the epilogue. Perhaps the most common response found in the largest number of contributions is the change in the structure of the organization. The word *structure* is employed in a number of ways, and some authors perceive even the disappearance of structure, with it being replaced by culture and/or process (see chapters 3, 4, 5, 6, 7, 8, 10, and 12). The most surprising and the second most common theme is that of networks and not just information networks—the surprise is only because it was not a theme at the conference itself but instead emerged afterward. In many instances the contributors perceive structures as being replaced by networks or new kinds of interdependences (see chapters 2, 3, 4, 5, 6, 8, and 11). Some of the most interesting of these are at the multiorganizational level. Not unexpectedly, organizational culture has appeared as another theme in several of the contributions. Readers particularly interested in one or another of these themes can read chapters 8, 10, and 11. The index provides more detailed cross-references for those who want them.

1
The New Rules of Competition

Jerald Hage

Recently, some essayists (Bell 1973, Toffler 1981, Naisbitt 1982) have suggested that we have entered a new age, which they have labeled "postindustrial society." Bell (1973), the first major writer on this subject, defined a postindustrial society as one in which a major part of the economic wealth is produced in services. He also stressed the growth in education and scientific research. Toffler (1981) put the accent on the demassification of society in what he labeled the Third Wave. Finally, Naisbitt (1982) discussed ten major trends, including information, high technology, networking, the creation of a global economy, decentralization, and the like, associated with this new era.

Most discussions of postindustrial society have not asked what new institutions are needed in a new society. Toffler (1981) perhaps pushed the furthest in this direction, but he devoted little attention to business organizations aside from his discussion of the electronic cottage. To my knowledge, there has been little consideration of what the new rules of competition might be, one of the most basic kinds of institution.

Even the new books on business organizations (Peters and Waterman 1982, Naisbitt and Aburdene 1985) do not stress how the marketplace may be changing except to note the importance of the service economy and the global economy. Nor do these books provide convincing arguments about what the new rules of success may be—that is, what kind of organization is needed for effectiveness.

Peters and Waterman (1982) look at large, successful corporations, many of which have started to experience major difficulties since Peters and Waterman published their book. What worked yesterday may well be outmoded today, depending upon the directions the future society takes, and experiments are not necessarily prescriptions for what business people should do. Naisbitt and Aburdene (1985) report some of the experiments that are occurring but do not make clear why they are most likely to succeed.

None of the recent books on business organizations or on what defines excellence have mentioned the importance of innovation in either products or production processes. Computers have been considered in various ways but usually not relative to the production process. Given Bell's original work (1973), this appears to be a serious, and perhaps even a fatal, omission. Although Bell emphasized the emergence of service economy as the major defining characteristic of postindustrial society, he also noted the growth in research, which has accelerated since he published his book.

There is an absence of causal reasoning in most of these popular books. We are not told how changes in postindustrial society may require new kinds of institutions or vice versa. A variety of experiments are occurring, but little is said about which ones might be successful and why. Although information and computers are emphasized, little is said about the causal forces that produce this growth in information. There is too much emphasis on a single, best organizational model and too little appreciation that different models may be appropriate in different sectors of the economy.

The assumption of much of this essay is that the growth in knowledge means that business organizations must constantly innovate and constantly upgrade their production process. These are the new rules of competition, and businesses that do not heed these new rules are doomed to fail. However, the rate of change in the growth in knowledge is quite different in different economic sectors of society.

To innovate continuously in a rapidly changing society requires new kinds of business organizations in some sectors. What kinds of new business institutions—for it is not necessarily only a question of organization but of other forms of social institutions as well—is open to debate. But the debate should center on the new rules of competition, on the character of postindustrial society, and beyond this on the global economy and what consequences it has for the structure and strategy of business firms.

The purpose of this introductory chapter is to suggest a single and coherent vision of what postindustrial society is and what its consequences for competition are. Not every contributor to this book agrees, and different authors play out different scenarios, but at minimum this single vision provides a point of departure that one can either reject or modify, depending upon the circumstances of a particular firm. Furthermore, this essay suggests there are several trends that reinforce each other and together are creating new environments for business organizations. Perhaps the most important characteristic of this new environment, besides the explosion in knowledge and in technology, is that, even for small businesses, the markets are global in reach. In the past, organizational researchers focused on the environment in a narrow or limited way (Lawrence and Lorsch 1967, Aiken and Hage 1968; for a general review see Hage 1980, chap. 12). Theirs is no longer a viable description, except for a limited number of traditional businesses.

A global economy might imply to some readers that there is one best way of handling the new environment. But this is not true! The second most important characteristic of this global environment is that within it there is room for many different kinds of organizations. Theory X and theory Y (McGregor 1960), the mechanical or organic organizations (Burns and Stalker 1961, Hage 1980, Tosi and Carroll 1983), or the prescriptions in *Theory Z* (Ouchi 1981) and *In Search of Excellence* (Peters and Waterman 1982) are all limited visions of what is possible.

In the past, the idea was the task environment, which involved the kind of technology and product mix found when the scope of the market was largely local or national. But since demassification (Toffler 1981) has occurred and service has become more important (Peters and Waterman 1982), the varieties of different products and service styles have proliferated, and in turn providing these varieties throughout the entire world results in one kind of economy of scale.

Signs of Change: Crises and Experimentation

Two pieces of evidence suggest that a watershed has occurred, which Toffler calls a "Third Wave" (1981). The first and most fundamental sign is the large number of *crises*. In the business world, these crises manifest themselves in a variety of ways. Not only is it the American economy that is being called into question, but all the basic societal institutions in the United States and in many other advanced countries are being criticized and found wanting. The second and equally important sign is that the discontent is being matched by an enormous amount of experimentation. Both of these indicators suggest that the old institutional forms and their rules of behavior no longer work in the new society. Thus, in the business world, new rules of competition are emerging. The best evidence is that many firms are being forced out of the market because they can no longer compete effectively. Table 1–1 shows the percentages of products produced overseas in 1982. It ranges from 20 percent in inorganic chemistry and 26 percent in games and toys to 47 percent in radio and television, 45 percent in office machines, 46 percent in oil field machinery, and 52 percent in general industrial machinery. Some of these areas, such as that of semiconductors, have caused concern, but the general penetration of different kinds of tool and machine manufacturers means increasingly that the goods sold in the United States might be produced elsewhere.

In these industrial sectors are some of the household names of American business. Perhaps most interesting is that many of these firms were quite successful in earlier decades, among them U.S. Steel, International Harvester, and Pennsylvania Railroad. Nor are these the only ones. Many of the heroes of *In Search of Excellence,* such a General Motors, IBM, General Electric, and AT&T are now closing plants, asking employees to take early retirement, and laying off both workers and middle managers. Previously, only the workers usually suffered when business declined but now the effects are reaching up

Table 1–1
Percent of Goods Sold in the United States
Produced Overseas, 1982

Product Group	Percentage
Motor vehicles	27
Steel mill products	19
Radio and television	47
Semiconductors	24
Office machines	45
Outer wear	66
Games, toys	26
General industrial machinery	25
Pulp mill products	32
Engines	25
Inorganic chemicals	20
Construction machines	41
Computers	24
Aircraft	25
Oil field machinery	46
General industrial machinery	52

the management hierarchy as well. The Fortune 500 largest industrial firms in 1986 lost 700,000 employees and declined 5 percent in total value and this during a period when many mergers were occurring.

In view of these firms' past successes, this tells us that their present arrangement or organizational designs, appropriate for the competitive rules of industrial society, are no longer effective. We need to search for new ones.

One might assume that the problem could be a lack of innovation in the United States, a failure to produce new products. Sometimes this is the case. For example, the Walkman, a successful product, was invented and developed entirely by the Japanese. Similarly, the Japanese have been ahead in the creation of the new generation of computer chips. But this is not the usual pattern. More typically, Americans invent the products but do not either sell them or decide to remain in business long enough to reap a profit. VCRs today are built outside the country, and the United States loses $5 billion a year on just this one product. Robots were largely developed in the United States, but many more are being purchased by Japanese manufacturers than by American. It is not so much a lack of American inventiveness as the failure to keep these products in production long enough for them to become profitable or to move them into production fast enough.

The magnitude of the failure of American business is measurable in a number of ways. One is the large trade deficit that is accumulating. For a time, people hoped that it would gradually disappear as the dollar declined in value. Increasingly, this explanation for the trade deficit appears less and less valid. Some argue that the real problem is that other countries have erected barriers to trade. This accusation is leveled most frequently at the Japanese, but it applies as well to the Common Market. Although trade barriers are part of the story, it would be foolish for American business people to believe that with lower trade barriers they would do better automatically. Clearly this would not save the automobile industry, the steel industry, the shoe industry, the rubber tire industry, and so forth. None of these industries exports (with the possible exception of the movement toward the world car). Lower trade barriers might help some of the high-tech firms, whether small or large, but not those firms that currently are doing poorly against the competition.

Paradoxically, support for the idea that there is a crisis is supplied by the success of books like *Theory Z, Reinventing the Corporation, In Search of Excellence,* and the like. They provide evidence that business people think that society and its rules of competition are changing. Managers are desperately looking for new formulas that can help them succeed. This search itself reflects the considerable uncertainty about what to do.

More striking is the current political discussion about the failure of American competitiveness. That this is becoming a political issue, and for both major parties, means that the United States is beginning to recognize the existence of a social crisis. Usually recessions produce political crises, not fears of competition. But the trade deficit is becoming a major political crisis. Nor is this the only issue in the debate. I suggest that the problem of competitiveness will increasingly dominate the political agendas of the two parties and that it will be one of the pivotal themes in the 1988 presidential campaign.

A second sign of the magnitude of the failure of American business is the lack of growth in productivity. Typically, we view Japan as the society that has achieved incredible growth rates in productivity, even during the past decade when it was much more difficult to do so. But the real problem does not lie there. The real problem is that almost all countries have been achieving much higher rates of productivity than was the United States until just 1987–88. Although Britain is held up as the sick society of Europe, the reality is that productivity growth in Britain has been much better than it has in the United States for the past decade.

This raises a number of issues about why American managers have failed in competing in the same way. A number of ideas have been advanced to explain why productivity has not kept pace in the United States. Perhaps the most popular notion is that because the United States is the richer country, it is more difficult to keep making advances. But again the facts are these: the United States is not the richest industrial country in the world anymore if we use as a measure the amount of income produced per capita (or net national product). Several Western European countries have moved past the United States. Furthermore, there is some indication that the dollar will decline in value even more; if it does this will increase the number of countries that are wealthier. (The fluctuations in exchange rates make comparisons difficult and these should be adjusted for purchasing power, but most would agree that the United States is slowly declining relatively in wealth, power, and prestige.) The lack of growth in productivity again suggests that some new rules of competition exist that are not being well understood in the United States.

Another reason frequently cited is the higher wages paid to labor in the United States than elsewhere. Again, the changing value of the dollar is altering the importance of this factor rapidly. But even in those industries where automation exists, many companies would be able to afford the high wages if they purchased the automated equipment. The refusal of the large steel companies to automate and the success of the mini-mills both are well known in the United States. Less well known is that in the shoe industry, one sector that has been particularly harshly hit, machines were available in the 1970s that could produce shoes in small batches with large productivity. Most of the shoe companies did not purchase these machines and instead have been going out of business. The same problem exists in a variety of the old industrial sectors.

A comparative study of Japanese and American businesses (Hull, Azumi, and Hage 1983) over the period of 1973–82, which examined many different industrial sectors, found that not only were the Japanese using more robots and progressing further down the road of automation, but they employed computers more extensively and intensively than did American industry. Another sign of the competitive crisis is that American industry has failed to use the equipment that provides higher productivity as effectively as some of its competitors.

Here too popular books have described some of the problems of American businesses. Two, Reich's *New American Frontier* (1984) and Shaiken's *Work Transformed* (1985), point to a large number of incorrect approaches businesses are using and help explain why productivity is low in the United States today, even with the purchase of new and highly automated equipment. Shaiken reports that the new equipment is frequently used as a control device and that workers' suggestions are not sought in understanding how the machines could be more effectively exploited. He reports a number of ways in which the machines fail to produce the gains in productivity they could. Reich shifts his attention more directly to managers' search for paper profits at the expense of solid investments for the long term. He notes the consequences of overemphasizing short-term profits rather than long-term growth. From the perspective of these two works it seems not that American business has not responded in certain ways, but that its responses in many cases have been incorrect.

Another finding in the Japanese/American comparison (Hull, Azumi, and Hage 1983) is that the Japanese use quality work circles both more extensively and more intensively than do the American manufacturers. One consequence is that on average the Japanese worker provides ten times the number of suggestions that the average American worker does. What the Japanese have done is mobilize human capital, the minds of their workers. How effective this can be is illustrated by the higher productivity in the Japanese-managed plant in Fremont, California, which has traditional equipment and production lines, than is found in most automated GM plants elsewhere.

The political elites are concerned about competitiveness in part because it has been called to their attention by the media. The large number of discussions in the newspapers and the weekly magazines means that thoughtful observers are recognizing that businesses are not effective and that in some way the economy has changed.

One interesting sidelight of the growing crisis is the re-examination of other major institutions in society besides business. This critical examination of basic institutions is further evidence that thoughtful Americans are experiencing a watershed and that at least some people are rethinking what new social institutions are required. For example, education is increasingly being held accountable for the failure to prepare people adequately. One aspect of the problem is seen as an insufficient number of students in science and in engineering. Many business deans believe that they must emphasize the management of production more than they have in the past and are building cooperative programs with schools of engineering. Indeed, many of the societies that are doing better in productivity and economic growth have larger numbers of engineering and science graduates. This raises the issue of whether in the future businesses should have higher numbers of scientists and engineers relative to managers and perhaps especially finance specialists.

Beyond this issue, the quality of education that American students receive is at stake. The recent reports and evaluations of both higher and lower American education are highly critical, suggesting that not much attention is paid to teaching students how to think and that perhaps too much emphasis has been placed on narrow career specialization. When American society decides it is in a crisis, education is typically taken to task. *Sputnik* shocked the United States into changing its educational system in the late 1950s. The loss of competitiveness will do the same in the late 1980s.

That managers buy the various books and help push them to the top of the best-seller lists and that political elites begin to discuss the basic economic issues are not the only signs of some profound changes. Another and equally important indication of the same phenomenon is experimentation in the design of new institutions, in this instance business institutions. In part, books like *Reinventing the Corporation* are successful because they document the many experiments that are taking place in firms and businesses. But as I have noted several times, these works lack theoretical perspective. Some experiments are likely to become examples of what can be done, but others are not, even if the firm is a success. Deciding what the right models are requires one to identify the new rules of competition, and to do this, one must understand the basic changes occurring in the society, especially those relative to competition. Then and only then can one evaluate the correctness of the alternatives that are part of the present experimentation.

Interest in books on changes in society and especially organizations, the increased failure rate of businesses and firms, and the considerable experimentation that is now occurring all testify to the fact that a major qualitative change has taken place—the emergence of postindustrial society.

Major Changes in Postindustrial Society

The growth in knowledge is the most fundamental and critical trend that is reshaping not only society but also the entire world. I use the word *knowledge* rather than *technology* or *information* for several reasons. These other terms are only part of knowledge and are not necessarily the most important. By *knowledge* I mean the ideas, theories or models, the tools and the machines, the methods and procedures associated with the tools and the techniques, and finally the skills and "know-how" associated with a specific product group or sector of society (Collins, Hage, and Hull 1986). The growth in science and in social science and their many applied fields constitutes the major explanation of the redefinition of society that is occurring. Scientific theories and models have broad applications for the production of products and the provision of services. They are quite different from the actual know-how involved in the first industrial revolution and even from that of the second (Landes 1969).

The stress on information is misplaced because it is only one aspect of knowledge. Some complain about the information overload and note the importance of the computer in generating constant streams of new information. But there is no information overload if individuals have theories, or at minimum, models. These summarize large quantities of information, reducing overload. One of the tasks of science is to create these new theories and models that allow individuals to handle the many new facts generated by research. The more abstract and comprehensive the new theories, the more applications in a wide variety of areas. Furthermore, the more abstract the theory, usually the broader the applications. The current work on superconductivity is one example, genetic theory is another, and the rapidly developing theory in computer science still another. In the social sciences, reinforcement theory, neoclassical market theory, and contingency theories of leadership and of structure are examples.

Another implication of the abstractness of scientific theory is its increased likelihood of interdependence. Theories in one specialty have implications for theories in another specialty. This is where business is concerned. As theoretical knowledge grows, so do the implications for the businesses. The explosion in scientific knowledge means an explosion in opportunities for businesses. Whether they are prepared to exploit these opportunities is another question; the monitoring of these developments depends upon the capacity of the organization and its associated information networks.

The new tools and machines refer to technology as it is commonly understood. Much has been said about the computer and more generally about microelectronics (Forrester, 1985), so we do not have to add to this discussion. Instead, the creation of new knowledge implies not only new products but also new technologies for producing these products. The most striking example of this is occurring in biotechnology, which, along with microelectronics, is probably the most distinctive new industry for defining postindustrial growth sectors.

One further point can be made about technology in postindustrial society. The technology of research will increasingly be as important as, if not more important than, the technology of production. In the technology of research, the place of machines is quite different from what it is in a production line; the machines and tools are best thought of as instruments, even if they are quite large. We are used to thinking of technology as the hardware of production— even the computer has this image. But the computer is not a machine in the normal sense of the term. It is not directly involved in the production process in the same way a robot is, but it is a technology that facilitates production processes. Computer-assisted design and computer-aided manufacturing (CADCAM) are aptly named. The computer assists the production process by handling a large number of machines in the production process, but it does not directly produce a product in the same ways as does a lathe, a stamping machine, a refractor, or other machines more directly involved. The same can be said for most of the equipment used in research, and the best term to describe this new kind of machine is *instrumentation*. Some of these machines are quite large and expensive. For example, the biotron at the University of Wisconsin occupies a whole building and can produce any climate known and some not known to humankind. This "machine" is much more expensive than many of our research tools and will become more important than the production processes found in biotechnology. Other examples of expensive research machines are telescopes, cyclotrons, accelerators, oceanology ships, deep-water submarines, supercomputers, and so forth. Although it is true that many of these instruments are associated with basic research that does not appear to have an immediate payoff, it is also true that the research and development more closely connected to industry requires more and more expensive equipment as well as close connections to basic research.

New knowledge means not only new theories and new technologies, but also new skills or human capital to handle these new theories and technologies (we will ignore the problem of the methods and procedures associated with either the skills or the technologies because it would be largely redundant). Many new fields, specialties, and subspecialties have been created in the various disciplines in the universities and colleges of the United States and elsewhere (Blau 1973). Many new degree programs have been created, and the United States has developed a mass college education system. Leaving aside whether or not the education is of high quality, the key point is that large numbers of people are receiving exposure to and even training in new theoretical specialties and applied fields reflecting the societal growth in knowledge.

Together these four aspects of knowledge—theories, machines, methods, and skills—define the new and critical resource now available to society. As this basic resource grows faster and faster, it alters the shape of society and its relationships with other societies. We will now look at two aspects of this growth in knowledge, namely the investment in research and development and the investment in human capital, to see what implications this has for competition and thereby implicitly what businesses must do if they are to survive.

The Explosion in Research and Development

The most distinctive and definitive trend is the growth in research and development not only by governments but by businesses as well. Unfortunately, Bell (1973) himself stressed more the shift to a service society than the enormous importance of research and development, although he did suggest that the stratification system was changing, so that scientists and researchers would become the most important members of society and would receive the largest rewards. Beyond this, the implications of this growth for competition are not considered in his seminal essay.

It is always difficult to date some historical moment when a discontinuous change and particularly one of special import has taken place. I would like to suggest that the major year relative to the futures of organizations was 1975, when the aggregate of American businesses increased their expenditures on research and development—most of this outside of military research—by 6 percent net of inflation. Since then, this expenditure has been growing at a rate of between 4.5 and 5.5 percent, irrespective of recession or expansion (U.S. Bureau of the Census 1984). This was a quantum leap in comparison with earlier figures. Furthermore, since this rate of increase has continued for more than a decade, its implications have become greater and greater. A sizable number of business leaders have decided that the basis of competition is producing new products or trying to add technological advances to existing products. This means a change in the rules of competitiveness in at least a number of industrial sectors, if not all of them.

Although it is true that a large percentage (some 75 percent) of the industrial R & D funds is allocated by the top twenty spenders—for example, GE, IBM, Hewlett Packard, AT&T, and DuPont—many small firms spend more than 10 percent of their sales dollar on R & D. The small high-tech companies, the Davids of industrial research, may be the more important ones in the long term. Yet it is not just the total amount that is spent by the company but more critically the percentage of sales dollars allocated to research that is essential for changing the competitive rules in any particular industrial sector.

How rapidly the United States economy is changing because of this shift is indicated in figure 1–1, which shows the trade balance in those industrial sectors where little R & D is invested and those where the R & D investments are large. A large chunk of the U.S. trade deficit is concentrated in those industrial sectors in which research and development have not occurred. For example (see table 1–1), 66 percent of American outerwear was made overseas, as was 19 percent of the steel mill products, 32 percent of the pulp paper products, 25 percent of the engines, 41 percent of the construction machinery, and so forth (U.S. Bureau of the Census 1986). Admittedly, these are specific product groups rather than the entire industrial sector shown in figure 1–1 and therefore they show much greater penetration. But regardless, two points can be made. First, there are some areas where much money is spent on research and development, and the United States is still not doing well, such as in semiconductors and computers, aircraft, and industrial machinery. Second, these are 1982 figures, and the situation has deteriorated since then.

The explosion in new knowledge manifests itself not just in new products that are on the cutting edge of technology, but also in new production processes that promise to reduce radically the cost of manufacturing, to provide much greater flexibility, and also to provide higher quality or dependability of product. Examples are production lines that have been automated; the marriage of the computer not only in production but in the processing of paper and the management of companies; CADCAM, or computer-assisted design and computer-assisted manufacturing; and the employment of robots for a variety of specialized tasks. The introduction and correct use of these advanced technologies are another aspect of the new environments being created in postindustrial society. It is not enough to invest in research and development. Managers must also be concerned about the constant updating of their production and managerial processes, exploiting the new technologies as quickly as they become available.

This is why our definition of *knowledge* is so important. We need not only R & D for new products, but also for new processes to produce these products. This is where the lower numbers of engineers and scientists may be hurting the development of American industry in postindustrial society.

It should also be clear that the situation varies from one industrial sector to another. Not all sectors spend equal amounts on R & D, regardless of whether it is product or process oriented. Similarly, the growth of scientific theory varies across academic disciplines, and in the various specialties within these disciplines as well.

The Explosion in the Level of Education

The growth in investments in R & D affects the input side of the typical business firm. The changes in the level of education affect its output side, shaping the

Billions of dollars

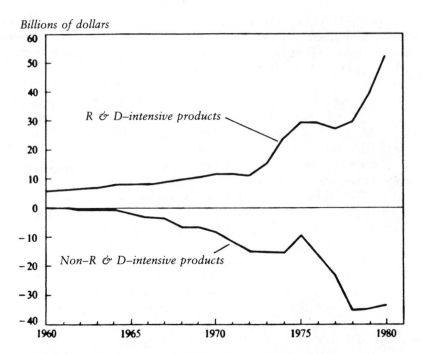

Source: National Science Foundation, *Science Indicators 1982* (Washington, D.C.: Government Printing Office, 1983), 21.

Figure 1–1. U.S. Trade Balance in R & D–Intensive and Non–R & D–Intensive Manufactured Products, 1960–1980

character of consumer demand. In 1950 only a small percentage of the population (15 percent) entered college. In the next two decades, the percentage of the relevant population—that is, those aged eighteen and nineteen—went up to above 50 percent, a threefold increase. In 1970, 11 percent of the population had four years of college education; by 1980, this had increased to 16 percent. In just another four years, it was 19 percent. We can make estimates of future increases by observing the present rates of enrollment in college and the dropout rates. Roughly one half of those who enter college eventually finish. Today, this means that about 30 percent of the population receives a college degree and usually by age twenty-five. Even if there is no increase in the number who enter college or in the completion rate, the proportion of the population with this level of qualifications will move toward 30 percent. As this book goes to press, the proportion has started to increase again. The large numbers of young adults entering college has gradually but inevitably changed the sophistication of the consumer, and this has implications for market strategy.

I agree with all the data that Toffler presents on the demassification of society, that is, the preference for nonstandardized products in his book *The Third Wave* (1981). The causes of this transformation lie in the much higher numbers of those graduating from college in the 1960s and 1970s; they are now transforming the nature of the marketplace, for college-educated people are becoming a larger and larger percentage of the population.

Demassification is not the only way in which the consumer is changing the marketplace. Quality is becoming more important than quantity relative to the price. This does not mean that there are no longer products whose price is very important, but only that in a larger and larger proportion of products, quality becomes a major consideration rather than the quantity for a given price. Organic meat and vegetables, designer clothes, compact disks, limited-production cars, and radial tires—these are only a few examples. This is obvious, and many American businesses are *now* quite concerned about quality, although perhaps not in the correct way.

Less obvious is that the average consumer appears to have developed a much more complex view of products and services, which manifests itself in the way the product is evaluated simultaneously on the basis of a wide variety of different and frequently conflicting criteria. Food is now more than just something to eat; taste makes a difference. Gourmet foods and restaurants are ever more popular. Health is another major consideration in that foods have to be produced with or without sugar, salt, preservatives, and so forth. Consumers are willing to pay large sums for organic foods. All of these changes have occurred in the last decade and reflect the major shifts in the consumer. I would argue that it means that the consumer is now much more complex in his evaluations.

What is producing this more complex view of the world and a preference for individualized life-styles? (These two perspectives are themselves interrelated because a complex view allows for the individualized differences to be appreciated and not scorned.) Education, especially college education, changes the way people perceive the world and therefore evaluate products and services. College graduates are more likely to see the complexities and interdependencies of products; they want products to have multiple attributes—for example, cars that do not pollute, that are safe to drive, that do not use too much gasoline, that have a variety of technological gadgets on them, that have a certain sense of aesthetics, and so forth. The best evidence for this carefulness in evaluation and critical attitude is the emergence of the consumer movement during the late 1960s. Nader's Raiders and the groups fighting to save the environment are products of the rise in the number of college graduates in the population. It was not the high school dropouts who joined these movements.

Another way in which the consumer has changed is in the preferences for particular kinds of products and services. There is a market for technologically advanced products. We have a high-tech society, and it is populated with high-tech consumers. In the 1950s, model changes involving face lifting were critical in the consumers' decision making. Now technological advance has appeal.

The consumer demand for quality, for complex products with a variety of attributes, and for technologically advanced products is not just a consequence of the higher levels of education. Other factors help to explain the changes in the consumer.

As one advances in levels of education, one not only develops more complex criteria of evaluation, but one also specializes in a particular discipline. Parallel to the growth of an educated public has been an enormous growth in the number of different occupational specialities. Whether in business administration, sociology, engineering, or any other subject, there has been considerable expansion of specialization during the past two decades. Disciplines shape people's values and ways of thinking. The movement toward occupational specialization creates the need for individual life-styles. Mass society depended upon a mass education system at the primary and secondary levels. Differentiation in learning only really started in college. Mass society also depended upon having many people do very similar kinds of manual work that demanded few skills. As society shifts from a manual to a nonmanual occupational system in which most of the occupations place a premium on skills (especially thinking skills, judgment, creativity, and the like), then the move away from mass society observed by Toffler (1981) is reinforced.

The consumer search for individual life-styles means that manufacturers and service providers have to develop a wide variety of products and services. The problem for large businesses becomes one of providing the variety with some control over cost, achieving economies of scale across small batches.

This does not mean that there are no areas in which mass products can still thrive. Fast foods is one example. But the dual existence of fast food restaurants and of gourmet and health food restaurants should not be lost to view. The postmodern consumer wants to save time and simultaneously enjoy high-quality and healthy foods. This problem is found in many areas. One item can well be cheap, the other expensive. Jeans and boutique clothes will coexist in the same closet. However, the high-quality product that helps define the individual life-style will become increasingly the most important part of the market and especially for the college-educated professionals, the "yuppies" of the world.

Behind both the expansion in higher education and the development of a variety of occupational specialities is the growth of scientific knowledge. We have to stay in school longer to learn what is known, and we have to specialize to handle the problem of information overload (there are cognitive limits; see March and Simon 1958). Theory alone does not solve this problem. In turn, this expansion in knowledge is itself caused by the heavy investment in research and development in the several decades after the war.

The emphasis on societal knowledge broadly defined now makes more sense. It allows one to see the interconnections between research and development, the growth in occupational specialization, the development of the technology of research, the emergence of the consumer movement, the shift in values toward quality, and the demand for individualized products as part of the same basic trend. *These are the new rules of competition.*

If we have identified some basic causal processes, then planners and managers can extrapolate trends in the movement toward demassification and do this sector by sector, depending upon the levels of research and development and education levels of the consumers. The process of industrialization did not occur in one decade but across a century or more. We can anticipate that the process of postindustrialization will also play out over a long time period of at least four or five decades before some new sets of rules emerge.

The New Role of the State

At the beginning of this chapter, I suggested that the problem is to define not only what kinds of new business organizations are necessary, but also what kinds of new institutional patterns. One key component in the postindustrial society, at least when we look elsewhere, is the role of the state. Japan Inc., has been held up to ridicule, but it is a fact with which everyone must contend. Nor is it limited to Japan; increasingly, more and more governments have decided that the state and business must be in partnership if there is to be continued growth in productivity and effective macroeconomic management. Furthermore, the same trend is developing in the United States, although it has not been recognized. A partnership between the federal and state governments and businesses is an important new rule of competition. Again, these facts have obvious implications for competition. American businesses and their managers are fond of seeing the state—that is, the central government—as the enemy. Throughout the past century, the government has frequently said no to many of the things that businesses would have liked to do. The pure food and drug laws, the legislation designed to protect the health of the worker, the many environmental laws that attempted to regulate pollution have all been seen as infringements of business freedom rather than as protection for society.

Regardless of the past, the relationship between business and the state is changing in many of the postindustrial societies that are competing with the United States. The first and most obvious role that the state plays in postindustrial society is that of providing funds for research and development, especially for large projects that many businesses would have trouble financing by themselves.

In the past decade and a half, Japan, France, and West Germany have moved past the United States in the percent of GNP allocated to research and development in nonmilitary research. Presently, the United States spends about 1.9 percent of its GNP on nonmilitary research, France about the same, while Japan and West Germany, the United States' two major competitors, spend more than 2 percent. Currently the U.S. government is concerned about this discrepancy and is projecting increases in the expenditures on basic research. Again, we have another sign of crisis, as viewed from the political arena.

Another indication of both political concern and of the need for cooperation between business and government can be seen in the existence of new centers for engineering research. Previously the federal government did not emphasize research and development on the processes for creating new products. Funding for the new centers for engineering research being started by the National Science Foundation is one half through the federal government and one half through a consortium of businesses. So far only about 20 have been started, but some 150 are planned. Many state governments are also funding research, frequently in partnership with business. For example, in the state of Maryland four biotech centers have been established with joint funding.

Foreign governments have become involved in partnerships with business because they have decided that knowledge and technology are the key to power, and I do not mean just military power. Perhaps the French put this most dramatically when they outlined twenty key technological areas in which their science and technology had to be dominant if they were to remain a major world power; a five-year plan (1970–75) was devoted to the problem of innovation. The Japanese have developed a national and political strategy for research and also for development and international competition. This is beginning to occur in the United States as well but with much less clarity. The federal government is establishing scientific priorities in specific disciplines, but it has not developed a coherent view.

The new attitude of cooperation between the state and businesses is also reflected in a series of new laws that alter competition. The antitrust tax laws have been amended so that competitors can do research together. Equally significant, tax credits are shifting in order to support research and development as well as capital expenditures.

If firms want to participate in the development of postindustrial society, they will have to create a partnership with government, not just in the planning of scientific research and technological development, but in the construction of products that are more environmentally neutral as well. In other words, although the federal government will continue in its role as regulator, we can anticipate a gradual evolution toward some partnership in the planning of legislation to protect the environment and in the enforcement of various regulatory practices. Once business and government start to cooperate in one area, they should start to cooperate in other areas as well.

Because this partnership exists in other societies that are the major competitors of the United States, the United States will be forced to engage in the same kind of activity. Japan, Inc., represents a model in some respects. That the model is being used is demonstrated in current concerns over superconductivity. Less appreciated is the collaboration of business and government in France, West Germany, Sweden, Norway, and many other countries that produce high-tech and high-quality products (Hage and Clignet 1982, Gruchy 1977). The same can be said for the new emerging industrial countries such as Korea, Brazil, Mexico, and Israel.

This cooperation does not mean state control or direction but instead a collaboration and a bargaining in which each side agrees to accept constraints on its behavior for the mutual advantage of both. I assume that business firms working alone cannot compete successfully against businesses in other countries that have collaborative relations with their governments. The days of the lone and successful business, whether General Motors or IBM or General Electric, are near an end.

Although Naisbitt (1982) discusses networking as an important trend, he does not consider the kind of institutional networking I have described above. However, he is right to place a great deal of emphasis on knowledge or information networking as one important kind of network. We now turn to another trend that Naisbitt (1982) observes, namely the global economy.

The Global Economy

As markets within countries become more individualized, they also paradoxically become more global. What is lost internally can potentially be made up elsewhere.

Since its borders are now open, the United States is subject to the competition not only of cheap labor from the Third World countries (as for example in industries making toys, cheap clothes, shoes, or other products where labor is a significant factor), but it is more critically facing the competition of advanced technical products from Japan and from France and West Germany, and increasingly from Korea, Brazil, and other rapidly developing countries. The amount of attention given to the competition with Japan over the new generation of computer chips illustrates the point. But it would be a serious mistake to assume that the competition is only with Japan. Other countries represent formidable competitors and at what used to be thought of as the American game: innovation.

The cost of transportation has helped make the world a global economy. In 1960, less than 3 percent of the GNP of the United States involved trade. In 1980, the figure reached 9 percent and since then has been steadily increasing. In several product areas imports account for 50 percent or more of the market. Steel, automobiles, machinery—some of the most basic industries—are areas in which 20–30 percent of the products are produced overseas. But the cost of these products is not the only issue. Frequently the consumer purchases imports because of their superior quality, design, or because of special utilities that have been added to the product. Foreign competition has often recognized more quickly the changes in the tastes of the American consumer. For example, American tire manufacturers never believed the consumer would pay more for the Michelin tire. The inroads made by Japanese car manufacturers because of perceived greater quality are well known. The same can be said for a wide range of products.

The reverse is equally true. If American business is to compete successfully, it must understand the tastes and needs of the consumer in other countries. Part of the failure of American business in Japan and in Western Europe has been an insensitivity to consumer needs and wishes. To achieve this appreciation requires knowing a great deal about the cultures of other countries.

This does not deny the place for global products such as the world car but only argues that there should be some individual variations in design to meet the specific tastes and needs of the people of particular countries. The global economy has received much discussion in the popular press, but it is not the only way in which markets are being internationalized. Equally important are the very large migrations of people which are internationalizing the United States internally, creating many new kinds of market opportunities.

The large and continual Asian and Latin immigrations and the radical shift in interracial marriages (which have increased from 10,000 to 100,000 in one decade) are altering the racial composition of the United States. These two parallel developments mean that American society is becoming both a multiracial society and one increasingly oriented toward both Asia and Latin America, as the European ethnic populations are balanced by new ethnic diversity. This implies a cultural richness and a number of special niches. But it also means an opportunity to build a global strategy if it is properly appreciated by business firms. These Asian and Latin cultural representations in the United States provide potential bridges to markets in these other countries.

Just as the economy is becoming global, so is American culture and in many ways. This internal differentiation requires an appreciation of the consumer needs of many ethnic groups. Furthermore, although in the United States' industrial phase one's ethnic past tended to be denied, it can now be displayed with pride. Again, the implications of this for business are many and obvious.

Strategic Implications

The new rules of competition imply automatically new strategies for the firms that want to compete in postindustrial society. Although we shall discuss these new strategic implications one by one, it should not be assumed that all firms should follow the same prescription. There will be considerable variation depending upon the specific niche the firm finds itself in. In the next three chapters, which form the first part of this book, the reader will find a variety of responses, all of which are viable, depending upon the circumstances of the firm.

Corporate strategy can be categorized both as a set of markets and as a set of inputs or resources needed to produce the desired outputs. Corporate strategy should contain the logic of a production function—that is, what resources should be emphasized in order to obtain the desired gains in productivity, quality, and, beyond this, growth. However, in addition to the inputs of labor, capital, human capital, and the like, I include technology as a necessary factor of production. Using this framework, we can make the following observations.

Market Strategy: Product Innovation

Given all that has just been said, a logical conclusion is that product innovation becomes increasingly critical as the best strategy for survival. In the past, large companies could make profits with either large market share or constant product innovation. Increasingly, the latter strategy becomes the more effective one. Given shorter and shorter product lives, the rate of innovation must be incrementally increased across time so that the sales level in real dollars remains a constant. Indeed, the strategic problem is to find product families that will endure for a certain number of years, even though within these families products may last only a year or two.

One of the major issues confronting many but certainly not all high-tech companies is the sheer bewildering range of potential products because of the advances of science. This is most striking in computer software, biotech, laboratory instruments, video, drugs, and telecommunications, to name only a few high-technology industrial sectors. Given this diversity, corporate strategy must consider families of products that have readily apparent niches. Single products and unrelated product lines have to be carefully thought through and either sold, handled in a venture capital situation, or managed in a joint venture product development situation, a strategic issue touched upon later.

Are there any directions in which products, regardless of technological sector, can be developed? The answer is a qualified yes. Certainly upgrading quality is a major issue. Quality here should be understood as durability, dependability, error free (at least a reduction in the amount of error), built to exacting specifications, or relatively pure, and so on, depending upon the nature of the product. Each new level of quality may not present a new product, but niches in markets are accorded to those products with higher quality. Frequently, they can command significantly higher prices.

Another direction that also may not qualify as developing a new product is to create the customized or individualized product. The more manufacturers can provide customized products, the more likely they are to create a niche for themselves. Earlier, I suggested some of the reasons for this shift in tastes away from a mass market; Toffler (1981) provides many examples. This has implications for technological development strategies, which are discussed later.

Still a third direction is the development of multiple attributes, besides quality, which customers want built into their products: safety, convenience, environmental neutrality, low operating costs, artful design, and flexibility are just a few. But they could all be captured under a single dictum: increase the complexity of the products' attributes. The interdependence of the world is increasingly recognized by the sophisticated consumer, and product innovation strategies must deal with this fact.

A fourth direction is the creation of products for the many cultures that exist in the United States and that in turn can allow the firm to build bridges toward various Third World countries in which American firms have traditionally been weak. Cultural tastes extend much farther than the boundaries of restaurants. For example, French drivers prefer nervous cars with good pickup, German drivers fast cars that are safe, Italian drivers stylish cars, and so forth. More and more cultural preferences should be built into a variety of consumer goods.

Culture is not the only way in which the population of the United States can be usefully divided. A fifth direction is the creation of different products for different age groups. The needs of different kinds of living situations for people at different stages of the life cycle have already become clear. The same logic can be extended to a wide variety of different products and services. The growth in knowledge and the differentiation of market into customized products and services on the basis of occupation, age, and cultural background create endless possibilities for product innovation.

Market Strategy: Economies of Scale in Diversity

Low productivity in the United States probably has several causes. One may be that there already is some product differentiation. The problem is of maintaining growth in productivity while greatly expanding the range of product diversification that exists.

Survival in a fast-paced world depends not only on new products but on process innovations that allow for the new products to be produced with some efficiency. Earlier I emphasized that the research evidence indicates that the United States has not stressed strongly enough continual improvement in developing better technical processes.

The basic issue confronting both small and high-tech companies is how to achieve economies of scale when there is a continual stream of products and when these products must be produced in multiple batches with different combinations of attributes. Obviously one needs to design extremely flexible production lines. The engineering research centers being created jointly by the

National Science Foundation, several universities, and consortiums of businesses represent still more opportunities for firms to find ways of achieving productivity with a great diversity of products. This strategy is most available to the large firms that can afford to contribute. It is not relevant for the small firms, although even there universities are beginning to confront the production problems of small firms. For example, at the University of Maryland, the Engineering Department runs a fermentation lab for small high-tech companies in biotech because such companies cannot afford to do experiments in this kind of facility.

This issue of productivity reaches its greatest challenge in the customization of products. Production managers need the concept of families of solutions so that their production systems can really provide customization with high productivity.

Another issue is that of creating an organizational climate or culture that stresses constant improvements in the way products are produced. Quality and quality improvement have been much stressed in the literature and rightly so. Quality is a production technology problem and needs to be recognized as such. But it is not just an engineering or machine problem. It is also a worker problem, requiring that workers and machines be combined effectively. Too often production lines are defined as sequences of machines, and not as sequences of humans with various skills and machines with various attributes. The human input is essential for upgrading quality—one reason for the effectiveness of Japanese manufacturers.

One of the United States' major problems is the movement of American inventions into effective production. Engineers design production systems but never consult the individuals who have the practical know-how. Culture or climate becomes critical in encouraging the use of workers in creating new production processes, the effective exploitation of new machines, and the constant upgrading of the productivity of the production line.

All this to say that process innovation is a critical component of any corporate strategy of survival. But the strategy involves the combination of both machines and workers. There has not been enough stress on productivity in the United States or on production management in the American business schools. I am suggesting that our very definition of productivity needs to change from measuring how much is produced at what cost to measuring how much diversity with high quality is produced at low cost (see Hage 1984).

The global economy provides an opportunity to achieve economies of scale. If the internal markets of the United States are dividing themselves into many small, customized markets based on culture, occupation, and age, then some economies of scale can be obtained if the same kind of market can be found in other countries at approximately the same level of development. This will perhaps require some adaptation to other cultures and societies, and it is a different kind of research from engineering—it is social science or marketing research but needed research nevertheless.

Resource Strategy: Mobilizing Human Capital

If constant change is the major issue facing both small and high-tech companies, then how does one prepare business managers for this world, and, more critically, what do companies need to do regarding career planning and personnel selection? The answer to all of these issues appears to be in the development of multiple specialties, either through joint majors in college or multiple degrees or job training. As the mind develops a more complex cognitive structure—that is, thinks in more than one way—then the individual is likely to be more creative and more adaptive to rapid change. Beyond this, careful thought should be given to the combination of science majors and business majors. Currently, combined engineering and management degrees are increasing in popularity. But in the future and especially for those companies that are more on the technological cutting edge, scientific training should be considered more and more a prerequisite. The main point is that double majors provide more protection and a more complex view of the world.

In postindustrial society, the mobilization of human capital or human resource management becomes increasingly important. People have the creative ideas that lead to the development of new products and new production processes. It is this creativity that has to be mobilized. In one sense, human resource management does not capture the correct idea. For me, the real issue is tapping the creativity of the people who work for the firm and then mobilizing it into a productive force that provides the process innovation and improves the economies of scale despite the small batches implied by customization.

Perhaps those with the most significant potential for increased mobilization are the workers on the production line. The United States has the highest levels of education among its production workers, and yet American firms do not effectively use their ideas. We have already observed that on average one Japanese worker makes ten times as many suggestions as does the typical American worker. As long as the Japanese are ten times as effective as the Americans in mobilizing this human potential, there will be little hope for American business. Nor is the problem simply one of quality work circles. It is much more complicated than this.

One element of any human resource strategy is the need to invest in continual education and upgrading. Ideas become obsolete faster than equipment. The problem, then, is continual upgrading. IBM provides an interesting example. It spends more money on education than it does on research. This implies that the secret of product innovation is not just research dollars but the amount of knowledge invested in the minds of the workers and at all levels of the firm. This policy of investment in people is also likely to pay rich dividends for the company in other ways by building trust and commitment.

Seeking creative researchers is another obvious personnel policy. Yet the real issue is to see product and process innovation as the job of everyone in the firm. How can one mobilize the creative potential—the tacit or unconscious knowledge—found in everyone? A good start is achieved through investment in education, but it is only a start.

In the previous section, I suggested that different disciplines had different kinds of information networks. One aspect of mobilizing human capital is not just education but proper networking. It may not be fruitful to invest all of the research and development dollars in in-house research. Companies have to learn how to tap external information networks and the ones most appropriate for the firm so that ideas in them can benefit the organization.

Cooperation as a Strategy

The importance of information networks, the development of engineering centers jointly sponsored by businesses that are competitors, the role of universities in supporting small high-tech firms during their incubation period—these developments point to some unusual ways in which cooperation becomes more important as a corporate strategy.

Where points of cooperation are most important? First and foremost, cooperation is most necessary in research and development. Complex problems require both corporations and universities to work together. German science and industry enjoyed a great advantage between the 1880s and the 1920s because of the close connection between scientific graduate work in the universities and industrial R & D labs. Both faculty and students moved back and forth easily. The new engineering research centers hold promise. But if they are to be effective, businesses both large and small need to have an attitude of cooperation. So do the universities—but this is a subject for another article.

The second area of cooperation is among suppliers and customers. The concept of cooperation means long-term relationships in which neither suppliers nor customers are played off against each other. This is necessary so as to have a flexible, adaptive structure across organizations to replace the rigidities of vertical integration. But as Williamson (1975) would argue, transactions are possible only where there is trust, and trust is built through stability. Customization is only possible by working with customers and maintaining service afterward for a long time.

The third area of cooperation is among small firms, whether part of a family in a large, high-tech case or not. The creation of product niches makes this possible and at the same time leads to the development of potential joint ventures with other firms, both large and small. So far, joint ventures are a phenomenon of the large companies, but as a strategy for small, high-tech firms it offers a great deal of flexibility and the creation of a coherent product line, without dampening the creativity of its people.

Conclusions

Seldom do writers make their assumptions clear. In this chapter I have argued that there has been a change in the ways in which business firms must compete. By assuming—and documenting the assumption—that the growth in knowledge, the rising levels of education, and expanding technologies will be with us for some time, as will the integration of the U.S. economy into the global economy, a clear business strategy emerges.

Businesses that want to survive must constantly innovate. Furthermore, by indicating how rising levels of education affect consumers' tastes and preferences and how the consequences of specialization lead to the demassification of society, the direction for innovation is clear as well. The movement is toward small-batch products in specialty markets with high-quality, multiple attributes and even customization.

But production innovation is only part of the answer. Firms must also search for ways of achieving economies of scale amid the diversity and of mobilizing human capital, especially that of the worker, to increase productivity constantly.

Cooperation internally should replace conflict between labor and management. Externally, cooperation with suppliers and customers should replace vertical integration and policies of domination. To beat Japan, Inc., American companies must compete as groups working together—across all the traditional lines that have divided them in the past.

I
Strategies and Structures

Probably the topic of greatest appeal to most managers is that of the preferred strategy and structure for survival. Presumably this explains the success of books like those by Peters and Waterman (1982) and Ouchi (1981). Because of these concerns, the members of the Center for Innovation have selected this topic for the first part of our book. However, we believe that this is probably the wrong way to phrase the question. Our first observation is that there are many strategies and structures and not just one best way. Our second observation is that it is extremely important for the managers to be able to diagnose their specific environmental context and on this basis select the appropriate strategy and structure. Of these two issues, probably the more difficult is the choice of structure. For this reason, the three chapters emphasize discussing alternatives and the factors that are associated with selecting one or another organizational form.

The major contribution of these three chapters is that they discuss alternative structures more than they do alternative strategies. As is well known, strategy is itself a relatively new topic in business schools. Indeed, it represents one of the new social technologies for businesses, allowing them to come to grips with an environment that is continually changing. Therefore, it is perhaps not surprising that there is greater emphasis on structure in the first part of this book.

The problem of strategy emerges in several different ways. Certainly it is discussed explicitly in chapters 1 and 9. The chapter by Rousseau focuses explicitly on a special kind of strategy, one for human resources, that some would argue is becoming the most important factor in the production of innovations and for the survival of the firm. The problem of strategy is also implied in the work on culture and especially in the contributions by Delbecq and Weiss and by Schneider and Rentsch. Creating cultures to achieve certain ends, such as service or interdependency, is another way of stating strategy.

But this does not make the first three chapters irrelevant to the question of strategy. Each of them makes at least one assumption about the environment and then indicates what the implications are for the structure of the organization. They thus complement the discussions of culture that appear later and reflect another way in which the organization can respond to its environment. Implicit in all these chapters is that organizations want to survive, and they need flexibility, innovativeness, and efficiency to do so, even if the mixtures differ, depending upon the context of the organization. With these performances implied as part of the strategic formulation of the organization, then connections between strategy and the contributions in this first part become much clearer.

Chapter 2 concentrates on the global economy, while recognizing that the speed with which this situation is becoming a reality varies for different firms and technological niches. In chapter 1, I provided a general strategy, but in chapter 3 this approach is qualified by the nature of the markets and by the technological context in which the firm or public service organization is located. Power in chapter 4 considers the broadest range of strategies that are tied to the relative stability or instability of the resources and the political situation in which firms find themselves.

The first two chapters of this section are the closest in theoretical perspective in laying greater stress on the contextual factors that are associated with technology and markets. In chapter 2, Galbraith and Kazanjian believe that the central questions in formulating strategy are the diversity and the extent and character of global competition. Power emphasizes stability or instability, and Hage in chapter 3 emphasizes primarily the acceleration in the growth in knowledge, as well as the extension of markets worldwide. These differences, while sometimes quite small, do lead to different insights about the appropriateness of particular strategies and structures. In comparing these chapters it is worth remembering that they are implicitly employing different time frames. Chapter 2 is discussing a current situation for some firms which will become more commonplace for many other companies. Chapter 3 looks a little further into the future and speculates a little more about what some future configurations might be, but chapter 4 attempts to go the furthest in speculating about what might be quite novel and interesting forms in the future. Needless to say, all four authors have in various ways extrapolated from current experience, but Power is right to admonish managers to think about the "unthinkable" in considering new kinds of organizational structures. Chapter 6 also provides insights into what structural alternatives in the future might be.

Traditional organizational theory and management science has concentrated too much on one or two kinds of modal organizations. (Those readers unfamiliar with the traditional views can read the first part of chapter 3 or the relevant parts of chapter 5.) Each of these three chapters proposes several more types than are currently found in the literature. Even chapter 2, which is concerned with the advantages of matrix structures, perceives a considerable variety of alternative ways that these can be constructed. Hage suggests that the typical typology of four organizations will evolve in a variety of ways, even as some types are eliminated or radically diminished in number. And Power goes so far as to suggest six new kinds of organizations.

This diversity of alternatives has several common themes, which is surprising since each selection was written independently and the themes had not emerged in the conference. The most prevalent theme is that of networks and the idea of a network organization. All three chapters discuss this concept in different ways and indicate some of the problems this concept may create for managers in the future because it is quite different from the typical way in which managers have functioned in the past. Although the concept of networks has been suggested in some of the work on organizations (Naisbitt and Aburdene 1985), these discussions go considerably beyond the present literature and indicate what a rich idea the concept of networks is and the many ways it can manifest itself in the organization. Power's essay in particular opens a number of interesting possibilities with quite inventive names. Again, these are not the only chapters to do this; the preface describes the other chapters that in one way or another touch upon the subject of networks.

All three chapters to some extent look at the mixed mechanical-organic form, although this term is used only by Hage. This form, sometimes called the multidivisional form or the conglomerate, is implicit in many of the examples in chapter 4. The same is true of chapter 2. The authors of these chapters and Hage discuss some of the pushes toward alternative forms of networks, such as joint ventures, close working relationships between customers and suppliers, strategic alliances, venture capital, and the like; while Power describes the different ways these networks might be knit together. Thus these chapters complement each other in several ways.

Power and Galbraith and Kazanjian also emphasize the role of information technology and how it is altering the role of the manager, while Power and Hage look at automation and the consequences it might have for the form of the organization. These themes occur again and again throughout the book and for understandable reasons: their effects are everywhere, and they define what probably are the most significant aspects of the effect of knowledge on organizations.

This does not mean that there is agreement on all issues. Power, for example, believes that under certain conditions centralization and formalization are likely, whereas Hage implies that this may be disappearing, except for firms managed through franchises. Hage indicates that research and development is being or will be decentralized in many operations; chapter 2 is not so certain that this is the case. This theme of centralization or decision making also reappears at various times.

2
Strategy, Technology, and Emerging Organizational Forms

Jay R. Galbraith
Robert K. Kazanjian

Recently, diversified multinational corporations (MNCs) have found that they must pursue strategies of increased diversity, while the individual industries in which they compete become more global in character. In addition, the capital investment for technology development required simply to remain competitive is increasingly burdensome. These conflicting challenges present new administrative problems. Effective strategy implementation and correspondingly high levels of economic performance will be contingent, at least in part, on the appropriate organizational configuration. In the following sections, we will detail these new challenges, which are highly consistent with the observations made by Hage in the first chapter, and describe why firms facing them must increase their capacity for lateral communication and coordination. In particular, we will argue that matrixes (or matrix variations) are one appropriate organizational response. Further, we will detail the emerging role of network organizations as a complex but potentially effective administrative innovation.

The basic premise with which we begin is that the firm has a variety of structural forms from which to choose when implementing a particular strategy. It is our contention that the choice of structural form makes an economic difference—that is, all structural forms are not equally effective for implementing a given strategy. (Empirical research support for this contention can be found in the work of Armour and Teece 1978, Nathanson 1980, Teece 1981, and Dundas and Richardson 1982.)

There are, however, other design variables in addition to structure to be considered if a firm is to marshal its resources and effectively implement its strategy. We subscribe to an information-processing view of organization design (Galbraith 1977), recognizing that specific organizational forms must be responsive to primary contextual factors. Increasingly, for large, diversified, multinational firms, those contextual factors are (1) the degree of diversity within the product-market strategy chosen by the firm, (2) the extent and character of global competition within each industry in which the firm is positioned, and (3) the requirements for technology development.

These factors together determine the task diversity and uncertainty with which the organization must cope. The firm must then match the people with the task through selection, recruitment, and training and development practices. The people must also match the structure. The structure, also chosen to fit the task, is specified by choices of the division of labor (amount of role differentiation), the departmental structure, the shape (number of levels, spans of control), and the distribution of power (both horizontal and vertical). Across the structure, processes are overlaid to allocate resources and coordinate activities not handled by the departmental structure. These information and decision processes include planning and control systems, budgeting processes, integration mechanisms, and performance measurements. And finally, the reward system must be matched with the task and structure through choices of compensation practices, career paths, leader behavior, and the design of work. These relationships are indicated in figure 2–1.

In total, all these choices must create an internally consistent design. If one of the practices is changed, the other dimensions must be altered to maintain fit. Similarly, if these strategic and technology factors change, then all the dimensions may need to be altered so that the form of organization remains consistent with the context. The process is one of constant readjustment. (This central theme is expanded upon in considerable detail in Galbraith and Kazanjian 1986).

Managing Diversity

It has been documented (Rumelt 1974) that there is a continuing trend toward diversification across all firms (not simply those that are U.S.-based). Additionally, as some of the studies referred to earlier demonstrate, many of these same firms have also pursued strategies of geographic expansion for some or all of their diversified product offerings. The primary challenge to these firms for effective strategy implementation has traditionally been the balancing of the forces of geography and line of business. More recently, however, new sources of diversity, around markets or technologies, have emerged as critical considerations in addition to geography and business line. Further, some firms have devised strategies that require that equal priority be given to two or more of such sources of diversity.

The result is an increase in interdependence among product divisions, business groups, area divisions, or whatever labels are used to name units. It is becoming virtually impossible to find clean, self-contained clusters of divisions or groups that can form profit centers. For example, the firms in the computer and communications industries must cope with the coordination of multiple functions when producing multiple products whose technology is changing rapidly, for multiple countries, and for multiple industries. Thus, one finds

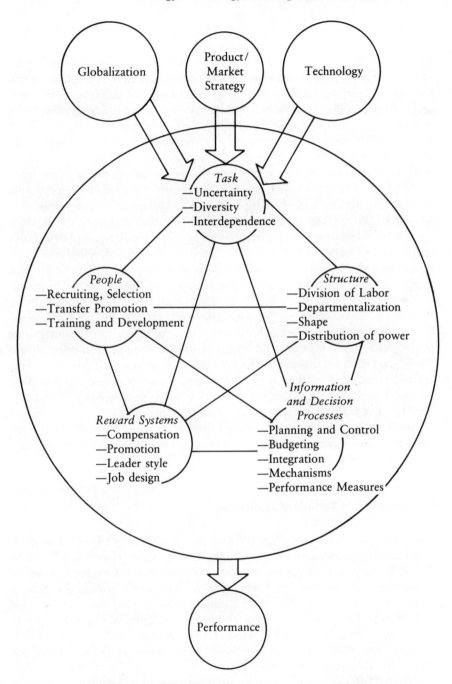

Figure 2–1. **Major Illustration of Fit among an Organization's Design Variables**

product managers, industry managers, functional managers, and area managers who focus upon each source of diversity. But multiple sources of diversity are not the only problem. It is when product, geography, and market are of equal strategic importance that the difficulty arises. In the past, firms could manage diversity by choosing to organize differently at each level of the hierarchy. For example, in figure 2–2, the electronics firm chose geography as the primary differentiating factor. Secondary emphasis was given to markets in an attempt to differentiate products going to consumers from products going to manufacturers. The next level differentiated between products. The product division was the basic profit center and was to coordinate the multiple functions, which were given fourth priority. The multiple sources of diversity were managed by the creation of multiple layers of management, each responsible for one of the sources. The level reflected the strategic priority.

The problem now is that geography and product are of equal priority, with technology so important that a single large research and development function is needed. All areas should sell the same minicomputer system rather than duplicate the development effort to create their own. Also, the minicomputer system needs to be compatible with the large-scale computing system, so that they can be arranged to handle electronic funds transfer for the banking industry. The result is that some functions cannot be relegated to a fourth-level priority. Geography is important, but so are industry and product orientations. There is a great deal more interdependence across products, industries, areas, and functions. Self-contained profit centers are impossible to find, because there is a great deal of interunit coordination that needs to take place. There is a need for more general management to provide the coordination. This is a critical administrative problem for the heavily diversified firm. How do you divide general management work so as to coordinate multiple sources of diversity, giving each equal priority?

Competing in Globalized Industries

The current challenge of competing on a global basis, beyond issues of managing diversity, is causing firms to fashion new strategies (Hamel and Prahalad 1985). These new strategies present tasks and priorities that require new organizational configurations, consistent with the logic of fit discussed earlier. A primary source of the challenge, which comes in many instances from Japanese firms (Kotler, Fahey, and Jatustrippitak 1985), come from competitors and customers who act on a global basis (Hout, Porter, and Rudden 1982; Levitt 1983; Fayerweather 1984). Not all industries or companies are experiencing this, but others are deep into these issues.

Global competitors have been around for some time. However, only in the past few years has the impact of global competition been felt across many

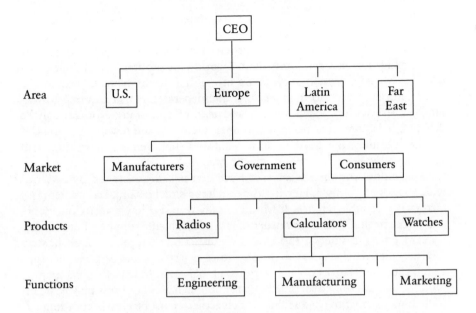

Figure 2–2. Standard Divisionalized Firm Emphasizing Geography

industries and the issue given a high priority. The effective competitor in such circumstances thinks and acts on a global basis. For example, a firm may enter a newly targeted market from an existing diversified position in other markets in other countries. This allows the firm to subsidize entry and start-up losses in that country market with profits from another country market (Hamel and Prahalad 1985). It is not uncommon for the global competitor to enter a new market by targeting a high-share, domestic company. The only response for the target company is to cut costs and prices and ask for protection. The entire battle gets fought in the targeted company's market with a significant portion of its revenue base under margin pressure. The attacking company, with a much smaller portion of its revenue under margin pressure, is better positioned to sustain the fight. The only effective response is for the target company to attack the attacker in its profit sanctuary, thereby putting a large portion of its revenue under margin pressure (Watson 1982). The global competitor, then, is one who is positioned worldwide within a business but can also cross-subsidize countries and businesses as it expands geographically or into new businesses (Hamel and Prahalad 1985).

The organizational implication of this interdependence is that companies must be capable of acting in an integrated fashion on a global basis. This ability to work across profit centers requires coordination processes such as integrating roles and other variations of matrix organization designs. For example, IBM has a profit center organization in the United States with a centralized sales and service organization. The rest of the world is organized geographically around countries and regions. But there are some fifty worldwide product managers who manage product development and worldwide profitability of their product line. Most of these managers are in the U.S. profit centers.

The organization to manage such interdependence also requires a planning process within which sources and uses of corporate resources can be debated. It requires that performance measurements and rewards be adjusted for the subsidies. But most of all it requires a management that thinks and acts on a global basis, not a domestic one.

The global customer is another force that is being exercised on a worldwide basis. For example, Hewlett Packard has a small personal computer (PC) factory in Grenoble, France. It would usually receive a low priority on supply and prices from a country manager of a semiconductor supplier. But Hewlett Packard puts pressure on the U.S. division of that supplier, which in turn pressures the French country manager. Other examples could be given, but they all indicate a need to act on an integrated global basis. Independent geographic profit centers cannot be the sole basis for organizing. Since firms may buy centrally for a number of product lines, such activity must be closely coordinated. Other companies may need a global account management system throughout their sales organizations. Such companies also need performance measurement and reward systems that accommodate subsidies across countries and businesses.

The Role of Technology

In recent years, technology has radically altered the basic character of competition in a number of industries. Rapid and revolutionary change in both product and process technologies have forced firms to increase their investment in technology simply to remain competitive. In some instances, the duration of product life cycles have been shortened, while the basis of competition has shifted from finance and marketing to product and process innovations. In the electronics industry, for example, the time-to-market for new products decreased dramatically as product life cycles collapsed down to three to five years. The automobile industry is currently experiencing similar pressures. In other cases, whole new industries, such as computer-integrated manufacturing, machine vision, and genetic engineering, have resulted from technological advances, with obvious implications for existing firms in established industries as well as for those firms founding the emerging industries.

As the investment in R & D resulting from these forces becomes substantial, individual country subsidiaries of firms find their resources to be inadequate. Given that technology development evidences clear economies of scale and scope and is applicable anywhere (the third law of thermodynamics is the same in every country of the world), the result is a move to more centrally directed and controlled technology development efforts. This reduces individual country autonomy but creates the need for technology integration, certainly across countries within a business, and in cases of firms working from a base of highly related technologies, across businesses as well.

Problems with Traditional Organizational Forms

The area divisional organization and the worldwide product divisional organization have both come under pressure as a result of the emerging managerial challenges of increased diversity and globalization.

When the universality of technology is combined with the homogenization of markets and the need for world-scale plants, geography becomes a less important basis for thinking about a business and for organizing profit centers.

The area divisions, or groups, and country profit centers of multinational firms have three primary issues with which to deal. The first is the homogenizing of markets (Levitt 1983) and the design of universal products for them. Geographic differences in markets and local adaptation of products lead to countries or regions being the basic profit centers. As local differences decline, the need for local adaptation declines, and with it the need for local geographic profit centers. Note that this view of global homogenization is not necessarily inconsistent with that of Toffler (1981) and others who have argued that there is a movement toward greater demassification and segmentation of markets. The result of greater segmentation is not different products for each country, but rather different combinations of products for each country. Additionally, economies associated with common components and other inputs continue to exist.

The effect of homogenizing markets is amplified when combined with the other two issues. One is drive for economies of scale and the increasing use of world-scale plants. Every country cannot afford its own manufacturing facilities. In semiconductors, it now costs over $100 million for the next plant. With the universal products being produced in world-scale plants, the decision making moves out of countries and regions and to the worldwide headquarters.

The worldwide product form of organization would have been the clear alternative means of organizing if it had not developed some problems of its own. The first is the relationship with more active host governments. Local governments do not sit idly by as manufacturing and technology development shift to other countries, and then import those products. They have shifted from using tariffs and quotas to industrial policies requiring local content, export, and local technology development. These policies require a relationship and negotiations with local government. This relationship is best handled by local country managers and geographic organizations. If the negotiations are not fruitful, then many advantages of worldwide products and sourcing will not be attained.

The organizations using the worldwide product structures have also under-performed in international markets. The product form was to lead to better use of new technology, newer products, and better transfer to international markets. However, they have not performed as well as companies with international divisions or matrix organizations (Davidson and Haspeslagh 1982). Instead of introducing new products overseas, the product organizations used licenses and reduced direct investment. The product divisions tended to be dominated by domestic management who saw international investments as more risky. Riskier still, in the eyes of domestic-oriented managers, were investments in new countries in which the company is not now doing business. Product-organized companies seemingly are poor at breaking into new geographic markets.

Emerging Organizational Forms

The effects of the economies necessary for manufacturing and technology development, and the need for responsiveness to local governments, lead companies to view their strategies as multidimensional ones. These companies must simultaneously emphasize geography for purposes of local responsiveness, and businesses for purposes of global integration (Hamel and Prahalad 1983).

The forces from global competitors, global customers, universal products, and requirements for large-scale technology investments all point to a need for more global integration. However, the countervailing forces from local governments are also strong. The global company is driven to participate in all key countries with a broad product line. These product lines and countries may not be open to companies without a negotiation with the local, host government. Also, independent worldwide businesses are not effective at opening up new geography. An international division can establish relations with host governments, invest in distribution channels, brand franchises, and build an infrastructure that no single business could afford. So there are still forces for local, country organization. Figure 2–3 shows the trade-offs that need to be made. The various businesses and countries will locate somewhere along this continuum.

The organizational result has been a move to matrixlike structures and mixed structures. For example, organizations that pursued area structures kept these geographic profit centers but added worldwide product managers. Colgate-Palmolive has always had strong country managers. But as they doubled the funding for product research, and as Colgate Dental Creme became a universal product, product managers were added at corporate headquarters to direct the R & D funding and to coordinate marketing programs worldwide.

Similarly, the product-divisionalized firms have been reintroducing the international division. At Motorola, the product groups had worldwide responsibility for their product lines. As they compete with the Japanese in Japan, an international group has been introduced to help coordinate across product lines in Japan.

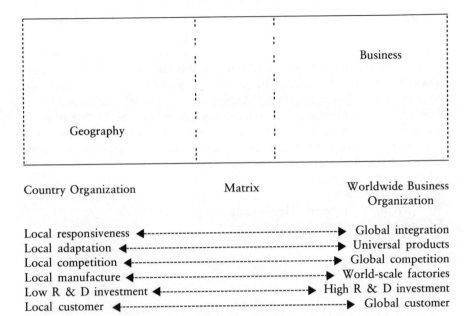

Figure 2–3. **The Local/Global Continuum**

The added organizational units vary in their strengths. Some are full matrix organizations, while others use integrating roles as worldwide product managers. Other organizations are using mixed structures. One company runs its pharmaceutical group as a worldwide entity. Pharmaceutical companies invest 15–20 percent of sales back into R & D. The products are the same in each country in order to meet medical claims made to ministries of health. The company's health, beauty care, and toiletries product lines are managed in a matrix of product lines across countries. The new countries in the Far East are managed as stand-alone country profit centers. Thus, the company mixes worldwide product, country, and matrix structures as the need dictates.

Research that appeared in the late 1970s suggested that matrix organization was responsive to the administrative problems of MNCs (Allen 1973, 1978; Lawrence and Davis 1978; Miles and Snow 1978). However, in the last decade, it appears that firms that use matrix designs have evolved beyond a very structure-reliant managerial approach.

The research findings of Prahalad and Doz (1981) lend further support to this view. They argue that the head office, working from a hybrid or a matrix structure, must use other mechanisms to influence behavior. These include: (1) data management systems-accounting, planning, budgeting, and MIS; (2) manager management mechanisms-management placement, compensation, development, career progression, and performance evaluation; and (3) conflict resolution mechanisms–task forces, planning committees, and integrative decision responsibility assignments. Bartlett (1983) came to similar conclusions. In his own study, he found that successful MNCs avoid a tendency to reorganize in the face of problems, but instead manage the complexity of geographic and market diversity through upgraded personnel, altered management systems, and multidimensional decision-making processes. The finding of both these studies, that firms are increasingly emphasizing process and system variables, simply suggests that the nonstructural elements of what are primarily matrix designs are becoming more important.

The Advent of Network Organizations and Strategic Alliances

Global strategies require companies to locate somewhere near the matrix organization if all the foreign-based assets and businesses are owned by the company. In a number of instances however, complete ownership and control will not be possible, and joint ventures, consortia, and cooperative arrangements are increasingly in evidence. These arrangements lead to a blurring of the boundaries of the firm such that the rather sharp contrast between markets and hierarchies (Williamson 1975) as dichotomous choices for the organization of work begins to erode. The result is an organization that is a network of various contracted relationships, joint ventures, partial ownership positions, and other strategic alliances. These are often pursued in addition to or in place of more traditional forms of organizing economic activity within the hierarchy of the firm, such as vertical integration. An initial categorization of such arrangements follows.

Contracting. In a number of industries, firms are entering joint manufacturing agreements through straightforward contractual relationships that do not involve the creation of any new organizational entity. For example, Westinghouse and Mitsubishi have agreed to cooperate in the manufacture of turbine generators to realize economies of scale unattainable by the firms individually. Each bids on discrete components with the low-cost producer chosen for each. Additionally, each assumes a different technology focus. Each is then in a more competitive position in the high-volume markets of the United States and Japan, and is well positioned independently to pursue other markets.

Contracting might also involve sourcing of components or products, which the firm might otherwise have produced itself, in an effort to round out the product line. The IBM PC was brought to market through the use of an independent business unit within IBM which contracted for much of the product components, serving more as a system integrator.

Joint Ventures. Beyond simple contracting, some firms have created new organizational entities to serve specific purposes. In some instances, these are joint ventures around a single functional activity. For example, because of the technology development expense required to stay at the forefront of today's rapidly advancing technology, RCA and Sharp recently agreed on a joint venture that will supply each with semiconductors. RCA will contribute product technology while Sharp will provide manufacturing technology. With each advance in semiconductor technology requiring a new $100 million plant, cooperation is warranted. Similarly, a joint venture for a semiconductor plant and application project has been created by Westinghouse, General Electric, and Toshiba. In this instance, Westinghouse will supply the plant, General Electric will contribute capital and aid in the distribution, while Toshiba will contribute technology. Similarly, Ford and Fiat have cooperated on a joint engine plant, and General Motors and Toyota are currently engaged in a joint venture in the manufacture of the Chevy Nova.

The number of cooperating parties in such joint ventures is not necessarily limited to a few, nor are such arrangements exclusively focused on manufacturing. The Microelectronics and Computer Technology Corporation (MCC) is an R & D cooperative with over twenty participating firms which focuses on technology development. A similar joint venture exists among European firms.

Some joint ventures are of the model in which a new, stand-alone entity is created by two or more parent companies to compete in a particular business. Corning Glass Works has traditionally engaged in a number of such joint ventures, with one of the most widely known being Dow-Corning. More recent joint ventures have been initiated with firms such as Genentech, MCI, and Kroger. In these cases, each contributes some knowledge, competence, or resource necessary to enter into a particular new business.

Another common use of such ventures is as a mechanism for entering closed markets in the international arena. Host governments may well require foreign firms to engage in joint ventures of various kinds with local companies if they are to be allowed to compete in that market at all. AT&T has more than forty such arrangements that facilitate its entry into foreign markets.

In all cases the motivations of the participants may differ from technology exchange, to the realization of economies of scale in manufacturing, to the acquisition of a position in a market new to the firm, but the mechanism is some type of joint venture.

Strategic Alliances. In some instances firms are engaging in what might be called strategic alliances that do not involve the creation of any new organizational entity but that may involve some joint ownership. For example, AT&T has a 25 percent ownership position in Olivetti, which facilitates distribution of AT&T products in Europe while rounding out AT&T's product line in the United States. Such arrangements are particularly visible within the automobile industry, with

Ford owning 25 percent of Mazda, GM having over 40 percent ownership in Isuzu and 50 percent ownership of a Korean auto manufacturer, and Chrysler increasing its ownership of Maserati—among other such arrangements for these firms. Such alliances are usually among firms within the same industry and are seen as one response to the pressures of global competition.

Similar alliances have been forged by firms that see a position in a related industry as critical to their continued competitive position in their core businesses (to be distinguished from a motivation to diversify). In many instances, these might be considered big company–small company alliances, and they are often driven by the big company's desire to gain a window on an emerging technology. For example, Procter & Gamble and GM each own 10–15 percent of a small artificial intelligence development firm. Ford has an ownership position in a small ceramics company. Most of the automobile firms in the United States have minority positions in machine vision firms, and many of the pharmaceutical companies have positions in biotechnology firms. In these cases the big company provides capital and in some cases a market for the initial product. In return, the small companies provide exposure to emerging technology that the big company may ultimately wish to bring in-house, or that is responsive to current or anticipated problems.

It is apparent, then, that the necessary capital costs and associated economies of scale in development and production, as well as technological and market risks in a number of industries, including computers, semiconductors, automobiles, robotics, and aircraft, will require extensive use of network arrangements and strategic alliances now and into the future.

Implications

The administration of networks of contracts, joint ventures, alliances, and wholly owned subsidiaries presents enormous new problems (Killing 1982), the resolution of which is related to the firm's capacity for lateral communication and coordination. A network is merely a matrix organization extended beyond the traditional bounds of the firm but without the ability to appeal to a tiebreaker. Further, we argue that it is an essential form for the conduct of diversified, multinational enterprises that aspire to be effective international competitors. Note that matrix skills then are critical to the effective management of emerging network organizations that may become a prime instrumentality of global strategy implementation.

Those companies that are acquiring expertise in matrix organization will be well positioned to manage networks and other nonhierarchical forms of organizing. Those companies that have backed away from matrix structure however, may be at a disadvantage in global competition. Or, they may become a local partner for a global company. It is our view that they will not be effective as a global company themselves.

The global pressures are seen in those companies that are experiencing the new competition. IBM is the best example of a global American company effectively responding to the current situation. It has worldwide integrating roles that manage product lines across geographic profit centers. They are to manage product development on a global basis. Regions manage the manufacturing, although worldwide sourcing from two plants is used. Sales and service are managed by countries. They also have extensive joint ventures and equity arrangements around the world, as well as research projects being conducted at universities.

Since they are now just emerging, network organizations will undoubtedly present implementation and managerial problems, some of which are currently unfolding. For example, the question arises as to the origin of the management talent for, let us say, a joint venture. Should management be drawn from one parent? Both parents? From outside? If a combination of all, then what should the mix be? Even more troublesome is the issue of ultimate accountability of the management of such a joint venture. What if the parent companies disagree about future directions or over specific activities? Which parent serves as the ultimate tiebreaker? According to what logic?

In the case of strategic alliances, problems of a different type emerge. When firms from the same industry are engaged in a cooperative venture, how do they cooperate on one set of tasks while simultaneously competing directly in various product/market arenas?

In summary, for diversified, global firms acting as a single entity, it can be demonstrated that in most instances, matrix designs are the appropriate organizational response to their strategic position. In the case of network organizations, however, there are far more questions than there are answers.

3
The Pathways of Evolution in Organizations

Jerald Hage

Previous conceptions of what constitute the most appropriate organizational forms are influenced by contingency theory, popular in both organizational sociology and management research, since the simultaneous publication of Fielder's contingency theory of leadership (1967) and Lawrence and Lorsch's contingency theory of structural differentiation and integration (1967). Contingency theories in sociology are usually built around different variables, most typically technology and size (for a review of these theories, see Hage 1980). Most of these theories, whether in management or in organizational sociology, have usually related the best choice of form to some aspects of the environment, typically what is called the task environment. In a number of them uncertainty has played a key role (Duncan 1972). These theories, however, usually specify only a few kinds of structure or design, usually four (see Perrow 1967, Thompson 1967, Hickson et al. 1969, Mintzberg 1979, Hage 1980, Tosi and Carroll 1983), because only a few environments are stipulated. These environments have been called large and small, uncertain and certain, dynamic and stable, and so forth.

These models provide a convenient starting point for a theory of the future. If we can stipulate how each of these environments is changing, then we can anticipate better the new organization forms required. The thesis of this chapter is that there are different starting points, which in turn dictate different pathways. Furthermore, pathways into the future can take several different routes, depending on whether the major changes are occurring in the tastes and demands of the consumer, in the technology available, or in both. Environmental effects on organizations, as many managers are well aware, are also unfolding incrementally in some instances, very rapidly in others. An important distinction must therefore be made between evolution, which is occurring in many industrial contexts, and revolution, or discontinuous change, which is occurring in some of them. By starting with models that were effective during the past thirty years, it becomes easier to ascertain how each model should or might transform itself. This kind of analysis allows managers to plan the evolution of the firm and, it is hoped, to proceed more rapidly along the best pathway for their businesses.

The growth in scientific research and especially in the investment in product research and development means the creation of many new environmental niches and the elimination of others. Consumers have become much more sophisticated in their evaluations, more demanding of quality, and more interested in personal service. The spread of automation, the development of franchises and of new ways of routinizing services, are all having a considerable effect on the environments of most businesses. The problem is in specifying the most appropriate organizational designs or situations under these new conditions.

Although both management and organizational sociology discuss contingency theory, they differ in the way in which they think about organizational structure or design or form (contrast a standard management text with Hall 1987). Management has been most concerned with the placement of departments and divisions and their coordination and control. Organizational sociology has focused much more on abstract concepts like complexity, centralization, stratification, and the like. This chapter adopts this latter perspective.

The first section examines a sociological theory about the most appropriate design and structure in four different environments, which are defined by the nature of their technology and the kind of market demand that they face. Although our perspective is drawn from organizational sociology, it is nevertheless close to that of many management theorists, including Tosi and Carroll (1983), Mintzberg (1979), and Daft (1983); it is also a synthesis of microeconomics and organizational theory. It does not represent the only way in which environments can be defined, but it does have the advantage of attempting to integrate a variety of disciplines and empirical findings (see Hage 1980 for an extensive review).

Given these four organizational types or models, each located in a specific kind of environment, the second section moves to a discussion of the pathways of evolution and revolution that are occurring in these environments. Several different organizational forms are suggested, not necessarily always on the basis of research on what is currently happening, but on the basis of the logical connection between the environmental changes and their implications for the most appropriate form. For example, traditional or craft firms are evolving in many different ways. Large mechanical-organic firms or the large, high-tech companies are changing fundamentally. And the small, high-tech firms also have a number of possible configurations.

My objective is to develop a *normative* theory about the futures of organizations, a theory about the links between the characteristics of the environment and the structure and design of the firm. Granted it has the disadvantage of not always being backed by current research evidence—I cannot point to the ten largest corporations for an example of what I mean—but it has, I believe, the advantage of possibly seeing further into the future. Some of the insights are drawn from a pilot study of small, high-tech companies, and others are drawn from the direction in which some firms are moving, so that the theory is not completely devoid of empirical support.

The major advantage of a normative theory is that it provides managers with a way of coding their environment and planning change. If the managerial team perceives a change in an environmental condition, it can begin to guide the organization toward the most appropriate form. This kind of futurizing, rather than projecting trends, as do most of the current writers on the future (see Naisbitt 1982, Toffler 1981, Peters and Waterman 1982), allows the greater likelihood of predicting discontinuous change and gives a more complex view of the variety of organizational forms and environments.

Four Types of Organizational Systems

Most managers probably view their markets as their single most distinctive characteristic. Markets can be classified in several ways. We can look at their size, product differentiation, the way in which price is calculated by the consumer, and so forth. With this in mind, markets—which is only one dimension of the environmental situation—have been classified on the basis of whether they are (1) segmented or specialized and dominated largely by tastes, (2) mass, with a largely undifferentiated product, (3) limited mass, built around large product groups, or (4) highly specialized, or even customized. Although microeconomics assumes that each of these markets is dominated by price, the way the price of the product is calculated by the consumer is quite different. In the mass market, the consumer searches for large volumes or quantities of a product relative to the price. In the semimass market, however, quality becomes very important. Furthermore, the meaning of quality to the consumer is complex. It may mean the durability of the product, the reduction in error, or savings in operating expenses. But quality may also mean the addition of other attributes. Rather than as a mere product, it might be evaluated on the basis of its environmental impact, its health impact, its fashion statement or aesthetics, its technological superiority or advance, or its capacity for saving time or providing convenience. The list of attributes is endless, and more critically, consumers want them in different combinations. Concerns about quality and the desire for multiple attributes change the nature of competition. Price and *price alone* are no longer the determinant of who succeeds in the marketplace.

In the customized or individualized product markets, a whole series of specific criteria or specifications play an important role in the purchase. The consumer wants to participate actively in the design of the product and is concerned about the quality of service provided both before and after the sale. Again, the computation of price in this kind of marketplace is even more intangible than it is in the one just discussed.

Obviously, the relationship between demand and price varies in each of these product markets. As quality, the variety of product attributes, and the customization of the product increase in importance, changes in price have less and less impact on demand. Prices become more and more inelastic because of consumer loyalty.

During the 1950s and 1960s, examples of the first kind of market were local firms such as gourmet stores, independent garages, cleaning firms, boutiques, and most local government services, ranging from fire and police protection to various welfare services. The second market was illustrated by the production of glass, cement, mass-processed foods such as soups and flour, tires, automobiles, steel, and so forth. Many commercial services, such as banking, insurance, and accounting belonged to this category. Similarly, the transportation services, especially the railroad and bus lines, were examples, while in the public sector, custodial mental health services and the army provided other illustrations.

The semimass markets were exemplified by drugs, chemicals, business machines, electronics, photocopy machines, ship construction, and so on. In the public sector, universities and hospitals were good examples.

Finally, the last category of firm included manufacturers of rare isotopes, precision instruments, robots, biotechnology, alternative sources of energy, and so forth. We think of the semimass markets as being the large, high-tech markets, and the specialized markets as being the small, high-tech markets.

We can also examine how many competitors there are in each of these market contexts. Traditional firms compete against a large number of other small firms, and they do so by providing for and meeting the needs of their customers. Their small size and lack of investment in heavy machinery makes them adaptive to changing tastes, which usually change slowly. In contrast, the mass markets are dominated by one large firm and several others. Market concentration is quite high, and investment in plant and equipment is also large. As a consequence, efficiency becomes the dominant performance characteristic.

In contrast, the large firms in the limited mass situation have to worry about quality and maintaining a balance between productivity and innovation in order to maintain their profits. Here rates of technological change are faster because of the greater reliance on basic science than is the case in the previous environmental situation (at least until now, for all of this is changing). Finally, the small, high-tech company focuses on customization and on a much faster rate of product innovation. Again, the small size allows for the flexibility needed to provide the individually designed products.

Anyone familiar with any of these different markets and their technologies knows how much change has been occurring in them during the past decade or two. My characterization is based more on the period of the 1950s and 1960s than that of the 1980s. In fact, this typology of markets can be used to describe the evolution of organizational forms in the United States during the nineteenth and twentieth centuries (for a brief review see Hage 1980).

The first stage in the industrial revolution led to the manufacturing of mass products (Chandler 1977), largely during the nineteenth century, while the second stage, which occurred between the two world wars, saw the rise of industries based more on product groups or families than on a few largely undifferentiated products (Chandler 1962). The fourth type of firm, what I call small high-tech, emerged in the post–World War II period. The second and third types of environmental situations rely upon economies of scale, whereas the fourth represents small-batch production.

Market size is closely associated with the presence of a technology that can produce economies of scale (Perrow 1967, Hull and Hage 1982). There are, therefore, four distinct technological configurations: (1) craft knowledge and machines that are handled separately, (2) an assembly line of machines and unskilled labor, (3) a continuous production process that relies more upon technical specialists, and (4) a firm in which machines are used more as instruments than as parts of the production process. The last two kinds of technology are based on science as distinct from craft or applied knowledge found in the two previous environmental situations and require large inputs of human capital. Descriptions of the first three kinds of production systems are to be found in Blauner (1964) and have figured in a number of research studies (most notably Woodward 1965). The last kind of production system, built more closely around teams, has received much less attention (but see Van de Ven and Delbecq 1976 for an application to groups, and Hull and Hage 1982).

The importance of new knowledge or of research and development varies enormously in each of these different situations. In the traditional or craft organization, the firm itself spends almost no money on research. In the mechanical organizations between 0.1 percent and 1 percent of the sales dollar is allocated to research, but much of it is more market oriented than product development oriented. Little basic research goes on. In the mixed mechanical-organic organizations between 2 and 8 percent of the sales dollar is allocated to research and a certain proportion of it to basic research. Finally, in the small, high-tech firms with the organic form, we find typically 10 percent or more of sales immediately allocated to research, and fundamental research assumes an even larger proportion of the research and development program.

The few types of market-technical complexes each have an appropriate organizational design and form. The large undifferentiated market, with the assembly line technology so important for economic growth during the 1880s through the 1950s, uses a mechanical or a bureaucratic structure, as outlined by Weber (1946) and Burns and Stalker (1961). The organic forms are for small-batch, high-tech markets and would appear to be the most important type today—although this too is changing. Both the traditional and the mixed mechanical-organic models are off this main diagonal.

The most important characteristics of the markets—the performances needed to achieve profits, the structure, and the inputs of these firms—are listed in figure 3–1. The basic point is that the mechanical structure consists of a large number of unskilled or semiskilled workers and many general managers

Traditional-Craft Model

Performances
  Adapted to local needs, tastes
  Mixture of quantity/quality
  Easy to start up

Structure
  Crafts, semiprofessions
  Centralized, but job autonomy
  Small administrative component
  Low formalization

Environmental Contingencies
  Moderate, but local demand
  Partially standardized service
  No economies of scale
  Simple technologies

Resources
  Crafts, artisans
  Simple technology
  "Family capital"
  Small size

Mechanical Bureaucratic Model

Performances
  Large quantity of outputs
  Efficiency: low cost per unit of output
  Productivity: minimum labor per
    unit of output

Structure
  Small variety of specialists
  Generalists as administrators
  Highly centralized
  Authority based on position
  Fixed leader
  Highly stratified
  Clear roles and responsibilities,
    high formalization

Environmental Contingencies
  Large demand for services
  Standardized service
  Economies of scale
  Simple technologies

Resources
  Unskilled labor
  Machine technology (where
    appropriate)
  Capital intensive
  Large size

Mixed Mechanical-Organic

Performances
  Quality and quantity
  Moderate innovation
  Moderate efficiency
  Productivity and adaptability

Structure
  Engineers, specialists
  Professional field agents
  Centralized and decentralized
  Some components mechanically
    structured and some components
    organically structured

Environmental Contingencies
  Moderate to large demand
  Multiple products from same
    technology
  Economies of scale
  Complex technologies

Resources
  Skilled workers
  Sophisticated technology
  Capital intensive
  Large size

Organic-Professional Model

Performances
  Custom-made products/services
  Innovation
  High quality
  Adaptable to changing conditions

Environmental Contingencies
  Small, but rational demand
  Nonstandardized service
  No economies of scale
  Complex technologies

Structure
  Large variety of specialists
  Professionals as administrators
  Highly decentralized
  Authority based on skill
  Shifting leader
  Highly egalitarian
  Nondefined roles and shifting
    responsibilities

Resources
  Professionals
  High technology
  Venture capital
  Small size

Figure 3–1. The Causes of Performance Levels

who perform routine paper work. Its power structure is highly centralized. At the other extreme is the organic structure, with a small number of employees, many of whom have college degrees (even Ph.D.s, depending upon the particular industry). Its complex structure is decentralized. The mixed mechanical-organic structure is typically found in the multidivisional company first studied by Chandler (1962). In these companies, the research and development is organized on organic principles, while the mechanical principles are employed in the production of semimass products. Finally, the craft organization relies upon semiprofessionals or crafts people who are given considerable job autonomy, while strategic decisions are concentrated in the owner, who usually has come up from the ranks. (More detail about the nature of the production process, managerial control processes, and the like can be found in Hage 1980.) The intent here is mainly to describe the previous four typical forms and their environmental situations in order to highlight the evolution from its starting point. Again, our major concern is the *future*, not the past.

Different Pathways of Evolution

The Futures of the Traditional Form

Since figure 3–1 is built around the market-technical complex, changes in either technology or the nature of the market would move a particular industrial group with a traditional or craft organization into one or another pathway of evolution. Some discontinuous change in the nature of the technology used by a traditional firm may occur, allowing the firm to develop mass production in an area where previously none existed. The most striking example of this has been in fast foods. McDonald's, for instance, developed an assembly line approach to the making of hamburgers and several other standardized food products.

Their success has been copied in a number of different areas where semiprofessional services (such as house selling and accounting) and other quasi professions (which are heavily routinized and as yet not dependent on new technology) have predominated. Franchising is in many ways a new form of mechanical organization and one that avoids some of the many problems of the mechanical form. Typically, the small size of the units encourages greater personal commitment. In addition, the manager is also an owner sharing in the profits. This has a considerable effect on the commitment of the management and thereby on the manager's relationships with the workers, all of whom he or she knows by name. Franchising is a useful way of handling services in a society that increasingly is characterized by services. One can imagine that this technique will easily be applied to many of the remaining stores on Main Street. It is indeed happening in chains of boutiques, health food stores, hardware stores, bookstores, and other specialty stores that used to be individually owned and operated. (By *specialty store* I do not mean the discounters, which are much more a characteristic of industrial society.)

Discontinuous change in the traditional form can also occur because of the development of new technologies. The most dramatic example has been the marriage of the computer to the linotype machine, which has eliminated the need for printers in many of the newspaper and magazine printing presses. It is next to impossible to predict when such discontinuous changes will occur. But when they do, the organization form must move from the traditional to either the organic or the mechanical form, depending upon whether the new technology requires the use of professionals, as it does in the newspaper and magazine business, or results in "deskillization," as it has in the assembly line production of prefabricated homes. Prefabricated homes provide another example of an area in which mass production technologies have made a sizable dent in what used to be a traditional market.

Some of the most interesting changes in craft or traditional organizations, however, have been occurring in the public sector side as a result of the investment in social science research. The police department, the primary school, and the welfare agency have been evolving toward organic organizations, or what Mintzberg (1979) might call professional bureaucracies. Concretely, this means that as the scope of work enlarges and new technologies are introduced into the organization, the organizational structure becomes much more complex and the power structure more decentralized. A dramatic example of this can be seen in the changes occurring in primary schools. Special education has meant that more teachers have been attempting to treat each student as an individual and to provide those students with programs that build upon their strengths. Alongside the classroom teacher, many remedial skills teachers have been brought in to help with particular problems. Specialists in library science are common, as are vocational counselors, psychologists, and many others. All are making the primary school more and more "high tech." This evolution will continue as the growth in knowledge about learning disorders increases and as the investment in research on pedagogy produces more results.

But changes in technology are not the only causes of this shift. Another is the changes in tastes. In many areas, the consumer wants the lowest price, encouraging the routinization of crafts. We have seen the development of chains of automobile repair facilities specializing in specific services that can be routinized and produced at low cost, whether it be an oil change, a muffler replacement, a tire change, or a tune-up.

One problem with discussing the evolution of craft organizations is that frequently several tendencies are occurring simultaneously. Simultaneously we observe the emergence of fast food chains and gourmet restaurants. Some consumers want customized homes and therefore seek individualized attention from builders and architects (Kidder 1985); others want low-cost housing and accept prefabrication or mobile homes. Thus it is possible for craft industries such as home construction to evolve in two different directions, toward the mechanical form for mass production and economies of scale, and toward the organic form for more individualized product design. Again, in both areas technological developments make this evolution more possible.

These parallel processes of evolution are another way in which many more environmental niches will be created in the future. We can have both customized service and routinized service relative to the same service. We can purchase cheap standardized products and expensive individualized ones. This is not only because different consumer groups exist, but also because the consumer has multiple needs. He wants both fast food convenience and tasty gourmet foods, both an expensive Porsche and a cheap Yugo.

Finally, I should briefly comment on a little-noticed trend that is affecting many of the small craft organizations. As products in other areas are built or provided with more quality, the craft is affected. A striking illustration is provided by the changes occurring in the quality of automobiles and the improvement in gas mileage. The movement from fifteen miles to a gallon (on average) to twenty-six miles to a gallon has meant that one half of the gasoline stations in the United States have disappeared during the past decade. Similarly, the number of garages has been reduced by the same proportion, because repair and servicing is now less frequently needed as the quality has improved. Under these circumstances, what does a garage owner do? He may either join a chain, such as Midas, to take advantage of franchising, or decide to specialize in customized service for imports or luxury cars.

There are then three basic drives that are gradually reducing the number of traditional or craft firms and agencies: (1) Changes in tastes, coupled with the development of rationalized production processes that allow for mass production of services and/or products. They lead to the movement toward the mechanical form, a process that has been going on since the industrial revolution. The most common new variety, however, is franchising. (2) Incremental and radical changes in the technology, usually coupled with demand for more customized services and/or products. These lead to the movement toward the organic form or the professional bureaucracy. This relatively new path of evolution will become more and more prevalent as the amount of research and development increases in a number of the basic human services. (3) Finally, the growth in quality in products, eliminating the need for many of the small craft firms that existed in the past. Their decline in number is also coupled in many cases with the growth in franchising.

The Futures of the Mechanical Organization

Except for some of the movements of traditional industries in the direction of mass production, the most dramatic changes in the American economy are occurring in the mechanical or bureaucratic form of organization and for several reasons. Consumers in many areas are now demanding products with quality, or at least perceived quality. In the opening chapter, mention was made of the trade deficit. In many instances, the deficit reflects the American perception of higher quality in European and Japanese products. For example General Motors produced a car, the J car, in the late 1970s that it thought would be competitive with Japanese models and priced it accordingly. The car sold poorly because it was perceived to be of low quality. In one area after another American businesses have been losing market share because they cannot—or in some cases are deemed unable to—produce high-quality products at competitive prices. Furthermore, consumers are increasingly interested in more product differentiation, which American mass production industries had previously been unwilling to provide. The examples of the new consumer preferences are everywhere and are well documented in books like *The Third Wave* (1981) and *Megatrends* (1982). Toffler (1981) correctly saw this movement away from mass society as one of the fundamental characteristics of our time. It has enormous implications for the mechanical form of organization. It means the end of the assembly line, except for the movement of some industries such as fast foods and franchises into mass products or services. Demassification, too, requires moving toward a new form of production process that must worry about achieving economies of scale across a variety of different products and must show more flexibility if production demand changes rapidly.

The spread of automation has corresponded to changes in consumer preferences in many of these same industrial sectors (Collins and Hage 1987). Automation allows for enhancement of quality and, when the production lines are designed correctly, for much more product differentiation at the same time. The flexibility of the production line is a key necessary characteristic. Clearly, a number of American companies are evolving toward the mixed mechanical-organic form as they attempt to cope with the new market demands and to exploit the newly available technologies. Computer-assisted design, computer-assisted manufacturing, completely automated factories, robots, and other technological advances are allowing for the possibility of designing production lines with a great deal of flexibility, which are simultaneously capable of achieving economies of scale across a much larger product group.

We can learn more about the ways in which the mechanical form should evolve by studying the mistakes that have been made by many American companies as they have attempted to evolve. These include the involvement of the worker, the investment in research and development, the importance of service, and other issues.

As yet, many managers do not understand that to produce quality they must involve the worker in the production process (Shaiken 1985). Quality and flexibility are best built into a production process by relying not only upon sophisticated technologies but also on the workers' skills and experience. Instead, many companies have been using the new automated equipment as a way of controlling the workers (Shaiken 1985) rather than involving them in the production process. Again, instead of mobilizing the human capital of the skilled worker to ensure greater flexibility, many companies have used the new automated equipment to replace skilled labor with unskilled labor. The worker is therefore left out of the equation.

This is a major mistake and for a number of reasons. The first and most obvious is that the greatest potential of the new machines is likely to be achieved only if the skilled worker helps management learn how to exploit the opportunities.

The second reason is the importance of the workers in moving new products into production. The success of high-tech companies requires a close tie between research and development, production and marketing. Lawrence and Lorsch's great contribution (1967) was to assert that as structural differentiation increased, so did the need for much greater integration. They stressed, however, the integration of managers. Although I do not disagree with their point I also want to emphasize that the integration of workers is as necessary for the production of new and innovative products. The more innovative the product, the more changes in the production process are necessary. As product lives become ever shorter, the necessity for rapid alteration of production processes becomes ever more the criterion of survival. This is best achieved with the cooperation of labor and not its active hostility.

Cooperation is won by retaining jobs when new equipment is introduced and by listening to and indeed actively seeking workers' ideas and advice on how to design the production process as each new product is launched. The design of the production line has been treated too much as a specialty of the engineer. As product lives shorten, there is no longer enough time to keep redesigning the production line. In any case, this is best done by having those who work in production cooperate with the engineers. Likewise, it requires the active involvement of the research and development people as well. All this means integration at the bottom of the hierarchy and not only at the top.

The difficulties of moving new products into production are perhaps best illustrated by the example of AT&T, which has an outstanding research laboratory but has not been able to exploit its innovations after selling its separate regional telephone service companies. So far, the company has not been able to move its inventions into production effectively.

Much has been made of the importance of service in books such as *In Search of Excellence*. Again, service is not just an issue of cooperation with the customer after the product is sold; increasingly it also implies cooperation with the customer in the *design* of the production process and the product.

Many of these mechanical companies have not increased their research and development budgets as much as they should. One could argue that despite the large increases in such investment that have occurred during the past decade in companies such as General Motors (whose R & D budget has jumped from less than 1 percent to upwards of 2 percent), research and development investment has not been sufficient in the firms that are in the process of evolving toward the mixed mechanical-organic form because of the greater differentiation in their markets and the availability of automation. If we use the percentages spent on research and development by the mixed mechanical-organic firms during the 1960s as our basis for comparison, we find that the old mechanical firms are far below the 2–3 percent of sale dollar that was characteristic then.

Why should U.S. Steel, Goodyear, and other companies that were and in some cases still are mechanical spend so much money on research and development? The reason is that the consumer wants high-tech cars, tires, foods, cement, and other products. Furthermore, research and development is necessary to provide the increasing variety of products needed and/or desired for the many groups described in chapter 1. As product lives continually decline, these companies must worry about developing new products to maintain themselves. Product differentiation means, for example, specialized kinds of cars such as four-wheel-drive Jeeps, convertibles, leisure vans, sports cars, and the like. The same holds for tires on the cars, containers, and even a seemingly basic product like cement.

Finally, research and development must worry about creating new production processes that allow for the economies of scale across this large product diversity.

Another important characteristic of the mixed mechanical-organic form which is not being adopted by many of the mechanical firms as they evolve is the multidivisional structure. New divisions should be created for new kinds of products groups and consumers.

For example, it would make more sense for Sears Roebuck to try to adapt its stores to the particular locations and the local needs rather than to attempt to have all stores appeal to all kinds of consumers. The same can be said for the automobile companies. Rather than consolidate their automotive divisions, as General Motors did, it would be better if they attempted to differentiate their product lines, marketing, and customer service.

In addition to effectively exploiting the new automated technologies and emphasizing both new product development and products that have higher quality and a greater variety of attributes, another change that the mechanical organizations have to introduce is reducing the size of their work force. Most of the large mechanical firms have already lost a third to a half of their employees and work force, but this is still not enough. One of the big adjustments that companies must make as they move from mass production to semimass production and to a concern about quality is the enormous downsizing of the company that is required. Automation reduces the need for unskilled labor, while the introduction of computers reduces the need for middle management. The reductions in the size of General Motors, U.S. Steel, the tire manufacturers, and now even AT&T have made the news headlines. Yet this process of attrition is hardly over.

Paradoxically, the more these companies are able to adopt the mixed mechanical-organic form and produce products of quality, the more they will be victims of their own success. If the quality of an automobile is improved so that the car lasts two years longer than the previous average of four years, this implies a 50 percent reduction in the number of automobiles that are required, assuming the same size market (unless there is an increase in income level and a willingness to own multiple cars). Today, in one area after another, one sees sizable layoffs as the improvements in quality make their influence felt on product demand. This is another reason why product differentiation and research and development become so necessary. They can potentially counteract the market demand lost through quality improvements.

One theme running through much of what has been said so far is that the managers in the mechanical organizations must learn how to decentralize their decision making. They must seek the advice of workers and achieve better integration between the different parts of the organization, most notably research and development, production, and marketing. Much of the original thesis of Lawrence and Lorsch (1967) applies: As there is an increase in structural differentiation—and we have indicated several different kinds, both new divisions and new departments, and multiple levels—organizations must increase their integration.

To summarize, the mechanical forms must add research and development departments and thus increase the complexity of their organizational structure. Relative to organizational design, they must create new divisions, each with larger product groups, that provide more service both before and after sale. The hardest part of the shift requires decentralizing their decision making and especially including the worker in the development of production lines that are flexible and capable of redesigning the production lines for innovative products. This means integration at the bottom of the hierarchy.

The Futures of the Mixed Mechanical-Organic Form

The two previous types of organizations have only a few pathways of evolution ahead of them; the mixed mechanical-organic form, on the other hand, has more possibilities. In the past, the two key features of the mixed mechanical-organic form have been a large research and development laboratory, usually located at central headquarters, and although R & D was centralized, the decision making in this part of the firm was decentralized. In contrast, production was decentralized geographically, but the decision making within this part of the firm was centralized. The other distinctive feature has been the existence of many divisions, each corresponding to a product group. Most of the firms discussed in the book *In Search of Excellence* represented this type of organizational form. However, as is clear from their discussion, a considerable amount of evolution has been occurring in these firms.

The first and most fundamental change is the decentralization of R & D units, which are now moved to each of the different divisions since each has quite separate needs. The role of the central research and development laboratory, even for fundamental research, is, therefore, being phased out. This change provides at least an opportunity for better coordination between research and development on the one hand and production on the other hand, and recognizes the need for different research programs.

The second and equally important change is the multiplication of divisions, which may or may not be related. There are a variety of conglomerates, usually classified in terms of whether their business is related or unrelated (see Donaldson 1985). The reality is that as product groups become more and more complex in their combinations of attributes, research and production programs in one part of the business increasingly have implications for other programs. The movements of the automobile industry toward robot production and toward the purchase of electronic firms represent two examples in which the distinction between what is related and what is not related becomes more and more obscure with the increasing interdependence of products. Under these circumstances the advice of "sticking to your knitting" given in *In Search of Excellence* is less and less relevant. Needless to say, some business groups are much farther apart than others, and there is some logic in growing organically as the possibilities of product development move firms into new research arenas. As this occurs, companies can purchase other firms that might provide the kind of expertise needed. However, this is *not* the only approach. More and more common is the development of joint ventures, a future form of the mixed mechanical-organic firm discussed later. But the point remains that as products and services are produced in varying combinations and with a variety of attributes, they inevitably involve a variety of industrial sectors.

To exploit these opportunities, however, means that central headquarters has to delegate ever more autonomy to the separate divisions and the profit centers within them. This has a parallel in higher education where academic departments in universities must be given increasing autonomy so that they can function effectively in a more complex environment. This process in education, labeled *decoupling* by Weick (1976), is equally apt for describing what needs to be done in the business world as well.

One interesting question is what the relationship between divisions of a multidivisional firm should be in the future. Control by central headquarters stifles initiative, but providing a lot of autonomy does not automatically provide synergy. We need to develop forms of integration between the divisions in a multidivisional company. For example, the best way of linking the many new research centers created by the decentralization of research needs to be explored. As the number of divisions grows, this problem becomes both more difficult to solve and yet much more necessary. One possibility is to create networks.

The third change and again one that has gone largely unnoticed is the decrease in the size of companies as they too put ever more emphasis on quality production. These declines are not as great as in the mechanical organizations, but they exist nevertheless. Even IBM and General Electric are beginning to lay off workers. What is not clear is how much central headquarters is being reduced in size as its control is given to the divisions and profit centers that are allowed to act with more autonomy. But I would argue that this is a necessary step if these aggregates of companies are to achieve flexibility.

One could argue that these three changes—the decentralization of research and development with its better integration with production, the proliferation of divisions, and the downsizing of companies—are "more of the same." In other words, they represent continued evolution in the direction taken in the past, with the possible exception of the decline in size, which is something new.

Are other changes occurring where one could more readily argue for a mutation in form or a more fundamental change? I believe there are. In the future and even now the mixed mechanical-organic firm will develop a number of new shapes and configurations that are not easily described by the term *multidivisions* but are loosely grouped under the term *networks of organizations* (see the chapter by Power). By *network* we mean that decision making is no longer part of some hierarchy but is shared among autonomous units. This is a new form of governance and is much more complex than even the decentralized or internal network form found in the organic model of Burns and Stalker (1961). As networks proliferate, the boundaries of the multidivisional organization become less and less distinct.

What will produce the variety of shapes and configurations is the kind of networks. There appear to be four basic kinds of networks, with different companies displaying quite different mixtures of these networks. Networks will be built around the production process, both backward to suppliers and forward to the customers, around joint ventures with other firms, around venture capital, involving former employees, and finally around research consortiums of various kinds. In turn, this allows for much greater variety in the pathways of evolution and in the types of successful forms. We can imagine different companies specializing in different types of networks. Although Naisbitt (1982) describes networking in his book *Megatrends* as one of the fundamental trends, he puts more emphasis on information and the sharing of resources than on the types of production and research networks I have just outlined.

There are two theoretical points to be made about networks. Networks represent the development of relatively permanent "action sets" (Aldrich 1979)—that is, networks concerned with accomplishing something together. These networks are built to last. Frequently, a network has the image of something fleeting; this is also true of Aldrich's action sets. In the cases below, the dominant characteristic is their duration. Organizations will have to learn how to cooperate, and how even to cooperate with competitors. The second point follows from the first. Since they are not part of the same hierarchy, many of the standard control mechanisms of central headquarters no longer apply. To make these networks work requires social interactional skills and not accounting skills. Negotiation is more important than being able to read the bottom line.

The first kind of network is the reorganization of the production process. In part, it is necessary because more flexibility is achieved by purchasing parts from suppliers rather than producing in-house. In fact, it reflects the need to have close coordination between supplier, producer, and customer as service and customization of the product define the market. Finally, and perhaps more commonly, rapid technological change forces companies to abandon the desire to produce the entire product internally.

Instead of moving in the direction of vertical integration, the mixed mechanical-organic firms gain much greater flexibility by moving in the opposite direction, toward the purchase of parts made by others. However, once this decision is made, it requires close cooperation with the supplier to ensure that the products are made to specification and adhere to quality. (It is this one aspect that deserves the name *network*; there is joint design of the product.)

But to integrate supplier, producer, and customer requires a team effort. This takes time to develop. As a consequence these relationships become much more permanent than neoclassical economics would suggest. Loyalty replaces price because loyalty pays off much better in a fast-changing world.

Nor is flexibility the only gain for the large, high-tech company that follows this strategy of networking. Another is much greater innovation, both in products and in process technologies. Two corporations are better than one—provided they have learned how to work together.

A second kind of network grows out of the increasing interdependence of products described earlier. As the implications of research and development indicate the desirability of moving into other industrial sectors, many large, high-tech firms are discovering that the best way of gaining the necessary expertise of production (or of marketing) is to create a joint venture with another firm.

We know little about how joint ventures are coordinated by the participating firms. One can imagine a variety of possibilities. But over time the network form of governance makes the most sense precisely because the future strategies of the joint venture itself will probably imply more collaboration between the two founding firms. As large, high-tech organizations become more and more involved in joint ventures with the same company, we can assume that they will increasingly move toward some form of coordination of their product development and production.

The number of joint ventures has been growing very fast, and as this process continues it should lead to a restructuring of the firm's decision making at the top. The boundaries between organizations will become less distinct as a larger share of the companies' entire production will be involved in joint ventures.

Joint ventures with other large companies are not, however, the only possibility. Many small companies, biotechnology being one example, have difficulty producing and marketing their products that require some production volume. One solution for the small, high-tech companies is to form joint ventures with the large companies so as to keep some kind of control over the production process. In turn, some large, high-tech companies rely upon the small, high-tech companies to do research and development for them in areas that do not require large resources. The small, high-tech company then produces the prototypes for the large, high-tech company.

Still a third kind of network, and one that differs somewhat from the joint venture although it shares many of its characteristics, is the development of joint research consortiums. The computer industry is the most striking example, but it is not the only case. The National Science Foundation, for instance, has launched a campaign to create some 150 engineering research centers jointly funded with a coalition of business organizations. The direction of these centers is being shared by the businesses and the universities involved. These represent quite a different kind of network but one that is critical for developing complex research projects that neither the firm nor the government could afford with its own resources. Freeman in his analysis of the economics of industrial innovation (1982) observes that what gave birth to the mixed mechanical-organic organization or the large, high-tech firm of today during the second industrial revolution was the large amounts of money that had to be invested in research and development. Developing a mainframe computer, nylon, cellophane, the telephone transmission lines, and many modern drugs could not be done cheaply. It required investment in large research and development laboratories over very long time periods. As the costs of some research projects keep escalating, firms are forced into joining forces either with the government or with their competitors and more typically with both. Presumably these joint efforts will feed more cooperation between firms in the same industries and may also increase the number of joint ventures within industrial sectors. So far, most joint ventures have been between industrial sectors rather than within them.

This process of evolution has barely begun, and it is difficult to imagine all of its ramifications. One can expect that there will be a number of conflicts as well, as different companies fight over who should gain access to which patents. It raises a number of interesting questions as to how to resolve these conflicts between autonomous units, each of which is contributing to the financing of the research. This is where the concept of network proves to be most useful: it draws attention to a new form of governance that is different from either markets or hierarchies (see Ouchi 1981, Hollingsworth and Lindberg, forthcoming).

Our fourth and last kind of network is venture capital among small firms being provided by a large, high-tech company. Some companies like General Electric have invested in the research ideas of their own scientists. As this occurs, one can imagine that larger and larger shares of the large, high-tech firm's profits will come from the venture capital that has been invested in small firms started by their own employees. What kind of relationship is to be maintained with these firms? Presumably not one of direct control but one of providing information and expertise of various kinds. Again, the network principle seems a more apt description of what is probably happening than do the traditional management ideas of coordination and of control. On the one hand, too much of an attempt to control the behavior and strategies of the venture companies will probably destroy them. Exxon destroyed all the high-tech firms it bought because of the heavy-handedness of central headquarters. On the other hand, totally ignoring the small firms is not advisable either, since the large firm has both former personnel and present capital invested.

All four kinds of networks say a great deal in contradiction to what managers learn in business schools. The first principle they are taught is the importance of clear boundaries and responsibilities. The world of networks means a movement away from the concept of single manager responsibility and toward group responsibility and decision making. Many managers will feel uncomfortable within this setting. However, if this analysis is correct, they will not have much choice. As has already been pointed out, the need for flexibility and adaptiveness underlies much of the discussion as to why networking makes sense. But networks are also being forced on organizations because the cost of "going it alone" is now too great, even for some of the largest of firms. Furthermore, the cost problem is not just one of money. It is also a question of human capital cost, *the know-how needed as well*! As the complexity of research and development, the integration of disparate technologies, and uncertainty and risk all grow, the managers in these companies are being forced into networks. They have, indeed, no choice.

Another favorite principle of most managers is the advantage of competition. But networks argue that growth can occur through cooperation even with one's competitors. Networks are built around long-term commitments, the sharing of decision making, and above all the lack of exploitation of the small by the large. The Japanese are demonstrating this as they cooperate to build the next generation of TV transmission equipment. Many managers will find it quite difficult to believe that more can be gained by active cooperation than by competition, at least within the national boundaries. This does not mean that there is not competition at another level. There is but at the international level. Increasingly this competition is happening between the networks of Japan, Inc., and those in the United States, and their counterparts in Europe, whether single country or common market based.

The Futures of the Organic Form

Although the organic form was first discussed some twenty-five years ago (Burns and Stalker 1961), it appears to be the wave of the future, since it was developed on the basis of an extensive study of electronics firms. What could be more representative of the future than electronics firms? Many of the principles of the organic form are probably relevant for firms today, especially those that are evolving toward small-batch production that produces customized products and services.

The most distinctive variables for describing the nature of the structure of organic forms are the network of authority, communication, control, shifting leadership, and a commitment to the advance of technology and/or science. Many of the ideas mentioned by Naisbitt and Aburdene (1985), such as networking, reflect the early insights of Burns and Stalker (1961).

But there are still some pathways of evolution for firms that were organic in the past several decades as they move into the future. The dominant theme in the evolution of the large, high-tech firm is the movement into a variety of production networks. But the dominant theme in the evolution of the organic or small, high-tech firm is the movement into two networks, one internal and one external, but shaped quite differently depending upon the specific scientific speciality involved.

As small, high-tech firms become dominated by scientific research, increasingly they will also begin to absorb the characteristics of the thought patterns of the particular discipline in which they work. For example, if the company works in the area of physics, and especially if it is one of the more theoretically oriented branches, the firm will develop more hierarchical patterns relative to many small, high-tech firms. In contrast, if the firm works in computers, it will place much more emphasis on horizontal linkages. This does not mean that in the physics firm decision making will be centralized but only that the patterns of interaction will be more hierarchical and that there will be lower levels of interaction vis-á-vis the average small, high-tech firm. These insights are based on two pieces of research on the characteristics of interaction in different disciplines (Shinn 1982, Shinn and Hage 1987).

Naisbitt and Aburdene (1985) emphasize the horizontal networks but do not appreciate that these can vary enormously depending on the kinds of cognitive processes employed in different disciplines. Among other descriptions the following apply: deductive reasoning based on mathematics or formal theory, inductive reasoning based on experimental data, reasoning involving simulation with formal analogies, reasoning involving simulation with geometric configurations or patterns, reasoning by analogies, and reasoning based on a quite specific phenomenon that emphasizes detail. Biology, for example, relies upon enumerative induction, construction or correlations, and eliminative induction.

Cognitive styles also entail implications about frequency of communication. To access information and technology, biology relies upon frequent communication between biologists and multiple publics, such as scientists from other disciplines, pharmacists, consumer groups, and so forth. Physics, however, is a self-referencing discipline.

One way of conceptualizing the pathways of evolution of the small, high-tech firm is to imagine a movement toward a series of variations on the theme of the organic firm where each variation is dictated by the nature of the cognitive processes of the scientific discipline, which then imprints on the flow of communication, the sharing of authority, and the choice of control mechanisms. To borrow an analogy from chemistry, we have a series of isotopes that, while sharing the same basic number of parts, differ in the configurations.

But although there are variations in the patterns of interaction, authority, and control, there will also be a striking similarity among the small, high-tech firms. This similarity is not much emphasized in the original Burns and Stalker (1961) model. I expect that structure to be replaced by process. Furthermore, the bulk of the work will be done by teams that should be called process teams as distinct from work teams. We are used to seeing work teams in various areas of highly complex work (Van de Ven, Delbecq, and Koenig 1976), but they are usually involved in research, production, or some other function. More distinctive is the importance of process teams, such as the product development team (which includes a member of the research group), the product development group, the production group, the marketing group, and the quality control group. Although Lawrence and Lorsch (1967) did discuss integration among managers, their examples did not cover the kinds of integration that one sees in the small, high-tech firm of today and especially at the worker level.

To go back to the original Burns and Stalker (1961) model, the small, high-tech firm has really two kinds of networks: one among the managers and another among the professionals or researchers, developers, producers—all of whom have college degrees or graduate degrees (see Hage 1974).

Another difference from the literature on organizations is the fact that structure disappears as the distinctions between positions, departments, and functions gradually erode because so much of the work time is spent in teams that are interfunctional and involve the processes associated with bringing a product from the research laboratory into production. This is not the kind of process that is discussed in the business literature. One might think of these as metaprocesses because they are not involved in production, quality control, marketing, and the like in the ordinary sense. Instead, they are processes that move products through a series of stages that correspond to these functions. The key problem at each step is for all functions to be represented in the group problem solving. This is yet another distinctive characteristic of these new kinds of processes; the emphasis lies not in decision making in the classical sense of the term but instead in group problem solving and creativity.

Megatrends (1982) discusses information networks, which for the small, high-tech company are extremely important. The fast pace of change—most product lives in biotech are less than one year—requires not just a monitoring of the environment but more importantly an integration with the environment. The extensiveness and intensiveness of the network is related to the nature of the discipline and its pattern of interaction. The disciplines that place greater emphasis on the logical deductive method of reasoning are more likely to have less extensive and intensive networks, while those disciplines that generate more of the knowledge from experiments without much theory are at the opposite end of the continuum.

Lawrence and Lorsch (1967) never discussed the problem of integration into the environment or the mechanisms that might be used to achieve this. Their concern was the problem of integrating managers with different temporal horizons. The group problem-solving process teams would seem to overcome the classical problem of integration as Lawrence and Lorsch conceptualized it. Now internal integration, while still important, must include integration into the extant knowledge production networks that are relevant to the firm.

Similarly, Burns and Stalker (1961) did not consider the problem of the shape and configuration of networks outside the firm. Instead, a single internal network was perceived as involving everyone. This is probably because of their focus on electronics firms during the 1950s when the growth in knowledge was much slower.

The distinctive characteristic of the small, high-tech firm of the future is that it will need external networks to keep abreast of the rapid growth in knowledge and to maintain its flow of product development. Again, the pattern and shape of the network configuration will be related to the nature of thought processes, which in turn are probably related to the rate of knowledge advance. Not only do small, high-tech firms vary in the pattern of their external networks, but the mechanisms that are used also vary a great deal. They are worth discussing because they are quite different from the typical managerial processes of control and coordination.

In their pilot study on small, high-tech firms, Shinn and Hage (1987) discovered that the following all represented patterns of coping:

1. The use of doctoral or postdoctoral students on internships as a way of keeping abreast of current developments in the university, with the choice

of the university depending upon whether it is on the frontier of the discipline

2. The use of consultants at the leading universities where the most basic research is being done

3. Search patterns among colleagues in other firms and in other organizations when a problem is confronted that is difficult to solve

Presumably there are mechanisms other than these which were not identified in the research and which need to be examined in future research on the problems and promises of small, high-tech firms.

If the four kinds of production networks in the large, high-tech firm provide four or more pathways of evolution then the eight reasoning needs identified by Shinn provide still more possibilities about the small, high-tech firm. Here have we considered their production networks in joint ventures with either large or small high-tech firms. The possibilities for complexity are growing rapidly! So, let me conclude by summarizing the various ideas developed in this chapter.

Conclusion

To survive managers must decode their present situation and determine in which type of market context they have been located in the past. Then they can more easily predict the pathway of evolution that they are likely to take. Rather than wait for some push from technology, market demand, or competition from overseas, they would be wise to begin the process of evolving now, if it is not already too late to do so.

The traditional firms are moving toward mechanical forms when routinization has occurred and when the consumer is interested in low price. This typically is being arranged through the franchise and is found in many of the commercial services. Another pattern is toward the organic firm, especially when the customer is interested in much more individualized attention and when the technology is growing more complex. This typically occurs in many of the semiprofessions involved in providing public services.

The mechanical form is also disappearing, mainly because most consumers want more differentiated, higher-quality products. In many industries the possibilities for automation exist. American firms, however, are having a great deal of difficulty adjusting, and they need to evolve much further than they have.

Perhaps the most interesting futures are to be found in those firms that many think of as having already stepped into the future, namely, the large, high-tech firms like DuPont, IBM, GE, the research laboratory of AT&T, and the small, high-tech firms that are largely unknown but are represented in the popular mind by the term *Silicon Valley.* The large, high-tech firms are moving to various kinds of production networks, whether with joint ventures, in venture capital investments with their former employees, in product development efforts with their suppliers or their customers, and finally in research and development, which though not a production network involves working with other producers. There are, thus, four major evolutionary or revolutionary pathways.

In contrast, the small, high-tech firms are involved in much more informal networks externally as they attempt to monitor the environment. These vary in both extensiveness and intensiveness. I have identified eight types of reasoning that would predict the shape of the networks. For the small, high-tech company with more than 10 percent of the its sales dollar being involved in mostly basic research, the future means the imprinting of the scientific discipline on the work processes. One of the most important pathways of evolution for the organic firm is away from structure toward process teams, such as the product development teams and the breakdown of the normal distinctions between position, department, and even occupation. Another distinctive pathway for the small, high-tech firm is the development of an external network, one that is essential for the creative process. Again, this is shaped by the nature of the scientific discipline.

Four kinds of industrial age organizations are moving into the future of postindustrial society in quite different ways. The overarching theme is that many more new kinds of organizational forms are being created. But in this new diversity, there is a great deal of order. Each form type is evolutionary in predictable directions and toward relatively known designs. If the members of the managerial team correctly observe the environmental changes, they can build their future securely.

4
Anticipating Organization Structures

Daniel J. Power

*T*ry to think ahead to the year 2015 and visualize your current work setting. What will have changed? What will be the same? Will you have the same job? Will you still be working? Will your current employing organization exist in 2015? Now, try again to look ahead to the year 2015 and visualize your encounters with employees of other organizations. Will your banker be providing the same services? Will your accountant be replaced by a computer program? Will your doctor work for a health services cooperative?

Current trends indicate that during the next twenty-five years the economic, political, and social environments of most organizations in industrialized societies will become increasingly diverse, complex, and dynamic. As a result, by the year 2015 many business and government organizations will be restructured and reconstituted by merger, divestiture, and/or liquidation. If managers discuss future organization settings and the work encounters and interactions that may occur in them, they can successfully anticipate needed changes in strategy and structure. Also, it seems logical that if managers try to anticipate a number of alternative future environments (see Hawken, Ogilvy, and Schwartz 1982), then they are more likely to design and structure "new" organizations that will be adaptable to a range of plausible environments. This chapter is speculative, but it is based on three explicit future scenarios and on major organization theories. This knowledge base was combined with a dose of imagination to anticipate six "new" organization structures.

In the academic literature, there is some disagreement about how to measure and categorize organization structures (see Blackburn 1982, Miner 1982, Pugh, Hickson, and Hinings 1969). But in general, the term *organization structure* is used to refer to the specific manner in which authority is distributed to managers (Weber 1946) and to how an organization is segmented into task units and the patterns of relationship among those units (Thompson 1967). In this chapter, the concept of organization structure is discussed in terms of the following major elements: the definition and composition of major task units, governance and reporting relationships, communication and information systems, measurement and reward systems, and planning systems (see Galbraith 1977, Nadler, Hackman, and Lawler 1979).

The next section of this chapter discusses a causal model of organization structural change. The major conclusion is that anticipated changes in the determinants of organization structure will require new organization structures. Then the third section discusses three environmental scenarios and the new organization structures that seem especially adaptive under each scenario. Six "new" organization structures are the major contribution of the essay, but no attempt is made to develop a complete typology of organization structures. The final section is a brief commentary on the future of organizations and on the need for new organization structures.

A Model of Structural Change

Modern organization theories (see Burns and Stalker 1961, Chandler 1962, Lawrence and Lorsch 1967, Mintzberg 1979, Thompson 1967, Weber 1946, Woodward 1965, 1970) discuss three primary factors or contingencies that determine the appropriateness of various organization structures. These theories and recent empirical findings (see Miner 1982) indicate that strong relationships exist among an organization's environment, its technical systems, its strategic actions, the appropriateness of its structure, and its performance and general effectiveness. In general, current evidence indicates that organizations operating in the same environments executing similar strategic actions and employing the same technical systems and resources will be more or less effective depending upon the appropriateness of their structures, including communication and information systems (Galbraith 1977, Miner 1982, Mintzberg 1979). In my opinion, current theory suggests that the existence of new environments, new technical systems, and new strategic actions will require new organization structures.

Articles in the popular press and various books on "the future" provide many reasons for believing that managers will encounter new environments and new technical systems in the next twenty-five years. I am confident that these same managers will innovate and create new strategic actions and will design new and more appropriate organization structures. Let us briefly examine anticipated changes in these primary determinants of structural change and the structural solutions that may be most appropriate.

New Environments. Many authors (Clarke 1986, Naisbitt 1982, Toffler 1981) argue that industrialized countries have entered a new era called an "information age" or "postindustrial society." The exact characteristics of this new age are disputed, but the assertion that a major social discontinuity has occurred is quite widely accepted. Industrialized countries are moving from a consumer/

products-oriented economy to a knowledge and service economy. This major change from past trends will create an extended period of great economic and social uncertainty.

Currently, leaders in industrialized countries are encouraging free markets and greater competition; they are removing barriers to megamergers that will create increased economic concentration; they are reluctantly removing trade barriers so many industries are becoming global in scope; and they are increasing research and development funds, encouraging the search for knowledge and speeding up the dissemination of new knowledge and products. Because of these major trends, I have concluded that most managers will encounter radically new and different organization environments in the next twenty-five years. The environment will likely be very complex, information intensive, rapidly changing, and dependent on advanced technologies. In my opinion, objective environmental uncertainty and complexity should increase for all organizations. Feedback about organizational performance should become increasingly ambiguous and delayed. More information will definitely be generated and disseminated in Western societies. In general, I have concluded that managers and planners will find it very difficult to use reactive management approaches in the future.

A number of authors have suggested structural responses to what they perceived as future new environments. Trist (1977) argued that "only organizations based on the redundancy of functions have the flexibility and innovative potential to give the possibility of adaptation to turbulent conditions" (273). Burns and Stalker (1961) argued that as the rate of technological and market change increases managers must develop more organic organization structures. They contended that these organic organization structures should include a "network structure of control, authority and communications," an emphasis on more lateral communication that resembles consultation, changing task groups, and dispersed responsibility and leadership. Bennis (1967) argued twenty years ago that new, complex, and turbulent environments would mean the demise of bureaucracies. Herbst (1976) suggested that autonomous work groups are the appropriate nonbureaucratic structure for dealing with turbulent environments. He suggested that large organizational structures can be created by linking autonomous groups and by creating a network of networks. Lawrence and Lorsch (1967) offered a similar remedy. They hypothesized that organizations in highly uncertain environments require a highly differentiated and integrated structure for effective performance. Finally, Mintzberg (1979) concluded that (1) the more dynamic the environment, the more organic the required structure, (2) the more complex the environment, the more decentralization that is needed, and, (3) the more diverse the environment, the more divisionalization that should exist in the organization.

New Technical Systems. Many managers will acquire, develop, and install radically different technical systems for their organizations during the next twenty-five years. Automation is expanding its scope of applications and diffusing rapidly to a wide range of companies. Toffler (1981) suggested that in the future new technologies would allow consumers actually to produce some of the goods they consume; we will become prosumers. Managerial work technologies are also becoming more widely accepted and more powerful. New computer and telecommunications technologies are speeding information flows, and managerial information loads are increasing. Executive workstations are becoming a major management tool, and these technologies are likely to change organizations and managerial work. Radical technological changes are occurring that can significantly alter organization management, production, and service delivery systems. In my opinion, current evidence indicates that the major technological innovations that will affect organizations are related to information processing, communications, and production technologies. All of these new technologies will help managers cope with new environments and will in turn create new environments. In particular, changes in information-processing technologies will help managers process much greater quantities of information and communicate with very diverse constituencies inside and outside of the organization, and these same technologies will create a need for such behavior (Power 1983, Power and Hevner 1985).

According to Woodward (1965), technological changes should lead to structural changes. She argued that if a new structure is not adapted to a new technology, the technological innovations will result in organizational failure. Regarding the organization's technical system, Mintzberg (1979) argued that the more automated the technical system the more formalized and bureaucratic the organization structure needs to be. And he argued that the more complex and sophisticated the technical system, the more that decisions need to be made by technical experts and the more that lateral communications and other liaison devices need to be used in the organization structure. Simon (1976, 116) argued that computers and automation are enabling managers to recentralize decision making and move away from decentralized structures. Huber (1984) argued that managers can design organizational structures that exploit information technologies and that improve organizational functioning and increase organizational effectiveness.

New Strategies. Chandler (1962) identified the theoretical link between organization strategy and structure. Chandler is a historian and he concluded from examining four case studies that changes in the economic, social, and technological environments at the turn of the twentieth century resulted in two major new business strategies, vertical integration and diversification, which required a new structural form called divisionalization. During the next twenty-five years, managers should encounter equally new and different environments, and they too will need to identify new strategies and make choices that exploit technological, economic, and social changes. It is likely that managers will adopt strategies exploiting information technologies for competitive advantage. Population increases and ethnic and cultural diversity will present new opportunities for further market segmentation and product niching. The creation of a more global business environment will encourage greater competition and possibly in some situations greater organization cooperation through international joint ventures and partnerships. A perceived need for new products and product innovations will further stimulate the development of new venture units in large corporations. Also, the global conglomerate organizations being created by aggressive managers in Europe, the United States, and Japan will dominate economic activity in some developing countries.

Some managers doubt that anticipating change and planning new strategies is possible because changes in the environment and especially in information technologies are occurring rapidly and the rate of change is accelerating. While it is true that an information explosion is both stimulating the need for strategic change and hindering some adaptive changes, in my opinion that feedback process means that both organization strategy and structural changes must be approached analytically and systematically. This chapter starts the discussion in that direction.

Anticipated Structures

In the next twenty-five years, managers will encounter a variety of radically different environment, technology, and strategy situations, and they will design and develop a variety of new adaptive organization structures. Identifying the full range of possibilities is beyond the scope of this chapter, but six new organization structures can be identified. Table 4–1 summarizes my ideas about the major characteristics of the new structures. The metaphorical labels that I use for the new structures are the "community," the "federation," the "octopus," the "mobile," the "tangled web," and the "skyscraper" structures. More systematic labels are also used in the following discussion to describe the structures. The actual frequency of occurrence of these new structures will largely depend on the broad social and economic events that occur in the new organization environments. As managers redesign their organizations, they should consider at least three plausible environmental scenarios: (1) a period of social and economic stability with slow growth, (2) a period of chronic social and economic disruptions, and (3) a period of conservative social changes and rapid economic growth. A future of social and economic stability and slow growth should encourage economic consolidation and the creation of much larger organizations and the widespread development of "community" and "federation" structures. Chronic social and economic disruptions over an extended period of time may increase the number of organization failures and increase the number of "octopus" and "mobile" organizations.

Table 4-1
Summary of Anticipated Organizational Structures

Anticipated Structures	Major Task Units	Governance and Reporting	Structural Elements Communication and Information Relationships	Measurement and Reward Systems	Planning Systems Systems
Hierarchical, community structure: "The Community"	Diverse sizes and tasks, semi-autonomous, 150–200 SBUs	Pseudo-market mechanisms and many bosses; an oligarchy governs	Real-time managed system, multiple media	Profit, bonuses, and equity	Coordinated operational planning, centralized strategic planning
Homogeneous, democratic structure: "The Federation"	Many similar task units	A representative democracy of owners, flat hierarchy	Real-time, dispersed system with central data bases	Quality, competence, volume, equity	Participative strategic planning, routinized operational planning
Hierarchical, replicated structure: "The Octopus"	Many similar operating divisions	An oligarchy governs; formal reporting	Duplicated operating systems, automated monitoring	Profit, long-term bonuses	Independent operational planning, centralized portfolio planning
Skeletal, multi-function structure: "The Mobile"	Discrete, general task units	Shared decision making, group reporting	Portable, redundant, streamlined	Event-oriented, equity	Frequent, contingency-oriented planning
Related, network structure: "The Tangled Web"	Ambiguous, overlapping units	Informal reporting, one or a few bosses	Accounting oriented, many systems, poor links	Task completion bonuses	Informal planning
Extended, hierarchical structure: "The Skyscraper"	Cascaded, well-defined task units	Explicit relationships, meritocracy	Centralized and integrated system	Multi-dimensional appraisal, varied rewards	Periodic, formal planning

Finally, a period of conservative social changes and rapid economic growth may stimulate the development of many new organizations and especially the proliferation of "tangled webs" and "skyscraper" structures.

Social and Economic Stability and Slow Growth Scenario

An extended period of social and economic stability and slow growth should encourage managers to consolidate and rationalize their organizations, but the goal of improving return on capital in a period of stability and slow growth will be difficult to attain. Technological changes that improve efficiency will be sought, and present trends indicate that many such changes will be adopted and they will improve efficiency. In a period of slow economic growth, it is likely such changes will increase competition, reduce prices for consumers, and create dislocations in labor markets. Managers will be encouraged by competitive pressures to make R & D expenditures, and organizations will adopt technological solutions very rapidly. Most features of this future environment scenario are very conducive to rapid technological change.

The following organization structures should proliferate and prosper given a stability and slow growth scenario:

Hierarchical, Community Structure. A large "community" of organizations can potentially achieve efficiencies in the provision of goods and services. In the community organization, two hundred or more functionally interdependent organizations will be grouped into a five- or six-level hierarchy in which individual organizations retain some autonomy. Both information system–based "market mechanisms" and many specialized "bosses" in finance, marketing, and planning will provide coordination and control for the managerial oligarchy that controls the community. Such a large grouping of organizations can be united with a sophisticated infrastructure of communication and information systems. The information system will facilitate coordinated operational planning by community members. Strategic planning will need to be centralized to ensure a broad view of the "community's" mission and strategy. Maintaining discrete organizations in the community should facilitate management control. Measurement and reward systems can be linked to the "profits" of each member organization. Stock options and other equity arrangements linked to unit performance should encourage the best managers to remain with the community.

Two current organizations, Allied-Signal and Alco Standard, may be forerunners of such an organizational community. Both companies are diverse conglomerates built by acquisition. In both companies acquired companies usually retain part of their identity and autonomy. In Alco Standard many of the component companies were family owned. In many cases family members continue to operate "their company" as a part of Alco Standard. One might anticipate that these family ties and ownership arrangements will help Alco Standard evolve into a full-fledged community of organizations that is governed and controlled by a coalition of owner-managers.

Homogeneous, Democratic Structure. Organizations without hierarchies may evolve in response to improved information technologies and an extended period of economic stability. Small business owners and professionals may merge their businesses and use information and communication technologies to share knowledge and more efficiently use resources. These federated organizations would be managed by the owners, using computer-aided voting mechanisms. Intelligent management support systems could aid owner-managers in implementing collective actions on pricing, inventory management, or investment of resources. Rewards would be tied to the volume of each task entity—for example, each medical office or physician. Also, in professional service federations the quality of work and the competence of each provider would also be assessed by a committee of owner-managers.

Many professional service firms—for example, large accounting and law firms and large universities—provide a structural model that is similar to a federation. These organizations differ from the envisioned federation in a number of ways. One major difference is that professionals are employees rather than "owners" of distinct productive entities that are part of the organization. These service organizations may evolve toward federations. The closest current example of a federation structure is the health maintenance organizations (HMOs) of "independent" physicians. Each independent physician has a private practice, and the physicians collectively own the HMO. Another example is a brokerage firm like Prudential-Bache Securities. At Prudential-Bache established account executives essentially run their own organizations under the corporate administrative umbrella. The federation structure may evolve from various current organization structures and relationships.

Chronic Social and Economic Disruption Scenario

A harsh social and economic environment will encourage managers to be much more cautious. In the next twenty-five years, much social and economic adversity is possible, including political instability, deflation, and chronic, runaway inflation. To cope with such developments, managers are likely to search for structural innovations that will increase organizational flexibility and resilience in the face of adversity.

Chronic inflation has especially significant side effects for businesses and social organizations. For example, redistributions of wealth will occur because of inflation, which affects the purchasing and savings patterns of individuals. Established markets will change in size, dominance, and profitability. Also, the political power of groups and interests is invariably altered by inflation. In many ways chronic inflation, political instability, and resource shortages result in rapid, unpredictable change. In such instances organization decisions must be made rapidly and some organization structures will impede rapid decision making.

Social and economic adversity will slow the implementation of some technological changes. For example, changes involving large capital expenditures for goods likely to become obsolete very quickly will not be as widely adopted in a period of economic turmoil as in a more stable or growth environment. Also, in this environment, the goal of wealth conservation will likely dominate business decision making. Finally, ten or fifteen years of environmental turmoil will eliminate many organizations that have inadequate resources, are poorly managed, and/or have obsolete products or services. Despite or because of the harshness of this scenario two new structures may evolve and proliferate: the hierarchical, replicated structure and the skeletal, multifunction structure.

Hierarchical, Replicated Structure. Managers may find that duplicating operating divisions and coordinating them using information processing and communications technologies is the most adaptive structure for the future. Such independent operating divisions can be treated as severable entities in times of localized crisis. This "octopus," or many tentacled, structure may help top managers explore diverse environments and cope with uncertainty. Structural relationships would have to be quite formalized to ensure that divisions were independent. Most major systems would need to be duplicated in each division. Top managers would manage the "tentacles" from a distance. Profits of a division and special bonuses could be used to control and encourage appropriate managerial actions in the divisions. Portfolio planning and risk analysis could be used to allocate resources to divisions. This structure is in some ways a very specialized multidivisional organization structure (Chandler 1962).

For many years ITT's phone company operations faced harsh environments in many foreign countries. Each phone company was structured so that it was somewhat independent and separable. Disruption of business in one country did not seriously harm the entire company. Such an approach can be used by managers of other types of businesses with multinational expansion strategies and for companies that operate multiple plants or facilities within a single country that is experiencing social and economic disruption. In the years ahead, new "octopus" organizations will likely be more efficient and better coordinated than are current multidivisional organizations because of new information and communication technologies.

Skeletal, Multifunction Structure. This structure should be visualized as a "mobile" organization. It is mobile both in the sense of being transportable or movable (at an economic cost and in a short period of time) and also in the sense of being responsive or changeable, like an abstract sculpture with parts that can move rapidly and easily in response to the slightest breeze. James Thompson (in Rushing and Zald 1976) speculated that complex organizations of the future "will be known not for their components but by their cadres, with each cadre devoted to mobilizing and deploying resources in shifting configurations, to employ changing technologies to meet changing demands" (245).

Creating an organization with a skeletal management staff and with transportable, movable production and service facilities may be very responsive in a harsh environment. This mobile structure requires innovations in production processes and changes in structures to cope with rapid turnover of personnel, skill mismatches, and communication isolation and breakdown. Mobile organizations will need structures and mechanisms similar to those found in military units operating under battlefield conditions. The structure needs to be easy to understand. Rules must be simple and easy to learn. Communication networks will involve small rings of people that are hard to disrupt. These operating units will be linked to a central unit that helps in resource acquisition and allocation of tasks, territories, and people. Permanent employees will be owners of the company. Promotions will be based on performance at specific events or "in crises."

A company like People Express had some of the characteristics of a "mobile"organization. At some cost and in a short period of time People Express could change its "hub" from the Newark, New Jersey, airport to another location. Also, it seemed possible that the People Express structure could divide amoebalike and create a number of replicated mobile entities. Expanding or contracting operations should have been much easier for a skeletal permanent organization like People Express, but the acquisitions of Frontier and Britt Airlines in 1986 taxed its organizational structure and culture. The People Express case suggests that growth by acquisition will likely be very difficult for future mobile organizations.

Conservative Social Environment and Economic Growth Scenario

Managers have more flexibility and are less likely to fail when the economy is growing. Also, a conservative social environment creates stability and predictability for managers. For our purposes, a "conservative" social environment can be characterized as one in which people are resisting many social changes, accepting traditional moral and political values, and conserving resources. Such a social environment may retard new product development, but it will not necessarily retard technological change, especially within companies. From an economic standpoint, in this scenario energy supplies will be abundant, resources will be widely available, and the population and the demand for goods and services will grow at a manageable rate. This environmental scenario is for many people "the dominant American optimistic view" of the future.

Most current managers are familiar with managing in a growth environment. They were either managing a business in the growth period from 1961 to 1973 or they have been trained to manage in that environment. Many current organization forms and structures are holdovers from that period. The economic shakeout of the early 1980s resulted in some retrenchment and restructuring of companies, including intentional understaffing, new financial incentive systems, and improved information and communication systems. Traditional structures should, however, continue to flourish in a conservative, growth environment. It is also plausible that new structures will be needed to exploit the very different possibilities for growth in the 1990s and beyond. Some of that growth may come from increased U.S. demand for goods and services—both higher birth rates and increased immigration can stimulate demand for housing, food, and other goods and services. Also, growth in demand for goods and services may come from expanding markets in less developed countries. The following new structures should flourish in a conservative, growth environment:

Related, Network Structure. Slow growth in traditional markets, the identification of new markets, improved information and communications technologies, and a conservative social environment may encourage some managers to change their organizations by "weaving" tangled structural webs. Interlocking corporations, structural decentralization, nested project teams, limited partnerships, and more traditional organizational forms may be combined to encourage innovation, protect investments from failures, and confuse regulators or social critics. These new structures will have ambiguous, overlapping task units and rely heavily on informal reporting relationships. Many different accounting systems will be used to segregate activities and funds. Planning will occur primarily in the mind of the entrepreneur/promoter. Tangled webs may help managers exploit limited growth, but they may also lead to enormous economic inefficiencies. Some limited partnerships and investment organizations of today are precursors of tangled web structures. Companies that exist only as shells with no real function other than avoiding taxes, companies that manage multiple limited partnerships, multiple-level holding companies, and other such complex legal mechanisms can provide a starting point for joining activities and people together in a tangled web.

Extended, Hierarchical Structure. Information technologies and economic growth may encourage managers to increase the number of upper-middle and top management positions. The structures will be such that those at the "top" supervise very few people and the number of management levels in the organizations is very large. The number of operating personnel may be a much smaller percentage of all employees than is currently found in many manufacturing companies. In this structure, Max Weber's (1946) bureaucracy has been stretched or extended. Explicit jobs and reporting relationships dominate this conservative neotraditional organization. Centralized and integrated communications and information systems ensure that everyone knows about everyone else's actions and performance. Managers often violate the strict authority hierarchy, and it is sometimes difficult to identify the "real" decision maker in the myriad organizational levels. A periodic, formal planning system provides a mechanism for ratifying negotiated allocations of resources. Managers in large financial institutions that are trying to defend traditional markets and services may move toward this skyscraper structure. New information technologies may allow managers in large financial institutions to automate much of the work at the operations level. The skyscraper structure will provide some upward mobility for managers, and automated services will provide the revenues to maintain an increasingly technocratic and bureaucratic managerial hierarchy.

Commentary

Anticipating the future of organizations is important and is a necessary activity for all of us. Trying to justify one's vision of the future is, however, difficult. My arguments about the future and my vision of the future will not be completely accepted, but that was not my goal. What is important is that my ideas stimulate managers to think about what structure is most appropriate for their organization. The environment is changing, technologies are changing, strategies are changing. Structural change seems to lag behind such changes, but structural changes will be necessary. The phenomenon of new structures following new strategies that Chandler (1962) identified will reoccur.

The direction of structural change is still somewhat vague, but some prior views about new structures and structural forms now seem less likely to be supported by future trends. For example, Weber (1946) was probably not correct when he asserted that bureaucracies would become the dominant form of organization in the future. And Bennis (1966, 4; 1967) prematurely predicted the death of bureaucracy, but we probably will witness the rise of new social systems. Also, it does not appear that James Thompson (1967) was correct when he anticipated that the primary organization structure of the future will be a fluid, ad hoc, flexible matrix form. The evidence does seem to indicate that the number of organizations with organic structural characteristics is increasing (see Burns and Stalker 1961) and project management structures are more common. Also, managers are creating more boundary-spanning units to deal with heterogeneous task environments (Thompson 1967).

A leading futurist, Alvin Toffler, also has a number of ideas about future organization structures. Toffler (1981) views future society as built around a network rather than a hierarchy of institutions. He concludes that corporations will undergo drastic restructuring away from standard old-fashioned bureaucracy and toward a wide variety of new-style organizations. He believes that where hierarchies remain they will tend to be flatter and more transient.

Supposedly these new organizations will do away with the old insistence on "one man, one boss" (372). Toffler also suggests that Third Wave production changes will make possible decentralization and smaller, more personal work units that may break up huge corporations into small, self-managed units (386). Toffler presents a rich set of ideas, but some of his ideas are inconsistent, vague, overly complex, and too idealistic.

Although many of my ideas about future organization structures are not radically different from what has been discussed by others, the grouping of the above structural ideas into a new framework may help planners and organization theorists. The most difficult issue that must be faced by planners and organization theorists when they discuss the future of organizations is what is a new, interesting, and/or innovative structure that is worth discussing. Much is uncertain about the future, but it seems certain that new structures will be tried by managers. Many managers will assume that grouping different people together into new work units, adding or removing levels in the managerial hierarchy, or improving the sophistication of communications and information systems will magically transform or rehabilitate an organization. Many of the new structures will fail. Also, many managers will avoid changes in structures because they fear that a new structure will be less effective or efficient. This managerial dilemma cannot be avoided.

To resolve the conflicts and manage the risks associated with structural changes, managers will need to search broadly for insights that may help them anticipate and assess the consequences associated with potential structure changes. Managers will also need to consider the new functions of future organizations. Structural forms should fit function, strategy, and environment. Most important, managers cannot rely solely on empirically derived typologies (for example, Pugh, Hickson, Hinings 1969) to define all structural forms when they are designing new organizations. Such an approach is limited to identifying forms that are extant at the time of the research, and it is further limited by perceptual and measurement problems.

More adaptive organization structures can help managers ensure that their companies will survive in "new" environments. And it seems certain for that reason that new structures will be developed for coordinating and controlling people, processes, and technologies. The greatest challenge for managers will be creating new structures that can withstand the unanticipated environmental shocks that will certainly occur in the future. Also, the increased complexity of the environment may mean that small organizations will be relatively less effective than very large ones. And a major ramification of new technologies and new structures is that some managers, engineers, and operating employees will need to be replaced and retrained. It is my hope that this chapter will help managers adapt to the future and help them create adaptive organizations.

II
The Impact of Technology and Knowledge on Managerial Roles

The first part of this book with its emphasis on structure has several implications for what the future roles of managers might be because it provided a context for the role of the manager. Galbraith and Kazanjian focused on several matrix structures, which have some obvious managerial implications. Less obvious are the connections in Hage's chapter on the pathways of evolution, but they suggest much greater unit autonomy and collective decision making at the same time. In chapter 4 Power suggested that managers can no longer afford to be reactive, but in the future, given the kinds of instabilities that he discusses, they must take a more active approach. Power also notes that technology increases both the quantity and diversity of information processing.

These themes are pursued further in chapter 5, in which Stephen J. Carroll attempts to predict how the role of different kinds of managers will change in the future. His chapter is unusual in that he analyzes the managerial role from several different points of view. Carroll considers the impact environmental changes will have on the various functions, or what he calls job activities, of the manager, and he looks at the generic goals, the key management skills, and the knowledge bases that a manager should have. The emphasis on knowledge bases contributes to the idea that increasingly the problem is to know what to do, a theme that appears often in this book. The roles of managers are thus viewed in quite complex ways. Finally, these roles exist at least at three levels and within five kinds of organizations. Thus, not only are there many more kinds of structures or organizational forms (as we have seen in part I), but now there are also many more kinds of managerial roles. Carroll thus advances the contingency theory of leadership (Fielder 1967), which has usually only considered types of organization or managerial situation, in several different directions.

The nature of these contingencies is considered as well. The first part of Carroll's chapter adds more depth to chapter 1 by offering more ideas about the nature of the pressures and changes that will face managers of the future. And although chapter 1 perhaps overemphasizes the importance of innovation, Carroll notes that the goals of efficiency, while perhaps less important in particular situations, still remain the objectives of many managerial roles, depending upon their situational context.

The theme of contingencies is examined further in the next two chapters, those by Ken G. Smith and by Andre L. Delbecq and Joseph Weiss. In chapter 6, Smith considers contingencies for deciding what might be the best way of maintaining innovation in an organization by institutionalizing entrepreneurial activity. In chapter 7, Delbecq and Weiss move outside the organization and suggest that there are some special ecological and social concomitants to the institutionalization of innovative activity associated with Silicon Valley.

The theme of the variety of managerial roles continues in chapter 6 in which Smith notes that increasingly the entrepreneurial role is becoming critical not only in small organizations but in large ones as well. Smith then observes that the problem of maintaining entrepreneurial activity starts almost immediately because growth leads to bureaucracy. The problem then becomes one of how to maintain entrepreneurial activity. The seventh chapter provides a great deal of concrete behavioral detail from interviews with key leaders in Silicon Valley about what is an entreprenurial spirit and sense of values.

To maintain this entrepreneurial spirit within an organization, Smith proposes three different kinds of structural solutions, each of them appropriate in a different context. His structural solutions should be compared with those in part I because they complement those ideas in several ways.

Especially interesting is Smith's discussion of the matrix solution. His ideas about combining professional managers like those described by Carroll with entrepreneurs as defined by Smith in the same group expands on the importance of matrix solutions, an idea advanced in chapter 2. Both the chapters by Smith and by Delbecq and Weiss pick up on the theme of teams and on some of the alternative ways in which these teams can be considered. One might wonder how close Smith's entrepreneurial team is to the engineering team in chapter 7. Furthermore, the engineering team should be compared to the process teams mentioned by Hage in chapter 3. All of these teams are quite different in concept from traditional ideas about work teams and perhaps constitute the heart of the matter for the managers of the future.

A very different and cultural solution to the question of developing entrepreneurship is suggested in the chapter by Delbecq and Weiss. They study the differences between the organizational cultures in Silicon Valley and those on the East Coast. They observe, however, that the organizational cultures are found throughout the entire Valley and therefore may not be so much a function of managerial leadership but instead have become institutionalized because of a set of unique characteristics that are unlikely to be duplicated elsewhere. Indeed, their chapter is basically pessimistic about the possibility of easily creating an entrepreneurial climate or culture in the absence of a whole set of environmental conditions.

Although the starting point of chapter 7 is the culture of entrepreneurship, the authors spend a great deal of time discussing the structural and process implications, and thus provide ideas about managers or leaders (in Silicon Valley no one likes to think of himself or herself as a manager!). For this reason, their contribution has been placed in this part and not with the other discussions of culture, which take quite different approaches (see in particular chapter 10). The themes of decentralization again emerge and should be compared with the discussions in part I. The comparative discussions of structure and process again provide a lot of concrete detail that makes the more analytical discussions elsewhere seem less abstract.

The theme of networking again emerges and is seen as a very special characteristic of Silicon Valley. Geographical context and job mobility thus facilitate the exchange of ideas. This is quite close to the problem raised in chapter 3 by Hage, who notes that the shape and configuration of networks outside the organization will have a great deal to do with how effective the small, high-tech organization will be. Hage suggests that this is affected by the cognitive processes of the discipline involved. With the computer basis of Silicon Valley in mind, Delbecq and Weiss provide evidence for this assertion, although they suggest other reasons for the extensive and intensive nature of the networks. The theme of networks is not involved in Smith's or Carroll's contributions, but one might ask whether this might be increasingly the critical aspect of the entrepreneurial task and the manager's role. Although akin to the idea of coordination, networking extends this idea in many ways. Furthermore, the type of networking discussed here is not the same as the macro kinds of networks that emerged in part I. But presumably the networks discussed in part II have implications for the type of networks discussed in part I.

Hage, Carroll, Smith, and Delbecq and Weiss examine both small and large high-tech firms as one of the important kinds of organizations. Indeed, this is one of the more or less constant themes in speculating about the future, with many of the examples taken from one or the other of these two categories, though more often from the large, high-tech firm. Given the focus on technology in the conference, this is probably inevitable, but it also may reflect another reality: most of the job losses are occurring in the older kinds of organizational structures.

5

Managerial Work in the Future

Stephen J. Carroll

Managers have been the focus of increasing attention in recent years in both the scholarly and popular literature. There appears to be an increasing awareness in American society that what managers do and how well they do it has enormous effects not only on their own organizations but on society as well. Since a nation's economy affects all other societal systems, business organizations in particular have substantial effects on humankind everywhere. In spite of the importance of management, there is still widespread ignorance about what managers actually do and how they do it (Carroll and Gillen 1987).

This chapter will describe the nature of managerial work as indicated by recent research on managers. Then we will focus on how the manager's job will change in the next several decades in response to a variety of trends and developments now occurring. Many new books (for example, Toffler 1981, 1986, Naisbitt 1982, and Didsbury 1984) have documented the significant economic, technological, political, and social developments that have arisen in recent years. Their effect on certain managerial practices and systems has been discussed to some degree (Carroll and Schuler 1983) but not in terms of managerial work itself. Also, only some of the current trends and developments can be expected to affect managerial work in a major way. Other trends and developments may affect society significantly but not managerial work itself.

Levels of Management

The various trends and developments will probably also affect the different levels of management in different ways. It will therefore be necessary to discuss how managerial work is likely to change at the different levels of management, since managerial responsibilities are quite different from one level to another. Top managers have the responsibility of relating the organization to the outside environment, including competitors, after receiving information from the organization's external monitoring systems (Tosi and Carroll 1976). They formulate the organization's strategic goals and plans. Middle management must translate these strategies into operating realities. The lower level of management serves as the organization's control function (Tosi and Carroll 1976).

Types of Organizations

Research has also established that there is a variety of different types of organizations in which managers perform their responsibilities. Organizations differ in the types of products and services they produce as well as in the technological processes they employ. The environmental pressures on organizations also vary by product and industry, and this will affect the work environment and demands faced by individual managers. In this chapter we have decided to speculate on some of the changes in managerial work in five types of industrial organizations, recognizing that these do not cover all of the various types of organizations producing products and services. However, they do account for a very significant number of employed managers. The five types of organizations that will be discussed to some degree are (1) large, very competitive manufacturers, (2) large, less competitive manufacturers, (3) large, high-technology organizations, (4) small, high-technology organizations, and (5) large service organizations such as insurance companies and banks.

With respect to the manufacturers, some organizations, such as automobile and television manufacturers, are facing intense international competition for sales of their products, which have traditionally been produced by large-scale, highly rationalized production systems. This has put great pressure on such organizations not faced with less competition from other manufacturers, such as those producing consumer durables (for example, refrigerators or washing machines). Such highly competitive pressures are forcing some manufacturers to make changes that are profound in their effects on organizations and their managers not faced by other manufacturers in a more oligopolistic situation. High-technology companies are faced with great change in the products themselves rather than just in the production technologies employed, as is the case with traditional manufacturers, and this has forced them to use technologies and management systems that focus on flexibility rather than on technical efficiency. Some high-technology companies are quite large, such as General Electric and Hewlett Packard, while others are much smaller, tending to produce a much more limited group of products. Robicon, a company in Pittsburgh that makes direct-current motor controls on a custom-built basis, is an example of a smaller high-technology company. The large service companies such as insurance companies and banks are actually much like traditional manufacturers in terms of their technology configurations and management systems, and are quite unlike smaller service organizations such as consulting, law, or accounting firms, which tend to constitute a type of professional bureaucracy.

These types of organizations of course do use a variety of organizational designs, such as those discussed by Hage in chapter 1 and in his earlier writings (Hage 1980). Certainly there is a tendency for organizations to evolve toward an organizational design that is functional for them given the nature of their products, their overall strategies, and the environments they inhabit. The small, high-technology types of organizations are likely to use an organic design, and the large, high-technology companies are likely to use the mixed organizational form (Tosi and Carroll 1976, Hage 1980). Most of the competitive manufacturing firms probably lean toward the mechanistic form, although those who emphasize a differentiation strategy (Porter 1980) are probably going to be of the mixed type, with some mechanistic units and some organic units. This means that in addition to the demands being placed on managers in business organizations because of the trends discussed in this chapter, additional demands will be placed on managers because of the design of their organization as well as its culture (Davis 1984). These additional elements add a level of complexity to this analysis which is beyond the ability of the author to discuss in one chapter, so differences among these five basic types of organizations in terms of organizational design and culture issues will be ignored for now.

The Nature of Managerial Work

Figure 5–1 provides a model of the manager at work as described in a number of empirical research studies carried out by a variety of authors and summarized and integrated by Carroll and Gillen (1987). This model rests heavily on the work of Kotter (1982a), who studied fifteen general managers for more than forty hours each. He conceptualized the manager's job as an attempt to carry out a "task agenda" that is constantly changing in an interpersonal network of associations, subordinates, superiors, and persons external to the organization. As figure 5–1 indicates, this "task agenda" of Kotter has been changed to a "work agenda" to incorporate the goals that managers have and the tasks necessary to carry out these goals, as well as the tasks assigned to the manager by others in his or her network to carry out their goals (Carroll and Gillen 1987). This work agenda represents inputs by the manager, by the organization, and by other members of the manager's network. The work agenda also represents the specific constraints, demands, and choices in a particular manager's job, as pointed out in the research of Stewart (1983).

The mental work agenda is then implemented in the daily observable interpersonal activities of the manager as described by Mintzberg (1973), and also in the thinking patterns of managers mentioned by Carroll and Taylor (1973). These thousands of daily activities can be classified under the eight

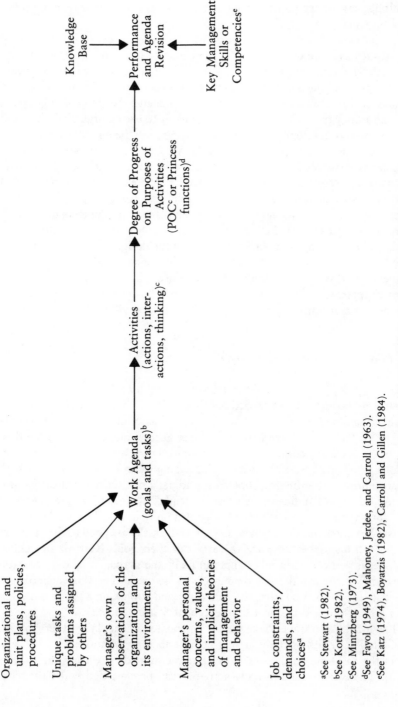

Figure 5–1. A Model of the Manager at Work

Knowledge Base

Key Management Skills or Competencies[e]

Performance and Agenda Revision

Degree of Progress on Purposes of Activities (POC[c] or Princess functions)[d]

Activities (actions, inter-actions, thinking)[c]

Work Agenda (goals and tasks)[b]

Organizational and unit plans, policies, procedures

Unique tasks and problems assigned by others

Manager's own observations of the organization and its environments

Manager's personal concerns, values, and implicit theories of management and behavior

Job constraints, demands, and choices[a]

[a]See Stewart (1982).
[b]See Kotter (1982).
[c]See Mintzberg (1973).
[d]See Fayol (1949), Mahoney, Jerdee, and Carroll (1963).
[e]See Katz (1974), Boyatzis (1982), Carroll and Gillen (1984).

functions of management examined in an empirical study of 452 managers by Mahoney, Jerdee, and Carroll (1965), and later validated in studies by Haas, Porat, and Vaughan (1969) and by Penfield (1975). These activity clusters can be called the "PRINCESS" functions since the initials of these functions of Planning, Representing, Investigating, Negotiating, Coordinating, Evaluating, Staffing, and Supervising spell out this acronym. Two other important elements in the manager's job are the knowledge bases from which the manager draws and the key management skills.

The key elements in the manager's job given this model are the focus of the goals under the manager's work agenda, the types of functions or purposes of the daily work activities of the manager, the knowledge bases from which the manager draws in performing his or her role responsibilities and the most fundamental or most basic management skills necessary to achieve high management performance. It is changes in these elements that we are concerned with in this chapter. These key elements are listed in table 5–1.

Table 5–1
Key Elements in Managerial Work

Job Activity Clusters:
Planning
Representing
Investigating
Negotiating
Coordinating
Evaluating
Staffing
Supervising

Generic Goals under Work Agendas:
Efficiency in resource use
Quality of products or services
Innovation or change in programs or outputs
Employee development or morale
Relations with rest of organization

Key Management Skills:
Goal setting and delegation
Problem solving– decision making
Interpersonal relations
Information acquisition and dissemination

Knowledge Bases:
Knowledge of organization
Knowledge of industry
Knowledge of technical specialty
Knowledge of managerial techniques
General knowledge (economic, political, social, and so forth)

In order to understand the table it is necessary to understand what is meant by these key aspects of the manager's job. The first category in the table is made up of the PRINCESS job activity clusters. These activities were validated in a study by Mahoney, Jerdee, and Carroll (1965). A later study of 103 managers in eleven companies by Carroll and Gillen (1984) indicated that these job activity clusters were very relevant to the jobs of 103 unit managers, with the possible exception of negotiating and representing. These latter two activity clusters are included here, however, because they would appear to be increasing in importance at present.

The PRINCESS activities are carried out for the purpose of achieving various objectives under the manager's goal and task agendas as indicated in figure 5–1. The tasks that managers carry out are typically steps toward the achievement of their own goals or the achievement of the goals of other managers, given the higher interdependence found in managerial work. (Focusing on just some of the many possible goals in a goal agenda, table 5–2 lists goals concerning efficiency in the use of resources, product or service quality, innovation and change in unit programs or outputs, employee development and morale, and relations with other units—these have been found to be key indicators of organizational unit effectiveness in other research [Mahoney and Weitzel 1969].) Obviously managers may have many other goals with foci other than these generic ones. In thinking about the goals of particular units in an organization it is useful to conceptualize these units as producing outputs in the form of products or services for other organizational units. Units are attempting to achieve in their own way many of the typical goals of entire organizations. They are held accountable for these performances.

Four key managerial skills are listed in table 5–1 as well. The first skill is that of goal setting and delegation, which has been identified as a key factor in managerial success in research carried out by Boyatzis (1982). Managers need skill in constructing their goal agendas and in influencing the goal agendas of others (Carroll and Gillen 1987). Also, most managers are forced to attend to the goals of themselves and others by the requirements of formalized goal-setting programs under a management by objectives format which are used by 75 percent of all U.S. companies with more than 2,500 employees (Bureau of National Affairs 1980). Goal-setting skills involve skill in choosing appropriate goals in terms of importance and relevance, in achieving understanding of these, and in obtaining and communicating information of relevance to their achievement. A second skill is that of problem solving–decision making. Managers are paid to find and correct problems, so problem-solving skills are important; in one study of 1,000 managers at Sohio this was the skill most associated with managerial success (Boehm 1981). Problem-solving skills include problem sensitivity, diagnostic skills, and the ability to find acceptable and practical solutions. Next, there are interpersonal skills, which are important to managers since they carry out their agendas in an interpersonal network from which they gather information and implement their agendas (Kotter 1982b).

Managers are also information processors. They constantly make inferences from bits of information in an ambiguous environment on the basis of the knowledge bases they possess (Carroll and Gillen 1987). These knowledge bases deal with the organization itself (culture, modes of functioning), with the industry and its customers, with managerial techniques, with technical knowledge of a particular field of study, and also with general knowledge about a world outside the organization. There is evidence that managers, compared with people in general, tend to be able to use such knowledge bases effectively. In addition they are able to sort the relevant from the irrelevant to a greater degree than others and tend to have longer future-time perspectives than do nonmanagers (Carroll and Gillen 1987).

Trends and Developments Affecting Managerial Work

Managers in industrial organizations have always had to face and react to changing environments. Some of these changes in the past have been very significant, such as the Great Depression of the 1930s, the demands of World War II, and the oil crisis of the mid-1970s. Some current popular books such as Toffler's *Third Wave* (1981) and Naisbitt's *Megatrends* (1982) argue that the total amount of change across all of an organization's many external environments has never been greater than at present, especially for American managers. The enormous publicity given to many of these changes in the popular press, by the U.S. government, and in various conferences held on some of these issues lends some credence to the idea that the present period of time involves more change for organizations and their managers than has been seen in a long time in the United States. Certainly many of these changes will significantly affect organizations, especially industrial organizations and especially the jobs of managers themselves. Some of the more relevant changes for the job of a manager are as follows:

The Growing International Competitiveness in Manufacturing

It is obvious that the United States has faced a significant loss in market share for many of its products. For the last fifteen years the United States has lost a greater percentage of its share of world trade than its share of gross national product. The U.S. trade balance worsens year by year, with the imbalance primarily caused by manufactured items. Of course, as indicated previously, some products have suffered more than others. The American consumer electronics industry has been decimated. Automobiles, tractors, steel, machine tools, and industrial power tools have faced ever increasing competition from abroad in the domestic market. More recent intrusions into the U.S. market by Korean, Taiwanese, and Hong Kong firms promise to intensify this international competitiveness. One reaction to this new competition from abroad, with its advantages in labor costs, is outsourcing. A large number of U.S. firms have now turned to overseas manufacturers for their products. This is turning some manufacturing firms into essentially purchasing and marketing organizations that some refer to as "hollow corporations." It is perhaps not surprising that manufacturing should be cut from the major subsystems of an organization, since it is in production that the U.S. firms seem to face the most serious competitive disadvantage.

Although international competition in manufacturing has greatly increased, it is not occurring in the area of services, where U.S. firms have an advantage. Indeed, the service-oriented U.S. economy now finds that it is having some difficulties in penetrating foreign markets with its comparative advantages in the costs and quality of its services, with some exceptions in banking and in the food service industry.

Changes in the Political-Legal Environment

Economic deregulation has been carried out in recent years in many industries that were formerly highly regulated. This has occurred in banking, in trucking, and in airline transportation, among other industries. This deregulation has forced companies that formerly were well protected and insulated from competition to become far more competitive and efficient than they ever were before. A large number of the weaker organizations in these industries have either gone out of business or have been acquired by the more efficient and competitive firms. These events have created great strains on management as they have struggled to survive. They have had to cut prices, expand services, and attempt to lower their labor costs by asking their employees for "give-backs," reducing the size of their work forces, and by cutting pay and benefits for newer employees through the creation of "two-tiered" pay systems.

On the other hand, the consumer and environmental movements have remained strong, and there continues to be a significant amount of legislation in these areas. Organizations are investigated and prosecuted for violations of regulations on worker safety and health and also for water and air pollution. In addition, the courts have increasingly held industrial organizations responsible for any accidents or harmful health effects from their products. Product liability suits have significantly increased in recent years and have become a major concern for organizational managers. This has increased the importance of activities designed to enhance product quality and reliability.

All of these environmental changes together have put great pressures on organizations to change their existing structures, systems, procedures, personnel, and other activities in ways that will minimize the occurrence of these threats to the industrial organizations. There is a search for new approaches to managing that can restore organizational health and viability.

Economic Pressures on Organizations

The increased international competition; the deregulation of certain industries that formerly had some degree of protection from completely free market forces; the changing tastes and preferences of the public, lowering demand for many traditional products; and the development of many new products, which have replaced older products—all these factors have combined to pressure organizations to lower costs and become much more efficient than formerly. Give-backs from unions to employers have become common in recent years, as have pay cuts for managers and even large layoffs of middle managers. Loss of market share often means that the breakeven point has to be significantly lowered if an industrial organization is to remain a viable entity. Such increased economic pressure has also led to crash programs to innovate and keep ahead of foreign and domestic competitors where product quality is an important factor in sales. Expenditures in R & D have started to rise as a proportion of company and national income since 1979, and this reflects this concern with product involvement and new product development. Older concerns of the 1970s with quality work life (hereafter QWL) and other human relations–oriented programs have been replaced by the new concern for economic survival.

The Growing Complexity of Organizations

Organizations themselves are growing even more complex for a variety of reasons. The bigger companies are getting bigger as size tends to increase with time (Tosi and Carroll 1982). In addition, many mergers and acquisitions are still taking place. These add great complexity to managerial work, since different organizations use different modes of functioning and have different sets of values. Often such differences reflect historical factors such as the values of the founder or the unique history of the organization. Clashes of organizational cultures create great uncertainty and ambiguity for managers, whose jobs are characterized by uncertainty under the best of circumstances. Organizations are also establishing relationships with other organizations that are quite different from those in the past. For example, organizations are attempting to establish long-term relationships with suppliers, with foreign companies in joint ventures, with banks and other supporting service organizations, with trade associations, and so on. Networks of organizations held together by mutual dependence are becoming the rule in the United States, as well as in the Asian countries where they have traditionally been more common. The internationalization of markets has also created pressures for elaborate structural arrangements to handle these new activities and areas of focus and attention.

Changes in the Social System

The growing diversity of the labor force has been documented by many (for example, Carroll and Schuler 1983, Strauss 1982). White males are now a minority and have been for a number of years. To a certain degree this diversity has created a balkanization of the work force, with the force sometimes fragmenting into diverse interest groups and with some reduction in cooperation and in the sense of a common organizational identification (Carroll and Schuler 1983). A growing legalism has put pressures on management to manage the work force with much more caution than ever before. The decline of the "employment at will" doctrine in the courts under common law principles has also greatly increased the risks of making poor hiring decisions. The courts now indicate that individuals cannot be let go except for certain causes. Staffing the organization and supervising the work force so that managers are sensitive to the needs of working mothers, minorities, dual-career families, and so forth, is much more difficult in many ways than was the case in the past.

The social environment has also changed with respect to living patterns, consumption habits, human values, and other factors as well. The high divorce rate, single-parent households, working mothers, and home versus work conflicts have also greatly contributed to a new set of workers' needs and expectations, and this has added to the complexity of managing human resources. These factors have also obviously had many economic effects as well, especially in those industries that are affected by life-style and living arrangement changes. Demands for products in the food processing, pharmaceutical, leisure and sports equipment, and other industries have changed significantly in recent years.

The Increase in Information and Intelligence Itself

There has been an enormous increase in information and the need for organizational intelligence itself in recent years simply because of the increased acceleration of change in all aspects of economic, political, social, and technological life. Under conditions of high stability, information demands on individuals are much lower than they are under conditions of instability. Because of the much higher uncertainty, a large intelligence industry and community has come into existence which has further added to the problem through its research and communication activities. In addition, there has been an exponential growth in knowledge itself in many disciplines, which in the case of electronics, chemistry, biology, and physics has fragmented these fields into dozens of subdisciplines, each with its own literature, which did not even exist in the past. The broadening of world markets and the increased economic interdependency of nations has added to the information needs of organizations and managerial personnel. No longer can managers operate in total ignorance of the world outside U.S.

borders. Finally, we must not forget the hardware and software systems that have given us the label of the information age. When it was not possible to have information of a certain type several years ago, nobody asked for it. Today, however, we expect that our new capacities for information storage and retrieval will give us all the information we want, and we tend to accumulate information beyond our needs and even beyond our capacity to use and absorb it.

The New Production Technologies

Computer-integrated manufacturing (CIM) and computer-assisted manufacturing (CAM) have replaced the numerical controlled machine technology of just a few years ago in the advanced manufacturing companies. These new technologies give such organizations far more flexibility and adaptability than they had formerly. The new technologies enable firms to have certain degrees of customization potential never possible before with more standardized technologies. The new computerized production technologies, while requiring very large capital investments, do significantly reduce the amount and type of production labor required. Such new technologies require fewer workers but workers with higher skill and intelligence levels who can perform their jobs to some extent independently, exercising judgment and discretion, and monitoring and evaluating machine outputs. These new production technologies also include computer-assisted design (CAD) systems that enable designers to design and modify products in a fraction of the time it took formerly. Since the computer can draw the objects and present them in three dimensions on screens and can instantly show the effects of design modifications on such factors as appearance, heat resistance, air flow, and other critical success factors, there is an enormous saving in expenditures for design and research personnel, or a given expenditure can result in a far higher payoff than formerly was the case. Certainly CAD greatly increases an organization's potential for improvement, modification, and change, and this will be even more the case when CAD is connected with CAM in CIM systems.

The new production technologies are also organizational to a certain degree. Just-in-time inventory systems greatly reduce plant space requirements and allow for much more efficient machine or equipment layouts. On the other hand these new inventory technologies require more complex organizational networking arrangements, and also have a tendency to create more pressure and strains on the organization and its personnel because of the reduction in slack resources that can accommodate or absorb unusual or atypical situations when they occur.

Other changes in production systems that are significant for management are the self-controlling and self-correcting mechanisms in modern automated or computerized systems in both the factory and office. The new high-technology production systems are capable of testing and monitoring while they perform their functions and of making the adjustments and corrections necessary to produce the results that have been previously specified. Computerized data entry and retrieval systems can keep track of operator productivity rates as well as errors, and can even automatically correct some errors such as spelling. They can provide remedial training to operators who make certain types of errors through the presentation of preprogrammed training materials presented on video screens.

Development of Decision Support Systems

The development of various new aids for executive decision making is occurring not just in the United States but all over the world. For example, one survey of thirty leading Japanese corporations indicated that 36 percent were already using advanced decision support systems for managers, and 46 percent of the group was evaluating these new technologies for implementation in their organizations (*Japan Economic Journal*, June 19, 1986). This is forcing U.S. firms to adopt these technologies to keep up not only with their domestic competitors but with those from abroad as well. The new decision support technologies can contribute to managerial planning and decision making in a number of ways. Some systems provide managers with up-to-date information several times a day on such critical factors as orders received, orders shipped, goods on hand, inventory levels, prices of the company's own product and those of competitors, and so on. Some systems enable one to project quickly the likely consequences in terms of financial indicators of taking various alternative courses of action. Others take managers through various problem-solving or decision or creativity heuristics, making it less likely that critical steps or factors will be overlooked and thus improving decision-making competence.

The Impact of Japanese Management Practices

The success of the Japanese in gaining ever increasing shares of markets once dominated by U.S. firms, their favorable productivity rates as compared with those of other countries, their achievement of high consumer satisfaction with many of their products, and their success in building profitable manufacturing plants in the United States at the same time that many U.S. manufacturing facilities have been moved to Asia, have all combined to spark a great interest in Japanese management practices. By 1983 more than fifteen books on Japanese management practices appeared on the market, and at least two of them (Ouchi 1981, Pascale and Athos 1981) have become national best-sellers. The first wave of these books largely attributed the success of the Japanese to their human resource management (HRM) practices, although some writers were critical of such practices (Carroll and Schuler 1983). Some

Japanese techniques, such as the use of the quality circle concept, became quite a fad with thousands of U.S. companies, which experimented with this participative management technique for improving quality and fostering innovation (Carroll and Schuler 1983). Lately some books have become more critical of the Japanese approach to management (Sethi, Maniki, and Swanson 1984). Other books have discounted the importance of Japanese HRM systems as an important factor in the success of Japanese mangement but have stressed the effectiveness of Japanese approaches to product planning, market research, the gathering of intelligence, coordination, labor relations, and international trade (McMillan 1985).

There is little doubt that all of these Japanese practices, especially the non-HRM practice, are becoming more widely known to American managers through these writings and the works of consultants. There also appears to be a tendency to consider some of these Japanese management practices as viable alternatives to traditional American approaches to these activities. It is quite possible that Japanese management practices will become more widespread and influential in American companies in the next decade or so, since it is managers in the pacesetter companies that appear to be showing the greatest interest in their use.

Research on the Management Process Itself

Interest in the subject of managerial and organizational effectiveness has increased enormously in recent years. Many new management guides and theories have emerged, only to fall from favor a few years later and be replaced by new ideas. The *Search for Excellence* (Peters and Waterman 1982) and other popular management books and articles (Hayes and Abernathy 1980) have all helped to create uncertainty and ambiguity as to how to proceed in the world of the manager. New behavioral technologies, management systems, and organizational structural possibilities have significantly widened the choices available to managers to solve problems, take advantage of opportunities, or attempt to reach certain end results. Much of this literature is beginning to affect management thinking, however. There is an interest in paring down corporate staffs to produce leaner organizations, to focus more on customer needs, and to build better relations with outside groups.

A new field of strategic management has emerged which has emphasized the benefits of planning and furthermore has produced many writings on strategy that provide useful guides and approaches to management in carrying out successful strategic planning (Porter 1980), especially on a competitive basis. Many managers now belong to planning groups and read this planning literature; this cannot but help to increase the importance of planning and the success of managers in carrying out the planning function.

The literature has been growing on product quality and how to improve it through the use of statistical quality control, procedures, the use of quality circles, the improved training of workers, the improvement of supplier relationships, the use of zero defects systems, and so on (Crosby 1979). The ideas of W. Edward Deming on quality improvement have now been implemented in many American firms, including Pontiac, Ford, Polaroid, and Campbell Soup Company. These ideas include making total quality control the responsibility of top management; looking for product quality problems in production system characteristics instead of in the behavior of the worker; clear communicating quality goals to the work force; training and facilitating high-quality performance by workers through appropriate supervisory behaviors and organizational programs; and enlisting the aid of the operatives in achieving quality standards. Acceptance of these ideas has been growing.

Differential Effects of Trends on Different Levels of Managers

The trends just discussed will not affect all managers in the same way. Managers at one level will be affected by trends differently from managers at another level. As indicated previously, managers at the top of the organization have the responsibility for relating the organization to its environment, for creating a direction or vision for the benefit of organizational managers, for resolving conflict among the various organizational political factions and organizational interest groups, for representing the organization to the outside world, and, finally, for identifying and developing the future top management of the organization (Carroll and Gillen 1987). The middle levels are much more concerned with linking the organizational strategies to operating activities through the development of specific action plans and through the development of needed changes in superstructure and infrastructure. They also serve as the means by which actual operating results get summarized, condensed, and clarified before submission to higher levels. The middle level managers develop the mechanism for the control of the organization as a whole. They also have important mentoring and development responsibilities with respect to lower-level, entry-level managers from the colleges. The lowest level of management must actually operate the system of people, procedures, and equipment on a day-to-day basis, monitor results, and take quick and appropriate corrective action when it is needed. The variation in the tasks of managers at different levels means that they will be affected differently by these trends and developments.

Top-Level Managers

Table 5–2 presents speculations on how the manager's job will change in the future for top managers. The table predicts the magnitude of change for each key element on the job in terms of a 1–5 scale, signifying that change will

Table 5–2
Differential Effects of Trends on Different Types of Managers

Key Elements in Managerial Work	Levels of Management		
	High	*Medium*	*Low*
Job Activity Clusters:			
Planning	+ 3	+ 1	S
Representing	+ 3	+ 2	S
Investigating	– 2	– 2	– 2
Negotiating	+ 4	+ 2	S
Coordinating	+ 3	+ 2	+ 2
Evaluating	– 1	– 1	– 1
Staffing	S	+ 1	+ 1
Supervising	S	S	– 1
Key Managerial Skills:			
Goal setting	+ 1	+ 2	+ 2
Interpersonal	+ 1	+ 2	+ 2
Decision making	– 1	– 1	– 1
Problem solving	– 1	S	– 1
Goals under Work Agendas:			
Efficiency	+ 2	+ 2	+ 3
Product quality	+ 3	+ 3	+ 3
Innovation and change	+ 2	+ 2	+ 2
Employee development	S	+ 1	+ 3
Relations other organizations or units	+ 3	+ 2	+ 2
Knowledge Bases:			
Knowledge of organization	S	+ 1	+ 1
Knowledge of industry and technology	+ 2	+ 1	S
Knowledge of a technical specialty	S	+ 2	+ 2
Knowledge of managerial techniques	+ 2	+ 3	+ 2
General knowledge (economic, and so forth)	+ 2	S	S

be very slight (1) to very significant (5). These projected effects are based on the author's subjective assessment of the *total* impact of the total effect of the trends previously discussed. The table first indicates that the demands on top managers for planning will increase somewhat because of the greater turbulence in the outside environment, and because of the greater risks involved for the organization given the rates of economic and technological change and the high level of competition. Top managers have always had to be involved in planning, but planning today is much more difficult than in the past and will probably be even more difficult in the future because of the widening of organizational markets and the enormous increase of information of all types that will be available. On the other hand, the demands on top managers for planning will be somewhat lessened because of the new planning technologies, such as suggested guides that will be published in the literature on strategic planning and because of software systems representing a considerable advancement over the spreadsheet format used today.

With regard to the trend toward increases in interorganizational relationships, top managers will have to increase their contacts with outside organizations, and many of these relationships will involve negotiations, as with suppliers, bankers, investors, customers, unions, government agencies, and so on. This will increase the demands on managers for negotiating and representing activities. With larger organizations and mergers caused by growth and acquisitions there will be higher demands on the top managers to coordinate organizational subunits. It is also expected that the new information technologies, such as electronic mail and executive workstations, will make it easier for managers to obtain relevant information and to evaluate this information. This will reduce demands on these managers for investigating and evaluating and also for decision making. The new decisions technologies will diminish the need for the intuitive and subjective decision-making modes of the past to some degree. These new technologies will also contribute to easier and more effective problem solving. However, goal-setting skills and interpersonal skills will increase somewhat in importance for top managers because of the more complex and larger organizations in existence in the future.

With respect to the focus of goals, the greater environmental turbulence and greater competition will force top managers to emphasize even more than at present organizational efficiency, product quality, innovativeness, and relations with outside key groups, such as investors and the government. Development of subordinates will probably receive about the same amount of attention as today.

The knowledge bases of the manager will grow in size because of the sheer increase in accumulated information, but the demands on top managers for a larger knowledge base will especially focus on top maangement's general economic, political, and social knowledge. With more competition and a technological environment changing more quickly, top managers will also be required to know more about their industry and current industry technologies than is presently the case.

Middle-Level Managers

There will of course be fewer middle managers in the future, and even today the ranks of middle managers have been significantly reduced by the need of organizations to have leaner structures and by the replacement of many middle-management positions with new information and communication technologies.

Table 5–2 indicates that with respect to the types of management activities carried out, middle managers, like top managers, will have to face greater demands for coordinating in larger, more complex organizations with more specialized units than at present. This situation will also require more time in negotiating as well, and middle managers in unionized plants may have to deal with the unions of their employees on a day-to-day basis. In nonunionized plants there will still be interest groups of workers based on gender, race, and other considerations which may have to be consulted before various new programs and plans are implemented. Middle management often has the task of implementing new organizational programs and systems. Investigating and evaluating activities, largely carried out for purposes of organizational control, may diminish somewhat in importance because of the new computerized control systems present in most organizations which make it far easier to obtain and evaluate information for purposes of tracking goal progress and unit performance.

Middle managers will have to become more skillful in goal setting and interpersonal communication in many organizations because of the increased complexity and wider scope of operations and in the types of products and services produced. Decision skills and problem-solving skills will be enhanced by the new decision aids and the new information systems available for controlling operations.

Like top managers, middle managers will have to concern themselves even more than at present with efficiency, product quality, innovation and change, relations with other units, and the development of subordinate entry-level managers. It seems likely that more formalized mentoring programs and more individualized performance appraisal systems will be used by middle managers.

Middle managers will have somewhat more extensive knowledge bases to work from but may especially need to have significantly greater knowledge of the technical specialties involved in their particular industry, such as electronics, chemistry, or biology. In the future it is likely that there will be greater demand for a technical undergraduate education for managers than at present.

Lower-Level Managers

Lower-level management will probably have to spend more time in coordinating activities. This will be especially important in the many types of organizations that will be attempting to align production more closely with customer needs. The controlling function of lower management will be lessened in importance because of the new computerized control technologies and the self-control mechanisms in the equipment that the operators use. Otherwise their job activities should remain much the same as they are today.

In other aspects of their jobs, like middle managers, many lower managers will have to deal with more complex production or transformation systems with more variable rates of output for a larger variety of products and services. This will increase demands on them for goal setting and interpersonal skills. Their decision-making and problem-solving activities will be made easier by the new information technologies and decision aids. Lower managers, like middle managers, will have to have higher degrees of technical competence than before because of the higher levels of sophistication in their products and the production processes used.

The goals of concern for lower managers will be increased attention to efficiency, product quality, innovation, relations with other units, and employee development. This last concern is included because the skills of the employees in many industries wil have to be upgraded so that they can deal with the complexity of new production processes.

Differential Effects of Trends on Managers in Different Types of Organizations

Highly Competitive Manufacturing Organizations

Highly competitive manufacturing companies are under great pressure to reorganize, change their current management philosophies and values, change their modes of functioning, upgrade their labor force skills and motivation, and follow the other prescriptions associated in research and current management books and articles with success in competing successfully on a national and international basis. Successful competition in manufacturing does require adopting many of the new manufacturing technologies, which give organizations higher efficiency and greater responsiveness to customer needs and changing demands. However, these also require large capital expenditures, a technical upgrading of the company's personnel at both the managerial and operative levels, and improved relationships and communications with suppliers and customers. Highly competitive companies must become far more efficient than they are at present, and they must also be continually involved in at least incremental improvement with products, services, and transformation processes. And as it is widely recognized today, they must especially attend more to the objective of making the highest quality products if they are to compete in international and national markets. Such organizations must also establish better relations with customers, unions, suppliers, trade associations, and other organizations. They must become technically more proficient.

Table 5–3 (developed on the same basis as table 5–2) indicates that these changes will require significant increases in the activities associated with planning and with representing the organization to outside organizations and authorities. The more complex organizations themselves will require more complex coordination approaches within the organization itself. Many American organizations are forming into complex networks of organizations not so dissimilar from the complex arrangements found in Asian countries, such as the Japanese enterprise groups and the Korean Chaebols (Hamilton and Orru 1987). Negotiating activities with outside organizations and even among the

Table 5–3
Differential Effects of Trends on Different Types of Organizations

Key Elements in Managerial Work	Types of Organizations				
	High Comp. Mfg.	Less Comp. Mfg.	Large High-Tech	Small High-Tech	Large Service
Job Activity Clusters:					
Planning	+ 3	S	+ 5	+ 1	+ 2
Representing	+ 3	S	+ 3	+ 1	+ 1
Investigating	− 1	− 2	+ 1	+ 1	− 1
Negotiating	+ 2	S	+ 4	S	S
Coordinating	+ 2	+ 1	+ 2	S	S
Evaluating	− 1	− 2	+ 1	+ 1	− 1
Staffing	+ 1	+ 1	+ 1	+ 1	+ 1
Supervising	S	S	S	S	− 1
Key Managerial Skills:					
Goal setting	+ 2	+ 1	+ 3	S	S
Interpersonal	+ 2	S	+ 2	S	S
Decision making	S	S	S	S	− 1
Problem solving	S	S	S	S	− 1
Goals under Work Agendas:					
Efficiency	+ 1	S	S	S	+ 2
Product quality	+ 3	+ 1	+ 4	+ 3	+ 1
Innovation and change	+ 3	+ 1	+ 3	+ 2	+ 2
Employee development	+ 3	S	+ 2	+ 1	+ 2
Relations other organizations or units	+ 3	S	+ 2	+ 2	+ 2
Knowledge Bases:					
Knowledge of organization	+ 3	+ 1	+ 2	+ 4	S
Knowledge of industry and technology	+ 3	+ 1	+ 3	+ 1	+ 2
Knowledge of a technical specialty	+ 4	+ 1	+ 3	+ 1	+ 2
Knowledge of managerial techniques	+ 3	+ 1	+ 3	+ 3	+ 1
General knowledge (economic, and so forth)	+ 3	+ 1	+ 2	+ 5	+ 2

various interest groups within the company will increase in frequency and importance. The increase in the number of specialized groups and in the diversity of products produced will require higher levels of goal setting and interpersonal skills. As indicated previously, the new control and decision technologies will decrease the heavy demands on managers for investigating and evaluating, but the demands on managers for decision-making and problem-solving skills will not change significantly because the new contribution by the new information technologies will be offset by the greater number of problems arising from the growing complexity of the organization itself.

As the table indicates, managers will be primarily concerned with issues of quality, innovation and change, employee development, and relations with other units. New managerial technologies are needed to improve accomplishment in these areas, and some of these new managerial technologies are known and being used by the Japanese, among others. American managers in the highly competitive manufacturing firm of today are gradually becoming aware of these new managerial technologies and are slowly adopting many of them, such as the total quality control programs advocated by certain prominent consultants in this area and implemented by pacesetter companies.

Less Competitive Manufacturing Firms

A very large number of American manufacturing firms are not facing international competition and have small market niches they have been exploiting for some time. Many of these firms are small or medium-size and have special location advantages or special technical skills or abilities for making specialized products such that they have not suffered from the severe economic and technological change faced by other American manufacturers. At present their primary task is to maintain past levels of performance and success and to engage in sufficient incremental improvement to keep their present position; this is likely to be their task in the future. Certain companies making specialized steel products and the well-known Lincoln Electric Company, which manufactures arc welders, would perhaps fall in this category.

As table 5–3 indicates, little change seems likely in the mangement activities, skills, goals, and knowledge bases of these companies. Some of the new decision aids and computerized information technologies will make some of their tasks easier than at present.

Large, High-Technology Companies

Large, high-technology companies are world competitors and obviously are facing great challenges today, since the level of competition they must handle has significantly increased and since they engage in difficult technological races with competent economic adversaries all around the world as well as within the domestic economy. General Electric, RCA, Honeywell, 3M and similar companies typically make a wide variety of products that are often related to a core of special technical skills possessed by the organization. They usually have extensive research laboratories, sometimes employing two thousand people or more, and they have many extremely complicated relationships with government organizations such as the Department of Defense, with foreign companies in the form of joint ventures, sometimes with thousands of smaller firms and suppliers, and with academic researchers and facilities. They tend to have very complicated organizations with many separate divisions, which often have little contact with each other. Their strategic decisions and research programs are usually quite risky, and it is not uncommon for such companies to be forced to write off unsuccessful programs whose losses can sometimes amount to more than $100 million.

Table 5–3 indicates that there will be increased demands on management in such firms for certain managerial activities, key skills, goals, and knowledge bases. First, these firms more than any other type face incredible planning difficulties, which are increasing in severity because of all the recent trends and developments described earlier. These companies face all the changes now occurring rather than just some of them, as is the case for smaller organizations and those in more stable environments. This has put great pressure on their planning systems and mechanisms, and these conditions are likely to continue in the future. The complexity and extensiveness of their outside organizational relationships will also make representing—a very important activity at present—even more important in the future; the same is true for their negotiating activities. Negotiating with foreign partners alone is certainly one of the supreme tests of one's capabilities in this area. As the government attempts to cut costs, the large organizations serving government markets will also face severe threats and risks from foreign partners as well as in the negotiating process. The growing complexity of these organizations will add to the already difficult coordinating problems they now face.

Again, as the number of products, services, and units increases, and as alternative uses of resources, time, and energy increase, goal-setting skills become more critical, as do the interpersonal skills needed to attain such goals. Because of these factors, managerial skill in decision making and problem solving will be needed to a high degree, but the new information and decision technologies will contribute to the ease with which these skills are exercised; this may result in an offsetting situation in which demands on managers for these skills will remain the same as at present.

In order to compete in world markets successfully with high-technology products, managers in these companies face high demands for product innovativeness and product quality and performance. This will require of them higher degrees of research knowledge in the various technical areas of electronics, physics, biology, chemistry, and other relevant fields not only at the more applied levels but also at the more fundamental or basic levels. Managers in these organizations also must become familiar with all of those managerial and behavioral technologies that are related to attaining higher levels of product innovation, quality, and reliability. Since innovation and quality are both at least partially dependent on human competence and on the use of specialization, more attention must be paid by such organizations to employee development and to organizational and unit relationships. With respect to other knowledge bases needed for successful competition in world markets, one must know all the present technological processes that exist in the industry or in the world, along with the relative benefits and costs. Thus, extensive knowledge of the industry and technology will be mandatory in the future for organizational success for this type of company. Competing throughout the world with high-technology products whether used for military purposes, producer goods, or as consumer goods means that one can be significantly affected by economic, political, and social forces. Increased general knowledge of the world around us will be even more important in the future for these large, high-technology companies.

Small, High-Technology Firms

Many thousands of small, highly specialized, high-technology firms exist. Often such firms employ individuals with specialized academic degrees with very high levels of technical knowledge; such firms also have organic or very flexible organizational structures and a committed and highly motivated labor force that needs relatively little direct supervision. The new manufacturing technologies, information system technologies, decision aids and support systems, and other technological developments may not significantly affect the mode of functioning for managers very significantly. These firms often do not compete on an international or even on a national basis and frequently have certain advantages or niches that give them some measure of protection. However, such firms often must be quite creative and adaptive to survive. For example, some of these firms will contract out their technical personnel when they have an insufficient number of projects to keep their human resources fully employed.

As table 5–3 indicates, such firms are not likely to change significantly in the future with respect to changes in demands made on their managerial personnel. Managers in these organizations have quite a demanding job at present, and there is some evidence that in general they must be more skillful than managers in more stable or bureaucratic organizations (Gillen and Carroll 1985). Such organizations will have to pay more attention to their planning and representing responsibilities and to increasing their knowledge bases, but they are not likely to need to change their management approaches to a significant degree.

The Large Service Organization

The large service organizations have been among the most successful of all American organizations in recent years. They have expanded their markets considerably, added millions of new jobs to the economy, increased significantly the scope and variety of services offered to the general public, and successfully invaded the markets of other countries where this has been permitted. Banks, insurance companies, food service companies, and testing companies are among the types of firms that fall in this category. Many of these organizations are highly bureaucratic in their systems and procedures and have highly specialized and effective training programs; they use elaborate monitoring and control systems to produce quality and reliable outputs at relatively low costs. Many of these organizations are also able to earn consistent profits. They have obtained these benefits through an emphasis on efficiency, quality, slow but gradual incremental innovation and change, and employee development. Obviously, there are considerable variations in performance among service companies in a particular industry, reflecting differences in the degree of adherence to these goals and in general management competence. There is often a high degree of competitiveness, however, among such firms of a particular type.

As table 5–3 indicates, there will probably be only limited change in the near future in the management of these organizations. Successful firms tend to try to continue what has worked in the past. They prefer to make changes slowly and to make improvements in a slow and incremental manner but fast enough to meet competitive pressures. They tend to do considerable planning and environmental scanning. As competition among large service companies increases, there will be even more emphasis on planning than in the past. With respect to demands on management, these firms respond to many of the same trends as do the less competitive manufacturing firms.

Summary

In general we see from this analysis that across various managerial levels and types of organizations consistency seems to appear in terms of likely future demands on managers with respect to how they carry out their responsibilities and work. Certain types of activities, such as investigating and evaluating, although perhaps of even more importance in the future than now, may be made easier by computerized informations systems, by software decision aids developed for different computer sizes, and by the growth of information and consulting organizations specializing in these activities. Other activities such as planning, representing, coordinating, and negotiating are also likely to increase in importance and difficulty in the near future. Although there has been a significant expansion in computerized technologies for planning in recent years, the activities of representing, negotiating, and coordinating have received far less attention and less emphasis than they should. We have seen too that across many levels and situations, managerial goal setting and interpersonal skills are becoming more critical. Also, demands for increases in knowledge of various technological processes and the subject matter of professional specialties are very likely for managers in the future. Certainly these demands are likely to affect significantly management selection and development, and here new computerized selection and development technologies may significantly increase in use. This review also indicates that much more attention in the future must be paid to the goals of product quality and reliability, innovation and change, and the development of human resources. There must be much greater use of current research that is relevant to the achievement of these ends.

In addition, there must be new research that can be converted to effective means of diagnosing organizational problems in these areas and creating practical programs for attaining these goals.

In this chapter I have only indicated how certain present and future trends and developments may change the demands on organizational managers at different levels and in different types of organizations. These demands on managers as a group will surely result in the creation of programs and systems for meeting these demands, along with changes in individual managerial behaviors. This is how management has always responded to such demands on it. If there is a need, for example, for more general economic, political, and social knowledge for particular types of managers or organizations, one would expect the creation or expansion of environmental scanning or search groups in the organization or trade association or something in the form of specialized consulting firms that sell their services to other organizations. This in fact has happened in recent years. As the demand for increased product quality and reliability grows, management must respond with organizational systems that facilitate this, such as longer-term relations with suppliers, more extensive training of the work force, the replacement of workers by robots, the use of quality circles and other quality participative management approaches, and other means to accomplish these particular end results. Increased needs for goal-setting skills might cause companies to expand managerial training in this area and to attempt to improve the quality of their formalized "management by objectives" or other goal-setting systems. When employee and managerial development becomes more important, formalized mentoring programs might become more common and so on. Predicting how all these changed demands on managers will manifest themselves in actual practice is beyond the scope of this chapter. These predicted changes obviously are nothing more than hypotheses to be validated by what actually happens in the future. The human mind is unable to grasp the interplay that exists among the components of our social systems or how these components interrelate to the physical world of nature and the universe. In spite of this it does seem worthwhile to attempt to see what lies ahead. Those nations and organizations that look to the future are more likely to survive than are those that do not.

6
Entrepreneurial Organizations of the Future

Ken G. Smith

Introduction

The entrepreneur and entrepreneurship have always been an important part of the U.S. economy. After all, freedom to put one's ideas into effect and freedom to enjoy the fruits of success are principles for which the United States stands. Many have argued that entrepreneurs are essential to the economy because they exploit waste as economic opportunity. Champion entrepreneurs like Carnegie, Du Pont, Sloan, Kroc, and Jobs have made significant contributions and are well known to most Americans.

Despite the historical importance of entrepreneurs to the economy, U.S. organizations today are decidedly nonentrepreneurial. These organizations are often described as inflexible, formal, mechanistic, and bureaucratic (Peters and Waterman 1982, Hayes and Abernathy 1980, Reich 1983, and Kantor 1983). The facts also indicate that these organizations are less innovative. For example, U.S. organizations initiated more than 80 percent of the world's major innovations in the 1950s; today the figure is closer to 50 percent, as foreigners acquire more and more U.S. patents. Furthermore, after leading the world in the percentage of GNP spent on nonmilitary research and development, the United States now ranks third (1.5 percent) behind West Germany (2.0 percent) and Japan (1.9 percent) (Lewis and Allison 1982).

Many are arguing that the problems with American organizations are managerial. For instance, Hayes and Abernathy (1980) contend that today's professional managers have the wrong priorities and orientation: toward finance and short-term profits, as opposed to innovation. Reich (1983) claims that these managers have resorted to "paper entrepreneurism": the sorting of numbers as opposed to true entrepreneurship. Some have argued that American organizations lack champions who implement ideas and create results. For instance, Peters and Waterman (1982) argue that excellence in the organizations they studied was related to a *champion* and to an *organization structure* that allowed the champion to succeed. They found that poorly performing firms lacked champions *or* a structure in which champions could succeed.

Given the lack of innovation and of American organizations, and the criticism of professional management, there is renewed interest in the concept of entrepreneurship. Many writers have argued that American organizations will need to be more entrepreneurial (Peters and Waterman 1982, Kantor 1983, Peters and Austin 1985). The entrepreneurial organization is described as flexible, ad hoc, and organic. It is characterized by innovation, confidence, risk taking, and an achievement orientation. In today's rapidly changing world the flexible entrepreneurial organization is likely to be the model of the future.

Even though many writers are suggesting that organizations should be more entrepreneurial, they give little guidance on how this can be achieved, and simply arguing that organizations need to be more entrepreneurial neglects the literature that suggests that entrepreneurs and bureaucracy do not go well together (Schumpeter 1934, Chandler 1962). If organizations are to become more entrepreneurial in the future, managers and researchers must solve the problem of how to relate the entrepreneur and entrepreneurial functions to the operations of large, bureaucratic organizations. One fundamental step in this direction is understanding the basic differences between entrepreneurs and entrepreneurial organizations and today's large bureaucratic organizations.

The Entrepreneur and the Entrepreneurial Organization

Let us begin by defining the concept of the entrepreneur. Most dictionaries define the entrepreneur as an organizer of an economic venture and especially one who owns, manages, and assumes the risk of a business. J.S. Mill (1848) is generally credited with bringing the term into common use among economists. According to Mill, entrepreneurial functions include direction, control, and risk bearing. Schumpeter (1934) expanded this definition by identifying the entrepreneur's essential role as encompassing virtually any kind of innovation. This could include innovations in process, product, markets, and marketing, as well as social and organizational innovations. Hartman (1959) differentiated entrepreneurs from managers and argued that the distinguishing characteristic of entrepreneurs is that they have the ultimate source of authority within organizations. Martin (1982) has provided perhaps the most complete and accepted definition of entrepreneurship to date. He notes that although any innovation can be entrepreneurial, entrepreneurs must also own *or* direct an organization, take risks, and be creative in transforming economic waste into economic opportunity.

While there are many different definitions of the entrepreneur, a consistent theme is that the entrepreneur and the entrepreneurial process are unique and special. For example, Robert Reich (1987) describes the entrepreneur as "personifying freedom and creativity." He notes that "they come up with Big

Ideas and build the organizations—the Big Machines—that turn them into reality. They take the initiative, come up with technological organizational innovations, devise new solutions to old problems. They are the men and women who start vibrant new companies, turn around failing companies, and shake up staid ones. To all endeavors they apply daring and imagination" (78).

In a similar vein Gilder (1984) writes, "It is the entrepreneurs who know the rules of the world and the laws of God. Thus they sustain the world. In their careers, there is little optimizing calculation, nothing of delicate balance of markets. They overthrow establishments rather than establish equilibria" (19). Most Americans are familiar with the names of such entrepreneurs as Peter Ueberroth, who single-handedly built a multimillion-dollar business and went on to organize the very successful 1984 Olympics, or Steven Jobs, who built Apple Computer Company from nothing and became a multimillionaire before he turned thirty years old.

Psychologists have identified some of the key characteristics of entrepreneurs. For example, in the United States, Italy, and Poland, McClelland (1961) reported a relationship between an individual's need to achieve and entrepreneurial behavior. He concluded that a strong need to achieve influenced the individual's decision to begin an entrepreneurial activity. McClelland's work was subsequently replicated by Komives (1972).

More recently, Liles (1974) argued that it was the entrepreneur's perception of a particular situation that differentiated him or her from others. Specifically, Liles argued that the entrepreneur's perception of control should be studied since this influenced the decision to start a business. McGhee and Crandell (1968) and Lao (1970) found that individuals with a strong need to achieve also had an internal locus of control. Rotter (1966) defined *internal locus of control* as a perception by the individual that outcomes are within his or her personal control and understanding. Shapero (1975), in a cross-cultural study, reported that entrepreneurs generally had a greater internal locus of control. Brockhaus's (1975) research supported this conclusion as he found that an internal locus of control was associated with a more active effort to affect events and outcomes. He suggested that it was key in distinguishing successful from unsuccessful entrepreneurs.

Hornaday and Aboud (1971) conducted the first major test of entrepreneurial values. Their study was supported by the findings of Decarlo and Lyons (1979), who found entrepreneurs to have a strong need for achievement, a desire for independence, and little need for support.

Entrepreneurs have also been found to be different in their backgrounds. For example, when compared with the general population, entrepreneurs, Brockhaus (1980) found, were significantly less satisfied with previous work experience. In fact, Brockhaus (1980a) found that successful entrepreneurs were more dissatisfied with their previous job experience than were unsuccessful ones. Comegys (1976) labeled this phenomenon "entrepreneurial cognitive dissonance." He suggested that when entrepreneurs quit their previous jobs and invest their entire life savings, they become supercommitted, which causes them to lose their objectivity.

In summary, the research on entrepreneurial characteristics suggests that entrepreneurs are unique individuals who are driven to achieve, are confident of their ability, are dissatisfied with their past, and who seek situations that allow them to achieve and be independent. Gilder (1984) more vividly characterizes them as "fighters, fanatics, men with a lust for contest, a gleam of creation, and a drive to justify their break from the mother company." Now consider the organizations these entrepreneurs develop.

There is keen interest today in the entrepreneurial organization, as evidenced by the sales of such books as *In Search of Excellence, The Change Masters*, and *Entrepreneurship and Innovation*. Drucker (1985) points out that the entrepreneurial organization always looks so small, so puny, so unpromising next to the size and performance of maturity of larger organizations. For Drucker two key characteristics of the entrepreneurial organization are small size and simple structure. Kantor (1983) describes entrepreneurial organizations as "always operating at the edge of their competence." These organizations focus more of their attention and resources on what they do not know rather than on what they already know. They measure themselves according to visions of the future, not standards of the past. Accordingly these firms are structured with "looser boundaries, crosscutting access, flexible assignments, open communication and use of multidisciplinary project teams" (148). Kantor describes how different employees at the entrepreneurial Chipco imagine their company: "As a family, a competing guild, a society on a secluded Pacific island, a group of people with an organization chart hung around it, a gypsy society, a university, a theocracy, twenty-five different companies and a company with ten thousand entrepreneurs" (132).

The literature concerning stages of organizational development is useful for detailing additional characteristics of entrepreneurial organizations (Greiner 1972, Kimberly and Miles 1980, Scott 1968). This literature presupposes that there are regularities in organizational development and that these processes lend themselves to segmentation into stages or periods of time (Scott 1968). There are numerous stage models, each containing an initial stage of development, often referred to as the entrepreneurial stage. Kimberly and Miles (1980), Smith, Mitchell, and Summer (1985), and Smith and Gannon (1986) found empirical support for this stage of organizational development. Firms in this stage were found to have strong centralized control, involving a powerful entrepreneur, informal organizational structures, and subjective reward systems. Smith and Harrison (1984) found leaders of entrepreneurial organizations to be "hands-on managers" who avoided rules and regulations and made things happen by getting directly involved in the action. This finding is consistent with that of Mintzberg and Walters (1985) who contended that entrepreneurs need to be deeply involved in the implementation of their company's strategy. In the studies by Smith, Mitchell and Summer (1985) entrepreneurial firms also employed judgmental decision making and face-to-face communication processes, and were managed by generalists as opposed to specialists.

It is clear from the above discussion that the entrepreneur and the entrepreneurial organization are uniquely intertwined. The entrepreneurial organization provides the entrepreneur a vehicle by which to achieve, control, and maintain independence. Many writers have noted how profoundly different these characteristics are from those found in today's large organizations.

The "Entrepreneurial Paradox"

Schumpeter was perhaps the first to note that the entrepreneur and the entrepreneurial organization spawned bureaucracy, which doomed the entrepreneur and his or her organization. More recently, Drucker (1985) described this phenomenon: "If entrepreneurship and innovation do not well up in an organization something must be stifling them. That only a minority of existing successful businesses are entrepreneurial and innovative is thus seen as conclusive evidence that existing businesses quench the entrepreneurial spirit" (150).

Gilder (1984) echoes this same concern: "Among the legions of lawyers, financiers, bureaucrats and masters of business administration strutting into the American economy from the nation's leading schools, nothing has been so rare in recent years as an Ivy League graduate who has made a significant innovation in American enterprise" (246–57). This dilemma, labeled for this chapter the "entrepreneurial paradox," can be explained by a theory on the stages of organizational development. In the early stages of organizational development the goal of the firm is often survival. At this point, it is crucial that the organization have a leader who has a plan and who can implement that plan (Greiner 1972). Drucker (1985) describes these leaders as having a vision for opportunity. Schon (1980) notes that a new idea or opportunity either finds a champion to seize it and make it happen or it dies. In contrast, organizational goals for larger, more developed firms are often very different and involve maintaining growth and managing complexity (Smith, Mitchell, and Summer 1985). Smith and Gannon (1986) describe how effectiveness for managers in larger firms means focusing on planning, coordination, cooperation, and delegation. Drucker claims that as a result of these priorities, managers in larger organizations only see what is presented to them; what is not presented is overlooked, and what are presented to most managers are problems, not opportunities.

Chandler (1962) was quite pessimistic about this paradox when he noted that there comes a time in the development of the organization when the entrepreneur is replaced by the professional manager. Greiner (1972) labeled this the "crisis of control." He noted that as the firm develops it reaches a point where the entrepreneur, because of his or her need to control and inability to delegate, stifles the organization's growth. Specifically, as the organization grows the entrepreneur becomes increasingly incapable of controlling every aspect of the organization. Consider the following entrepreneur's comment: "As the two companies I started grew, I planned that each company would have its own professional manager and that I would kind of oversee their activities and continue with my entrepreneurial activities . . . It failed miserably. No one could run the companies as good as me but as we grew I couldn't control everything. I simply got in the way of my companies' growth."

There are a number of case documentations such as this one. It seems that many entrepreneurs reach a point, as their firm develops and grows larger, where their personal needs run counter to what the firm requires to continue to grow effectively and survive.

Designing Entrepreneurial Organizations

An understanding of the entrepreneur and the entrepreneurial organization, as well of the entrepreneurial paradox, reveals important insights into the process of designing organizations to be more entrepreneurial. Specifically, three factors must be considered: (1) the entrepreneur must be selected/trained and integrated into the design, (2) the design of the organization must fit the characteristics of the entrepreneur, and (3) the organization must be structured in such a way as to prevent the entrepreneurial paradox from occurring. Three organizational designs are proposed and described in this section.

The Entrepreneurial Core Design

One future entrepreneurial organization involves designing the unit around the core entrepreneur. This design is identified in figure 6–1 and is similar to Peters and Waterman's (1982) skunkworks. In essence the entrepreneur is the president and general manager of the unit, division, or organization. Since the entrepreneur has a strong need to achieve, control, maintain independence, and directly influence outcomes, these factors must be considered in the design. Two elements crucial to the success of this design are the degree of entrepreneurial autonomy and the organizational size.

First, the core entrepreneur and his or her group, unit, division, or organization should be autonomous. The entrepreneur should be allowed to take risks, suffer losses and gains, and influence outcomes directly. In short, the entrepreneur should be allowed to fail or succeed on his or her own. Clearly, in larger organizations complete independence may be counter productive to total organizational effectiveness. Thus, an important question is what the correct degree of independence is. Peters and Waterman write that skunkworks

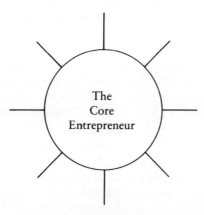

Figure 6–1. The Entrepreneurial Core Design

involve socializing employees to be entrepreneurs but at the same time maintaining control where it counts. This can be a very difficult task and is likely more one of balance. However, it may be best for organizations to recognize that entrepreneurship brings different kinds of benefits and that attempting to control it will be counterproductive.

A second, related factor that must be considered is the size of the group, unit, or division. In theory the unit should be small. If the entrepreneur is personally to control, be independent, and be directly involved in implementation, the unit must be within his or her control. Here the important question is, what is the optimal unit size for the entrepreneur to control effectively and at the same time maintain innovation and flexibility? Peters and Austin (1985) suggest a maximum size of one thousand employees, but this is likely to be too large for most entrepreneurs. The answer to this question will probably vary with organizations, technologies, entrepreneurs, and markets.

However, this core design is not meant exclusively for small organizations. Moreover, it may represent a form of entrepreneurial decentralization in larger traditional organizations. And although the design has been fairly well documented by Shils (1982), integrating the entrepreneur into the decentralized structure is not well understood or researched. Most often decentralization is attempted without considering the characteristics of entrepreneurs. Specifically, organizations usually attempt to make their present management more entrepreneurial by simply changing to a decentralized structure. Thus, the first step in successfully implementing this design may be identifying or recruiting personnel with entrepreneurial characteristics.

This design may also be integrated into the basic strategic business unit (SBU) design. At the corporate level is an entrepreneur who innovates products, services, and processes that can then be passed on for professionally managed units to control and implement. An example of this design is a company called

IDEAS, Inc. IDEAS is controlled by an entrepreneur who does not enjoy management. Thus he designed the organization to be small and independent. Although IDEAS is a small, innovative company, it owns a portfolio of stock in other companies that it initially started and has subsequently spun off. As IDEAS developed new products and processes the company formed venture companies, retaining minority interests in these new ventures but avoiding getting actively involved in management. This allowed the entrepreneur to spend his time innovating in the small central core.

This design captures Peters and Waterman's notion that behind each success is a fired-up champion. They describe the champion as being obnoxious, impatient, egotistical, and perhaps a bit irrational in organizational terms. This would suggest that this design is not likely to evolve from management above but rather from the champion's demands from within the organization. This design may also evolve from entrepreneurs' facing the entrepreneurial paradox.

The strengths of this design are that it is simple and that it provides organizational flexibility, control, management efficiency, ease of implementation, and entrepreneurial motivation. The weaknesses are its limited size potential (limits organizational legitimacy), lack of coordination in larger organizations (different entrepreneurs may pursue different goals), lower levels of employee motivation and creativity (as a result of strong centralized control), and limited economies of scale (because of small size).

The Entrepreneurial Structure Design

Another entrepreneurial design involves multiplying the number of entrepreneurs in the organization as the organization increases in size to overcome the entrepreneurial paradox and the resulting "crisis of control." This design, identified in figure 6–2, is aimed at satisfying the core entrepreneur's needs to achieve, control, take risk, be independent, and directly influence outcomes, and at the same time overcoming those factors that inhibit the organization's ability to grow very large. Specifically, a team of subentrepreneurs, with a set of values and beliefs *similar* to that of the core entrepreneur, directly manages and controls the unit, division, or organization. The emphasis here is on a strong but centralized entrepreneurial culture. The culture would allow all the subentrepreneurs to understand and agree on the organizational priorities as established by the core entrepreneur. Such priorities would include informality, flexibility, control, and achievement.

Three factors appear most important to this design. First is the extent to which the team of subentrepreneurs retains some management expertise. Schollhammer (1982) has suggested that there are different types of entrepreneurs. However, there has been little research on this issue. The literature suggests that entrepreneurs have a difficult time managing and vice versa. It would seem important to determine the extent to which there are different types

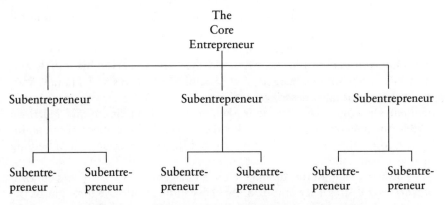

Figure 6–2. The Entrepreneurial Structure Design

of entrepreneurs, such as an administrative entrepreneur, and the extent to which these administrative entrepreneurs can balance the demands of entrepreneurship and management.

Second, the subentrepreneurs would need to have a set of values similar to that of the core entrepreneur. However, as entrepreneurs they would also require the opportunity to achieve, control, and so forth. Thus, to a certain extent, they would have to accept the vision of the core entrepreneur and within this context fulfill their own needs. Hambrick and Mason (1984) suggested that heterogeneity in the top-level team is conducive to innovation. Thus an important question is, to what extent would value consensus among a team of entrepreneurs be conducive to innovation and flexibility?

Finally, it would seem important that the core entrepreneur have strong leadership qualities in order to inspire and control the subentrepreneurs. Entrepreneurs have been described as leaders in the sense that they provide direction (Greiner 1972, Smith and Harrison 1984). The vision and the conceptualization of an opportunity and a plan to seize that opportunity seem to be important leadership acts. While this may be true, the profile of the entrepreneur is hardly one of an inspirational leader. Thus, with regard to this design, it would be interesting to investigate the extent to which leadership characteristics are congruent with entrepreneurial characteristics.

Although this design has not previously been identified, it has been used. The previously quoted president of Marine Supply Company, Inc., was unsuccessful in delegating to professional managers. This president was successful, however, in recruiting subentrepreneurs who had values and beliefs similar to his own to control the organization's growth. Interviewing these subentrepreneurs was like interviewing the president. Surprisingly, this was an extremely aggressive and innovative organization, although many of the innovations were provided by the company's president. This design has also been used by other entrepreneurs. Charles Revson of Revlon was described as a forceful entrepreneur who controlled everything in his billion-dollar organization. Revson controlled his organization by hiring a team of people with values and needs very similar to Revson's. It has been said that Revson carved his initials into everyone with whom he worked. Ray Kroc of McDonald's and Thomas Watson of IBM were also described as hiring "look-alike" teams to control and maintain the aggressive attitude in their organizations. Smith and Harrison (1984) documented that these "look-alike" teams had the effect of maintaining the core entrepreneur's influence around the organization and of helping them overcome the entrepreneurial paradox.

The advantages of this design include management efficiency and control, organizational simplicity and flexibility (depending upon the foresight of the core entrepreneur), and entrepreneurial motivation. Some disadvantages include organizational tunnel vision (everyone has the same perspective), poor employee motivation (as a result of tight centralized control), and lack of creativity at lower levels of the organization.

The Entrepreneur and Management Matrix

Professional managers and entrepreneurs appear to be very different, yet each brings specific and unique benefits to the organization. This design, depicted in figure 6–3, is aimed at obtaining the benefits from both kinds of people. In a nutshell, it is team entrepreneurism, only the team includes both professional managers and entrepreneurs. With this design, managers would be responsible for coordination, communication, motivation, and cost control. Entrepreneurs might be responsible for strategy formulation and implementation, innovation, and performance. The essential elements of this design include a team composed of both entrepreneurs and professional managers, a loosely defined organizational structure, and a differential reward system.

Integrating entrepreneurs into new entrepreneurial structures has not been systematically evaluated. As has been noted, most organizations making structural changes have simply attempted to make their organizations more entrepreneurial by changing job assignments and rewards. This design requires entrepreneurs to be identified, recruited, and systematically integrated into the organization. One important question is, what should the ratio of managers to entrepreneurs be?

This design also requires that all reporting relationships be loosely defined. More specifically, it seems important to let the natural tendencies of entrepreneurs and managers take their course. Defining responsibilities would make the organization bureaucratic and too structured. Bureaucracy and structure are enemies of entrepreneurs. Kantor (1983) claims that the tidy world of "clearly defined structures" does not exist in innovative organizations. She argues that instead individuals operate in an environment that "contains vague

The Entrepreneur

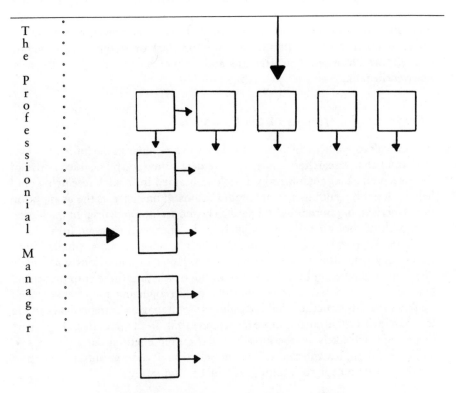

Figure 6–3. The Entrepreneurial Matrix

assignments, overlapping territories, uncertain authority and a mandate to work through teams rather than to act unilaterally" (138). Such a design promotes team independence but a mutually dependent team. However, ultimately someone should be responsible. Should that be the entrepreneur, the professional manager, or some specifically defined voting team? A voting team is likely to make the organization bureaucratic; giving control to the entrepreneur is likely to create a disgruntled coalition of professional managers; and giving control to the professional manager is likely to have some reaction among entrepreneurs.

A differential reward system would also be required with this structure. The opportunity to achieve appears to be the driving force behind the entrepreneur. Professional managers, on the other hand, seek mobility and security within the firm. Any combination of entrepreneurs and professional managers will require a differential reward system. It may be best to motivate entrepreneurs with stock ownership or a profit-sharing plan and professional managers with constant advancement within the firm.

The strengths of this design include the benefits of both entrepreneurship and professional management. Thus, the organization would likely be efficient, innovative, coordinated, and results oriented. The weaknesses might include management inefficiency, duplication of effort, lack of accountability, and increased formalization. The strengths and weakness of each design are summarized in table 6–1.

Entrepreneurial Designs of the Future

It is difficult to predict which design will be most popular in the future. It seems important that researchers study in more detail the specific characteristics of the entrepreneurial organization. Insights obtained from such research would help in designing entrepreneurial organizations. If one accepts the assumption that American organizations will need to be more entrepreneurial in the future, then each of the three designs is likely to be employed in some form.

The entrepreneurial core structure is in operation in many smaller high-technology firms today. It is also present in larger organizations with rogue divisions. However, in both cases one wonders whether these entrepreneurial structures are the result of rational choice. Recognizing the strengths and weakness of this structure could be valuable to managers/entrepreneurs trying to make their organizations more entrepreneurial. In the next five to ten years this design will likely be the most popular entrepreneurial design. A key to its successful implementation will be the selection of the core entrepreneur and for that entrepreneur to recognize his or her limitations.

Table 6–1
Strengths and Weaknesses of the Three Entrepreneurial Designs

	Strengths	*Weaknesses*
The entrepreneurial core design	Organizational flexibility and control Management efficiency Ease of implementation Entrepreneurial motivation	Limited size Lack of coordination mechanism Limited economies of scale Lower levels of employee motivation Lack of employee creativity
The entrepreneurial structure design	Management efficiency and control Organizational simplicity and flexibility Entrepreneurial motivation	Tunnel vision Poor employee motivation Lack of creativity at lower levels
The entrepreneurial matrix	Efficiency Innovativeness Coordination Results orientation	Management inefficiency Duplication of effort Lack of accountability

The entrepreneurial structure is likely to evolve from smaller firms (perhaps with the entrepreneurial core designs) that have strong entrepreneurial leaders able to recruit subentrepreneurs with similar values and beliefs. Because a strong entrepreneurial culture is so crucial to this design it seems unlikely that larger, nonentrepreneurial organizations without an entrepreneurial orientation could implement this design. But this design offers a number of benefits (primarily its efficiency and tight entrepreneurial control) to developing entrepreneurial firms seeking to overcome the entrepreneurial paradox. It will probably be a number of years before many firms implement this design. Even then, however, the design will likely result in less innovation.

The future of the entrepreneurial matrix is more uncertain. Although theoretically perfect (as are most matrix designs), the design may be impractical to implement. Identifying entrepreneurs and professional managers who can work together offers considerable challenge. This design could best be implemented by larger, nonentrepreneurial firms but would probably require the recruitment of entrepreneurs. This design could also be implemented by smaller entrepreneurial firms seeking to overcome the entrepreneurial paradox by recruiting professional managers. It would make sense to implement this design slowly. If this design did not bring the desired benefits, it would be very easy to attribute poor results to the design, when in fact the problem might be the entrepreneur/manager selection. If future environmental conditions continue to require entrepreneurial organizations, the entrepreneurial matrix may be the most appropriate design of the future, despite its problems.

It has been argued in this chapter that the future of entrepreneurship lies in making organizations more entrepreneurial. Three entrepreneurial designs were suggested. These designs were based on integrating entrepreneurs into the structure and capitalizing on the basic characteristics of these entrepreneurs. Obviously, this assumes that entrepreneurs can be correctly selected or trained. However, this may be the ultimate design problem, for it is often only by an entrepreneur's accomplishments in life that he or she can be identified.

7

The Business Culture of Silicon Valley: Is It a Model for the Future?

André L. Delbecq
Joseph Weiss

I n 1979 the senior author of this chapter moved from the Midwest to Silicon Valley. At that time both "high tech" as an industry and Silicon Valley as a geographical region had attained mythical status in the business press. The success of Silicon Valley, with many companies showing annual growth rates of 100–300 percent, stood in stark contrast to the industrial Midwest, which was suffering from a severe recession. "Smokestack" America looked with envy toward Silicon Valley. The questions were frequently asked, What makes Silicon Valley dynamic? Are there lessons for the reindustrialization of older American industries? Should other regions seek to spawn "little Silicon gulches?"

The purpose of this chapter is to focus on Silicon Valley as a business culture, to try to capture those elements of the business culture that differentiate this region from other business regions. In our view, regional differences are worthy of examination when exploring the compatibility of certain types of enterprise or industrial niches with geographical locations.

As Toffler (1981, 22) stated: "Today as we look at Kyusu in Southern Japan, or Scotland, or Quebec, or Texas, we find regional economies that have become as large and complex as national economies were only a few decades ago. . . . More and more these regional economies break out of national economic frameworks and demand to go their own way." This idea that regions are critical influences is shared by Garreau (1981, 1) and Naisbitt (1982, 116–34), both of whom argue that North American regions have distinct cultural prisms through which the practice of business is viewed. Nor is this simply a recent theory. Political and sociological writers (Vance 1952, 124–25, and Elasar 1972) had earlier argued the same point.

The Elan of Silicon Valley

Two stories can illustrate the sense of contrast immediately felt by someone moving from a conservative Midwestern region to Silicon Valley. The first story concerns a young entrepreneur,[a] and the second story concerns the action of a board of directors.

When the senior author first arrived in Silicon Valley to accept the position of dean of the School of Business at Santa Clara, within two weeks a young man arrived in his office carrying a business plan. The would-be entrepreneur was twenty-one years old and had not yet graduated with his baccalaureate engineering degree, but he intended to start an electronics business. He asked, "Would you help me meet the appropriate individuals so that I can raise half a million dollars to begin my company?"

In truth, in light of my Midwestern ethics the request seemed bizarre. However, being new to the region, I took the business plan to a member of the business school's advisory board who had spent the last decade in Silicon Valley, and asked for his advice. He read the business plan quickly but thoughtfully, and suggested that he set up a luncheon with a venture capitalist, a real estate developer, a senior entrepreneur who had established a similar company six years before, and a representative from a local accounting firm. The result of the luncheon meeting was that the young engineer was subsequently partially funded through a venture capitalist, partially funded through a bank loan, guided through the rental of appropriate industrial property by the local developer, and provided counsel by two outside board members (one of whom was present at the first luncheon). This past year the business initiated at that luncheon was sold for $15 million.

I recall telling this story to then Speaker of the House "Tip" O'Neill at a meeting on the Georgetown University campus and seeing the Speaker's face grow reflective. I remember his comment: "It couldn't happen in Massachusetts!" That it did happen and happened swiftly and smoothly illustrates one of the first cultural lessons I learned in Silicon Valley. Entrepreneurship and all business plans are taken seriously. Age, whether the would-be entrepreneur is twenty-one or sixty-one, is not a critical variable. The Jobs and Wozniak Apple Computer "shoestring" initiation formula continued then and continues now as a regular part of life in the Valley. Clearly, Silicon Valley is a business community that sees one of its major tasks as enabling entrepreneurship.

The second story is about a board of directors meeting also in Silicon Valley dealing with developing a critical market strategy. There were eight directors at the meeting. The discussion proceeded with vigor, and varied points of view were expressed. The strategic direction originally recommended by the chief executive officer was subjected to many suggestions for modification. When I left the meeting, there appeared to me, as an outside observer, to be no consensus. I felt some compassion for a CEO who was subject to such varied pressures. Three weeks later when I met with the CEO, I asked him how was he going to reexamine the issue of the market strategy at a subsequent board meeting. He replied, "What do you mean? We dealt with the marketing strategy at the

---

[a]Throughout the chapter, *entrepreneurship* refers to the initiation of a new business endeavor.

last board meeting!" I was stunned. "But there was no consensus, there was no agreement, there was no mandate given!" He looked at me with a perplexed frown. "There's never consensus. The risk is mine. The board gave me their advice. Everyone understands that having listened to their advice I will have to make my own synthesis and get on with it. If we waited until we had consensus, we would be out of the market!"

These two stories illustrate how the business culture of Silicon Valley clearly operates at a different pace. Businesses are established in a matter of weeks. Businesses rise and fall monthly. Entrepreneurial decisions internal to more mature firms seemed equally rapid. In one single year, one-half of the members of my advisory board of the School of Business changed positions. Three were initiating new businesses. Critical decisions were made without consensus. Product life cycles averaged two years, while product development cycles averaged four years. What is the business culture, "the rules of the game" as perceived by these business elites, that allows Silicon Valley to move at such a rapid and unique pace?

An Interview Study

What follows is a descriptive report. It seeks to capture the spirit of the Valley. However, it makes no pretense of providing a definitive answer. It is based on interviews with a small number of electronics firm executives in Silicon Valley.[a] The executives and background data are presented in table 7–1. Interviewees included John Sculley at Apple Computer, Robert Lorenzini and Brad Wait at Siltec Corporation, Irwin Federman at Monolithic Memories, Kenneth Oshman and Gibson Anderson at Rolm, William Terry and John Flaherty at Hewlett Packard, and Robert Fuhrman at Lockheed. Paul Wythes, the general manager of Sutter Hill, a venture capital firm, was also part of the sample. The executives were in their forties. Their average tenure with their companies was eighteen years. Four of the executives had either lived or worked on the East Coast. Three had attended college in the East. All had traveled between the coasts carrying out their professional duties.

The size of the companies in the sample, as measured by fiscal year 1984, ranged from $40 million (Siltec) to $4.71 billion (Hewlett Packard). The age of the companies (measured by date founded) ranged from eight years (Apple) to thirty-eight years (Hewlett Packard), with the exception of Lockheed which was founded in 1932.

The technology of the companies focused mainly on the manufacturing of electronic components, including silicon products, semiconductors, and

[a]This report is part of the larger study that included interviews with ten executives from firms along Route 128 in Massachusetts, which will be the subject of another publication.

Table 7–1
Demographic Profile of Executives and Firms: Silicon Valley

Name	Company	Date Incorporated	Sales (FY83–84, —in millions of dollars)	Title	Years with Company	Age	Degree	School
Ken Oshman	Rolm Corporation	1969	300	President and CEO	16	40s	Ph.D.	Stanford
Robert Lorenzini	Siltec Corporation	1969	40	President and CEO	16	40s	MSME	Stanford
Irwin Federman	Monolithic Memories	1969	185	President	13	40s	BS	Brooklyn College
Robert Fuhrmann	Lockheed Missiles	1932	6490	Group President	27	50s	MS	Michigan
William Terry	Hewlett Packard	1947	4710	Executive Vice President	27	50s	BSEE	Santa Clara
John Flaherty	Hewlett Packard	1947	4710	Manager, Corporate Personnel	29	50s	BSBA	Northeastern University
Gibson Anderson	Rolm Corporation	1969	300	Director, Human Resources	14	40s	MSEE	Stanford
Brad Wait	Siltec Corporation	1969	40	Vice President for Finance	1/2	40s	BSBA	Berkeley
John Sculley	Apple Computer, Inc.	1977	335	Chairman and CEO	3	40s	MBA	University of Pennsylvania
Paul Wythes	Sutter Hill Ventures	1962	—	General Partner	22	50s	MBA BS	Stanford Princeton

Notes: Executives's average age: 40s.
   Average time with company: 18 years.
   Number who lived and/or worked on the East Coast: 3.
   Number of Doctorates: 1.
   Number of Master's Degrees: 5.
   Number of Bachelor's Degrees: 4.

integrated circuits. Software development was also a major product. Lockheed, by exception, is a defense missile contractor.

Deliberately, the informants selected were not "young entrepreneurs." Rather, we sought seasoned regional executives. The question that concerned us in doing the pilot interviews was how the culture of the Valley influenced the mature and maturing organizations. By selecting mature executives in maturing companies we hoped to identify the attributes of the business culture of the region well after the start-up phase.

Open-ended questions were used, beginning with this query: "Are there differences between the way high-tech businesses operate along Route 128 and in Silicon Valley? Use your experiences and observations to explain any perceived differences." This question was followed by a series of semistructured follow-up questions that asked executives to compare management practices in the two regions regarding variables such as workplace formality, risk taking, intrapreneurship, networking, workplace communication, work force values and life-styles, dominant functional units, compensation systems, and so on. The interviews lasted between one and a half and two hours. All were tape-recorded in the executives' workplaces and later transcribed verbatim. The transcriptions were analyzed for content by four judges to determine themes that emerged spontaneously during the interviews.

It is important to note before reporting on the cultural attributes that we are reporting only on themes that were consistent across the interviews and that we think have value to management and organizational scholars.

In summary, this report is presented modestly as the shared interpretations by four analysts of interviews with experienced executives.

Entrepreneurship and Risk Taking

Any reader sifting through the pages of transcripts or listening to the tape-recordings would have no problem identifying the number-one cultural theme that all informants agreed upon as the central driving force of Silicon Valley: risk taking and entrepreneurship.

It is important to remember that we were interviewing senior executives in established, maturing firms. Yet, over and over when asked to describe the central cultural drive of the business setting in Silicon Valley, these executives emphasized risk taking and entrepreneuship. Here are some of the expressions of this cultural value:

Oshman (Rolm): The genesis of Silicon Valley lies in a business style which is entrepreneurial. Companies in Silicon Valley and their managements are characterized by an open-mindedness regarding the future, a welcoming of change, a belief in trying things to see if they work, experimentation. This is achieved by relying on delegating to people in a decentralized management style, a reluctance to depend on consultants or staffs for important business decisions, and a positive value toward innovative approaches.

Terry (Hewlett Packard): When I think of the West, I think of individuals who are dynamic! Willing to take risks! That's the critical characteristic of Silicon Valley.

Wait (Siltec): You immediately sense the focus in this Valley is on entrepreneurship. The companies here are the most entrepreneurial I have ever worked with, very different than those in other parts of the Bay Area. The style of top executives in the Valley is clearly entrepreneurial and unless you can meld into that entrepreneurial style you can't succeed.

Lorenzini (Siltec): I see Silicon Valley as being filled with experimental people. Being experimental *is* the prerequisite.

Federman (Monolithic Memories): People actually talk about being entrepreneurial, about the value of intuition. The central characteristic is that managers in Silicon Valley are willing to take more risks. They are more intrepid and eclectic. They are less respectful of constituted authority. I think that all of these characteristics reflect the one word *entrepreneurship*, which is the essence of Silicon Valley.

Sculley (Apple): I just sense that Silicon Valley tilts more toward zany ideas. I think it is a place that values change for its own sake. I think the regional culture values energy and excitement associated with originating new things; it attracts people who look for radical change.

Pages of the interviews are sprinkled with quotations reflecting this spirit. All the informants agree that trying something new, taking risks, being entrepreneurial is at the heart of the business culture of Silicon Valley. The mythic stories are not simply associated with start-up founders beginning in garages (like Jobs and Wozniak of Apple). They include executives who leave one company and move on to found another. This sense of entrepreneurship penetrates even the area defense firms. Listen to Bob Fuhrman at Lockheed:

> The sense of experimentation we have incorporated into our program management in Sunnyvale couldn't have occurred if we had kept our operations in Burbank. There was a spirit of experimentation, a willingness to engage in new, decentralized programs here. That was counterculture to the conservative defense industry in Los Angeles but was natural here in Sunnyvale.

We next asked the interviewers to speculate on how this particular entrepreneurial cultural emphasis emerged. The informants stressed three themes in explaining why entrepreneurship was so dominant, and why risk taking was such a highly valued element of the local business culture: (1) the West is seen as populated by "frontiersmen," (2) experimentation is valued for its own sake, and (3) technological push is important. Exemplary quotations reflective of the first theme generally followed the logic expressed by Federman of Monolithic Memories:

> To a large extent many of our employees are transplants. I am too. I came from the East. We have all made breaks in our lives. It's not surprising, along Route 128, to find that one is involved primarily with people who have been brought up in New England, perhaps right in Boston. The percentage of native Californians one would find in a California meeting in Silicon Valley is radically different. Our companies are composed primarily of people who have abandoned familiar surroundings, left their friends, and struck out for new adventures. They have already taken great risks and are unabashed at further risk taking.

A second theme was the pride in experimentation for its own sake. An exemplary quote can be taken from John Sculley of Apple:

> Silicon Valley offers a free form approach. I'd be really surprised if the next great industry emerged from the East Coast. I think it's more likely to come from a place that has no traditions. There aren't any traditions that I can see in California. There are no villages. There are just shopping centers. One day a company is written about in the business news and acclaimed as phenomenal. Six months later it's gone. It doesn't exist. It's not the people who disappeared. It's just that that particular new idea has disappeared. Another new idea will be emerging in another company.

The third theme was technological push. Given housing and labor costs, both of which disadvantage firms in the area as "low-cost producers," and a desire for "big wins" (which we will return to under our discussion of rewards), the big win or success was seen as associated with a breakthrough at the early phase of the product life cycle, when profit margins are high. The hope for the big win pushes the cultural emphasis on entrepreneurship as a path to fame and wealth.

Which of these themes is the more dominant? Most frequently mentioned was the belief that those who shake off their past and come west demand and value both independence and change, a refrain that will continue throughout the interviews. The technological push and early product life cycle niche does not, by itself, appear as frequently or as repetitiously in the interviews.

Structural Implications

If this theme of entrepreneurship and risk taking is a core value in the culture of the Valley, one would expect that it would have an impact on structure, on process, and on reward structures in area companies. The interviews are clear that indeed such effects are present. The most dominant and frequently mentioned effects are related to patterns of communication, decision making, decentralization, mobility, and reward.

Decision Making

All of the informants agreed that they perceived decision making in their companies to be more intuitive and less formal than in the companies they had worked for or presently work with in the East. Again some exemplary quotes:

Sculley (Apple): I'd say that decision making in the West reflects the entrepreneurial tradition. The discipline of formal analysis and data evidence is prescribed in the East. Also, the process and channels in the organization are carefully defined. The work starts at a lower level and moves through various levels of management. In this process decisions tend to get sanitized as they move through levels of management. In the East, management has the right to say no (but really say yes), so as the project moves up people at each level want to add their little comments. It tends to be a longer process and a somewhat less innovative process, although it is certainly a more thorough process. By contrast, I see decision making in Silicon Valley as more creative, more insightful, more eclectic. The focus is on new markets, new products, new ideas. It tends to be based on less thorough analysis. Nowhere in Silicon Valley do I find the intense market and internal performance analyses characteristic of the East Coast companies I am familiar with.

Federman (Monolithic Memories): Decision making in the East was always more deliberate, more analytical and more quantitative. More classical in its analysis. In Silicon Valley, great value is placed upon the intuitive process. While one can be skeptical, and posit that as an excuse for not doing homework, there is no question that we have come to value the net sum of experience as it expresses itself in intuition. We're more willing to take action based upon modest quantitative data.

Lorenzini (Siltec): Decison making in Silicon Valley is clearly more experimental. I think we're more willing to try things that may or may not work. Sometimes it will work very well and sometimes it doesn't work at all, but there is a spirit of trying something new that is different here on the West Coast.

One of the more charming anecdotes told to illustrate the style of communication was told by John Flaherty from Hewlett Packard. Earlier in his career he had worked for a firm (which he saw as typical of East Coast firms) which was subsequently purchased by Hewlett Packard. He talked about the first major presentation that he made with the new West Coast managers. He had been asked to prepare an analysis in support of a proposal. He had only been able to obtain some very preliminary data, which was not decisive. He had presented the results hesitantly.

And then the freewheeling, open-shirt, short-sleeved managers said, "What do you think might work?" I hesitantly indicated that I was in favor of a change, although I couldn't prove the case. I was told to "go do it and see what happens." That just never would have happened in the culture of the firm under Eastern management.

If there is a tendency to be more intuitive, to be more spontaneous, to make decisions based on less analysis, the question is what drives this culture. The informants returned to earlier themes. The first reason was the press of technology. The emphasis on entrepreneurship required the decision making to focus on the cutting edge of technology. In itself, this early technological emphasis implies that there is less certainty. In the absence of certainty, one reaches toward intuition. It is also true that if one wishes to capture the early phase of the product life cycle, the window of opportunity is minuscule. Because of the rapid pace of technological advance associated with these firms, all the participants agreed that a heightened sense of time pressure and accelerated pace was associated with decision making. It was clearly felt that it was better to take a chance and experiment than to wait and be more certain but miss the window of competitive opportunity. In the words of John Sculley:

> The essential observation I would make about our technology-driven companies in Silicon Valley is time compression. Things happen more rapidly. There are fundamental changes made in a short period of time. A major product can have a half-life of just a few years. You can establish a new product in a matter of months. All of this heightens the pressure to act quickly on the basis of limited evidence. The essential stake for the firm in Silicon Valley is being at the cutting edge of technology. This is entirely different from the focus on market share in established industries. In this industry (high tech) no one has any idea what share of the market is. There is no accurate way of measuring the market. Much of the time we are *creating* the market, not *sharing* the market. We can't even forecast correctly several months out because there is no way that you can use history to give you a trend line.

A second aspect of a willingness to accept nonconsensual intuitions was the need for independence of engineering and technical "champions." Since no one could be sure, others had to allow a champion freedom to "make the future happen" as a result of the champion's and the team's sheer energy. If the champion was not given support for the dream, there was always the possibility that the champion would join another competitor or form a start-up. Thus intuitive, nonconsensual support was reinforced by the champion's need for independence and wish to be an entrepreneur.

Communication

Another concomitant of an intuitive style of decision making was the presence of communication structures that are eclectic and decentralized.

Flaherty (Hewlett Packard): The West Coast is simply more casual in its communication style. It's easier to communicate with all significant others. It's less pretentious and there are fewer status barriers. Once you're given a mandate in a project group on the West Coast, you can talk to anyone in the company at any level that might be useful in carrying out your project.

A wonderful story was told by one manager who talked about his experiences in an East Coast company where he had worked on a project team and had wanted to discuss an idea with the vice president. He indicated that it took him three weeks to make the appointment, two weeks before he was ushered into the office, that he made sure he wore a pinstriped suit the day that he had the appointment, that no decision was arrived at as the result of the meeting since his revised project report had to be reviewed by several other officers in the organization, and that as a result timely action was never taken. He contrasted that with a recent circumstance in Silicon Valley, where an idea had occurred to him while he was jogging. He turned around and in his sweatsuit rushed into the CEO's office during the lunch hour, shared his idea, and was given permission on the spot to go forward with the adaptation.

One should not assume, however, that the informality of communication implies a form of decentralization that "deals out" key executives. On the contrary, the intuitions of the key executives are seen as critical to a firm's capacity to respond intuitively to market demands.

Flaherty (Hewlett Packard): At Hewlett Packard as well as other companies in the Valley, there are still key entrepreneurs who really control much of what goes on. It's because you have the entrepreneur to talk to that you can bypass an awful lot of structure. Once one moves beyond the period of time when these entrepreneurs turn over their businesses to professional managers, I think decision making will change in Silicon Valley.

This emphasis on the critical role of the entrepreneur was echoed by many of the informants. Key executive-entrepreneurs were talked about as charismatic, as understanding what was happening in technology, as being very close to the developments in the marketplace. As a result (and we will return to this theme when we deal with networking), while communication was informal in the sense of access, and decision making appeared informal by often bypassing the need for traditional rules of evidence, key executives (often founding entrepreneurs) served as critical checkpoints in the testing of ideas for rapid decision making.

Oshman (Rolm): I think it's very difficult in some of the large Eastern companies to know what's happening. Communication is formal. There is so much staffwork done before top managers see anything, so much report generation that you're not really involved intuitively in key decisions. This may be a function partly of size, but it's also a function of culture. It seems to go with the territory. There is an absolute desire to be highly informal on the West Coast. Individuals find it easy to communicate quickly. This informality allows us to share consensus and move rapidly.

Wythes (Sutter Hill): The communication patterns are clearly different in Silicon Valley. There is far more openness and much less worrying about whether someone goes around you. There's not only a tendency not to follow channels, there is a deliberate attempt to stimulate a wide variety of ideas. Innovations bubble up in unexpected places. Champions receive support from unexpected sponsors. People have no sense of an organization chart in Silicon Valley. On the other hand, there are wise entrepreneurial sponsors who filter the intuitions and provide informal mandates for progress.

Decentralization

Decentralization was an elusive variable for the informants to describe accurately. Everyone agreed that the critical investment is an investment in the right people (meaning entrepreneurially oriented risk takers). Everyone agreed that individuals (no one ever used the word *subordinates*) are granted relatively long leashes and that loosely coupled task force groups, program groups, and design teams are a critical part of the structure of companies in the Valley. On the other hand, there was enormous energy associated with maintaining communication between the decentralized team and the executive entrepreneurial elites. There was a constant discussion of communication events, of meeting people by the pool, while jogging, in the hallways. It was clear that while formal controls over decentralized units were relatively absent in comparison with traditional corporate America, informal communication was extraordinarily intense. The exact manner in which this was carried out is somewhat difficult to describe.

Federman (Monolithic Memories): It's possible for a Bob Noyce and a Gordon Moore to walk around Intel in open shirts. John Sculley can wear a plaid shirt to work and walk among his crazies. Having visited most of the companies in this valley, I am always struck with the continuous interaction between senior executives and their people at all levels of the organization.

Lorenzini (Siltec): The most important communications that occur in our company are informal, the ad hoc meetings that occur when we walk around the plant. Structured meetings held between 2:30 and 3:30 P.M. on specific topics really are atypical.

Wait (Siltec): Even as Rolm becomes a larger organization, there is a pattern of communication and decentralization that is different. Top management actively deals with problems several levels below the vice presidential level. We had a meeting this morning spontaneously associated with a major customer change. Our CEO wanted to get the story firsthand. There is a willingness of top level executives to be involved.

Sculley (Apple): Today even in Apple, where we have several thousand people at our Cupertino headquarters, people still expect that the leadership of the company should be out with them there on a frequent basis. Consequently, I spend a great deal of time every day with engineers in their different groups just talking with them. Further, top management plays an important role in informal communication of events. There are things called communication meetings which I never heard of before I came to California. On occasion I have gone out in the parking lot with six or seven hundred people. Recently with our reorganization, I went over and spent an hour and talked to two thousand employees at the De Anza College center. You wouldn't find the chief executive officer of an East Coast company engaging in that behavior.

Finally, again one should not assume that these are patterns only associated with newer firms. Listen to Bob Fuhrman at Lockheed:

> I think in the West there's a very clear sense of team management. You can't be successful without teams. Despite all the formalities of government paperwork, there's a sense that top management must operate through teams, and we communicate freely with every member of the organization.

In summary, the critical unit of organization in Silicon Valley seems to be a loosely coupled engineering team. The team, however, is not an independent "skunkworks." It is a set of individuals with a strong sense of entrepreneurship joined around a project mission associated with a technology-driven change who remain in contact frequently and informally with multiple levels and functions within the company through intense informal communication. None of the executives talked about organization charts, channels, or procedures as controlling mechanisms. Rather, they talked about allowing a spirited group of individuals focused on a developmental endeavor "to have a go" at their ideas. In turn, the team feels free and obligated to stay in touch with company leadership. Likewise, company leaders felt obligated to maintain frequent communication with the teams. In closing, it's worth reminding ourselves that this pattern was true in the largest organizations, as well as in the newer and younger organization. Bob Fuhrman, speaking for Lockheed Missiles and Space Company, commented:

> Entrepreneurship is located in program groups at Lockheed. The program is the center of loyalty and the center of innovation. I think in the older firms in the aerospace tradition there is much stronger functional management. The overlying aircraft firms tend towards very strong functional management groupings. We feel this stifles entrepreneurship. Individuals are loyal to their function

(engineering, marketing management) as opposed to creatively aggregating resources to get an innovative job done. I'm not sure we could have carried this off (decentralized programs) if we had remained in Burbank. Moving from Burbank helped us pick up the spirit of innovative program teams which have facilitated our success here in Sunnyvale.

Mobility

If this loosely coupled structure and emphasis on entrepreneurship has a cost, there seems to be agreement about this essential cost. It's not the cost of failure. In the culture of the Valley one can fail, rise, and begin again without embarrassment. Rather, the cost is employee turnover; indeed, the Valley is a frenzied place of labor mobility.

Deeply rooted in the Silicon Valley culture is the belief in small, flexibile organizations. Fuhrman speaks about the fact that a contribution of the culture in Silicon Valley has been to create flexible program management by means of confederations of small organizational teams that have substantial autonomy during the life of their program. These smaller organizations provide the excitement and the basis for innovation. But there is another story associated with small, flexible organizations: in the mythology of the Valley the team hopes to share in a big win and big dollars. If this opportunity is not available inside, it is seen as associated with leaving the current employer.

Lorenzini (Siltec): The stories that everyone has in the back of their minds is that people have made millions of dollars by starting their own successful companies. It's really difficult to match that increase in net worth internally in a normal organization. Inevitably you have employees moving to other organizations and setting up separate projects with large equity stakes, or founding new businesses.

Hardly anyone in the Valley can't tell the stories of Jobs, Wozniak, Bushnell, Packard, Hewlett, and other entrepreneurial heroes. Deep in the mind of each employee is an implicit belief that one can be an entrepreneur at twenty-three, or an entrepreneur at fifty-three. There is no age, social strata, or status that precludes the possibility of a new beginning. There are two types of new beginnings: one is the classic entrepreneurial start-up company. Another is the possibility of going with another organization where equity rewards will be more closely tied to the entrepreneurial adventure that your prior company couldn't fit into its strategic plan.

Oshman (Rolm): One of the realities of Silicon Valley is that you can walk right next door and get a new job. There are continuous job offers for anybody at any level who is any good from other companies in the area. There is the added competition from venture capital ready to finance new ventures. There is a great deal of money available at all times to finance any reasonable idea. As a result, if you don't recognize innovation in your own organization, a venture capitalist will.

Rates of turnover in the firms in Silicon Valley frequently reported at 17–20 percent often seem scandalous compared with the national data. Seventeen percent turnover rates among scientific and technical participants in organizations are not unusual. Managers as well as engineers move from company to company, or from company to start-up.

Most of the informants felt that the role of universities (MIT scholars or Stanford engineering spin-offs) was overplayed. The general consensus was that the major spawning grounds for start-ups were other companies, as opposed to spin-offs from universities. The willingness of people to leave companies and to initiate start-ups while giving Silicon Valley an edge in the development of entrepreneurial activity has also demanded a unique pattern of rewards.

Reward Structures

Oshman (Rolm): There is a difference in the reward structures for our people. Key employees don't care about things like pensions. They don't have a concern about long-term appointments. They have great self-confidence. They are very independent people. Therefore, things like guaranteed pension programs and unusual medical programs are not very important. They really are not worried about paternalistic or egalitarian kinds of rewards and compensation. They are very happy *not* to get a reward if they fail, but if they *succeed* they want a very significant, tangible, and unusual reward. People here believe in entrepreneurial rewards, and they want a shot at it.

Sculley (Apple): I admit when I first came from the East I saw mobility as a lack of loyalty. I've been here long enough to see that it really isn't a lack of loyalty. It is simply the mores of the Valley. Here it is accepted that people aren't going to spend their entire career with you. We don't have a pension program and no one particularly cares, because nobody expects to be here until he or she is sixty-five years old. I think that's probably true of many companies in the Valley. The world in which Apple employees live is a world in which they come from little companies, move to a larger company, then move back to another little company. I think you can cope with this as long as you understand it. The ground rules are different. But it does create a labor pattern that is unique.

All of the informants talked about discussions with colleagues from lower organizational levels who came to visit concerning the possibility of either joining another firm, or joining a start-up group. None of the informants attempt to penalize talented people who leave their own organization. They expect loy-alty from people while they are part of the organization, but they understand that part of the culture of the Valley is a sense of freedom. If the executives perceive that one of their people has a technical or scientific opportunity that cannot be realized in the priorities of their own company, their attitude is: "I think they should move. I moved and started this company [or this program]. They deserve the right to move and start their company [or new program in Company X]."

To be sure, as much as possible the executives would like people to find opportunities for entrepreneurship inside their company. But a certain percent-age of the time they realize it is not possible, and they see part of their obliga-tion to assist in the continuous spin-off process that has created a unique and prolific genealogy in Silicon Valley.

Sculley (Apple): The mobility among people strikes me as radically dif-ferent than the world I came from out East. There is far more mobility and there is far less real risk in people's careers. When someone is fired or leaves on the East Coast, it's a real trauma in their lives. If they are fired or leave here, it doesn't mean very much. They just go off and do something else. There is no penalty or very little penalty associated with that. I think the imper-manence that you see in the walls of offices, the mobility of the physical ecology itself is entirely different.

If I want to go back East to start a company the infrastructure that you have to tap into doesn't exist or is difficult to find. Where do you go to find accountants who understand start-ups? Where do you go to find lawyers? Where do you find people who can just move into an open space, create the office for you, set up your furniture, and get you going? The whole attitude of facilitating start-ups here has a tremendous bearing on labor policy. Out here the way Silicon Valley companies are managed reflect the start-up mentality. For example, one of the things that struck me when I came to Silicon Valley was the impermanence of all the facilities. The walls are all temporary because everyone knows that the configuration will be changed six months later. And my experience at Apple has been that everything does change in six-month increments. The idea of permanent walls with windows and doors that was part of corporate American is not part of Silicon Valley.

Organizations respond in two ways to this challenge. The first is to do what is possible to keep the individual inside the organization to benefit the strategy of the firm. As a result, compensation programs emphasize stock options and the opportunity to share in substantial earnings associated with major breakthroughs. By contrast, there is much less emphasis on job security and pension plans. Making money is important in the Valley. The chance to "win big" has to be built into the reward structure internally, or talent will seek to "win big" externally. Some companies have even gone so far as to share in the underwriting of entrepreneurial businesses started by their former employees. While the feeling is that the "jury is out" with respect to this practice, the pattern of exceptional labor mobility has become part of the culture of the area.

Additional Factors at Work in Silicon Valley

Networking

There seem to be three facilitators of networking as a critical variable in the Valley. The first is that the area is compact geographically. With mountains on one side and the tidal flat marshes of the San Francisco Bay on the other, individuals are accessible to each other geographically. The second facilitator is that key figures are still very much part of the communication hub. The third is implicit in the mobility, discussed earlier. People have many contacts with prior employers.

Sculley (Apple): The heritage of this Valley is that it's been driven by a few individual gatekeepers. In this Valley there are probably a half-dozen or a dozen leaders who started their companies, are still associated with their companies or with the industry, and provide a network. You are either in the network or you aren't in the network. The network is a very small one. These individuals all talk to each other, see each other quite frequently, know what's going on, and provide guidance to many start-up enterprises in the area. I think this network represents a key aspect of the character of the Valley.

The network however, is not simply associated with elites. It is also part of the scientific and technical culture that allows engineers to stay close to developments in technology and close to potential adaptations by clients.

Lorenzini (Siltec): There are people gathered together once a month or once every two months to discuss every area of common scientific interest in the Valley. Around every technological subject, or every engineering concern, you have meeting groups that tend to foster new ideas and innovate. People rub shoulders and share ideas.

This kind of networking (while somewhat infamous in the literature of international espionage and the leaking of "secrets") is part of the stimulation for the constant and rapid-paced change. A company president in San Diego indicated that the thing he missed most in leaving Silicon Valley was this informal networking:

> The institutionalized luncheon circuit made it possible for companies to serve as faculties to each other regarding technologies, customer developments, and market potentials. In San Diego we can't share any secrets. I miss the forum of communication that was characteristic of the Valley.

Market-driven Technology

There seems to be a consensus that a final driving force in the Valley is technology. The Valley in many ways has become one vast R & D park. Many firms have moved their manufacturing overseas or to other parts of the country both because of land scarcity and the cost of labor. Nonetheless, they wish to keep a corporate foot in the Valley for two reasons: (1) it possesses a fluid talent pool close to the cutting edge of new technologies, and (2) it is a source of endless idea generation regarding new niches that meet new customer needs.

Lorenzini (Siltec): It's obvious that our only advantage is truly understanding customer needs as the primary driving force. This means that we must constantly force engineering and manufacturing to listen even if it means grabbing the manufacturing guys by the necktie and repeating again, "listen." It's critical to balance the marketing function, which has to have enough power and ability to shape priorities, along with the technological and manufacturing wizards.

Observers of the companies in the Valley who have a perspective on other parts of the nation express the idea of the market and technology link even more strongly.

Wythes (Sutter Hill): With respect to parts of the organization that initiate priorities, Silicon Valley is much more market driven. Apple created a market that didn't exist for personal computers. Firms are engaged in the design of technologies for which markets don't even exist. I think the rest of the country is far more concerned with market share, or far more concerned with decreasing costs through better management in order to penetrate or capture a particular product line. By contrast, Silicon Valley still emphasizes new products driven by new technologies and the creation of new markets for new technologies. The Valley obviously has less of a manufacturing advantage. This is clearly a weakness in the West. However, the Valley has an instinct for innovation and entrepreneurship around the initiation of new products and market innovations. This will have to be its comparative advantage. It will have to be more market and technology driven because it has no unique advantage with respect to decreasing costs or penetrating traditional markets.

The Future

We have tried to capture the business culture of Silicon Valley. There is no implication that this particular culture constitutes the only fertile humus for technology. The business culture of Route 128 in Massachusetts as a geographical region is entirely different. It is more formal and orderly, has greater employee stability, focuses on long-run market share, and achieves decisions through a more ordered analytical process.

It is not the intention of this chapter to study the normative. It is, rather, to examine the hypothesis that workplace behavior is influenced by regional and environmental variables that create a "business culture" specific to the region. We believe that the interviews attest to this reality.

Nor would we portray the culture or environment of the Valley as laudable in all regards. For example, with respect to environment, everyone agrees that a major weakness is that the sheer physical ecology of the Valley is beginning to constrain its potential. The double-edged ecological sword poised to limit future growth is housing and transportation.

Federman (Monolithic Memories): Housing is a stumbling block, especially for people who grew up in the Midwest or the East. There is a quality of neighborhood and house to which they aspired that is not achievable here. It is rewarding to live on two acres surrounded by trees. Stable neighborhoods are attractive rewards. While we in Santa Clara can create exciting equity packages, even that enrichment often fails to deliver some of the basic wants and/or needs.

Increasing population density, an impacted transportation network, increased pollution, and a high cost of living are all taking their toll.

A more radical threat is the maturing of the electronics industry itself, and increased international competition. Doomsayers say that a Silicon Valley focused on electronics will see an aging and maturing cycle not unlike that of machine tools and automobiles. Optimists argue that although certain types of products may mature and take on attributes of a commodities oligopoly, the electronic revolution is still in its infancy, and "user-friendly" adaptations to meet new needs will be virtually endless—indeed, new products of an entirely new generation are being developed. The optimists argue the flexible, fluid, market technology–driven, innovative culture of Silicon Valley will allow future generations of entrepreneurs to replicate the Silicon Valley success story independently of the fate of selective older companies or of the semiconductor industry, which is only a single aging facet of the Valley's industry base.

However, regardless of one's prognostication of the future or personal evaluation of the pros and cons of the culture of the present, there is no doubt that it would be difficult to replicate in other regions the unique business culture that exists in Silicon Valley in 1986.

Summary

Finally, is Silicon Valley business culture a model for the future? Many authors argue that a loosely coupled, fluid organization is a prerequisite for organizations that wish to focus on innovation. Silicon Valley is a laboratory that exemplifies both some of the advantages and disadvantages of such organizational models. It is clearly not a culture for all businesses or for all individuals, but it deserves careful scrutiny as we look toward the future. Certain attributes are supportive of early phases of product life cycles: labor mobility among scientific and engineering personnel, who move easily to new challenges as older product challenges are met, a support system for entrepreneurship and risk taking, extensive communication networks at a cosmopolitan industry level, loosely coupled project teams in close communication with overall company strategy, and a tolerance for risk taking and concomitant failure.

It remains to be seen, however, whether a region can sustain itself as a specialized subculture focused on innovation completely independent of more stable and traditional business structures that can maximize dollar flows at maturing stages of product and industry development.

III
The Impact of Technology and Knowledge on Nonmanagerial Roles

The distinction between managerial and nonmanagerial roles is important—even if in the future the differences between managers and nonmanagers disappear—for two reasons. Automation will eliminate many unskilled jobs, computers many skilled and managerial positions, and most important, both workers and managers will increasingly be involved in quality work circles and other kinds of problem-solving groups, such as process teams and task forces. As the differences between top management and the worker decrease, both in skill level and in the amount of contribution to the firm, we should see an erosion of status differences. Our emphasis on nonmanagerial roles is an attempt to counterbalance the many books on management in the United States that ignore the role of the worker in the production process, despite the attention paid to the success of Japanese management techniques (as noted in chapter 5). We thought that the worker's role should receive equal time.

Although managerial and nonmanagerial roles are distinct from each other, some of the same themes emerge that we have already observed. Carroll observed in chapter 5 that the knowledge bases of managers will increase; Klein and Hall in chapter 8 and Tuttle in chapter 9 in different ways suggest the same thing. Both Schneider and Rentsch perceive implications for both selection and training as a consequence. One of the themes that emerges in the chapters by Tuttle and by Klein and Hall is the destruction of jobs and the movement toward process that is the steady decline in importance of job descriptions, titles, and even occupations.

The chapter by Tuttle also offers a useful connective to the overemphasis on innovation in chapter 1; Tuttle observes that productivity is still and will continue to be a major driving force in the alteration of jobs. Tuttle also emphasizes the importance of job security. In this regard, his contribution can be contrasted with that of Rousseau, who notes a number of new methods for reducing dependence on labor. Similarly, the theme of flatter structures emerges in chapters 8 and 9 as it has previously in a number of other issues.

Consistent with this idea is the notion that many jobs will enlarge. Although this is not discussed relative to managerial roles, one would expect it as a consequence of flatter structures. Finally, the theme of participation parallels that of decentralization and teams discussed in parts I and II and may be the only way of making the resulting new structure work.

All three chapters stress the common themes of selection, training, and reward systems as ways of handling the problems created by environmental change, despite the fact that their objectives are quite different. In this regard, they look forward to part IV, where the themes of motivation and human resource management are discussed. In particular, they seem implicitly to agree with Latham that the problem of motivation remains very much the same and with Lengermann that the problems of control are still there. Certainly Rousseau's chapter on human resource management also stresses selection and training as core activities.

One of the most important themes in any discussion of the impact of technology on nonmanagerial roles is automation in production processes and in the office. The first two chapters in part III consider some of the effects of these changes, but they do so in quite different ways. Klein and Hall note a number of negative consequences of these trends and suggest the kinds of work innovations that might reduce their impact. The chapter by Tuttle takes a more global approach and looks at the effect of several different kinds of technological changes; he then analyzes the effects for each of three different kinds of employees: staff, production, and support personnel. Klein and Hall discuss some of the many ways in which technological change may manifest itself, while Tuttle observes a parallel trend toward smaller-size plants. The two chapters thus complement each other in several different ways.

Both chapters 8 and 9 discuss some of the changes that are occurring in the larger environment. These complement and provide in some areas considerable detail on the broad brush/stroke approach employed in chapter 1. For example, although demographic changes are mentioned there, Klein and Hall elaborate on the many changes that will unfold over the next two decades.

Chapter 10, by Schneider and Rentsch, defines both climate and culture and then indicates what must be done if management wishes to create either a climate or a culture. Unlike the discussion of the culture of Silicon Valley, which mainly focused on management, their analysis looks much more at creating a culture for the lower-ranking employees in the firm. It emphasizes not what is but instead what might be. With a careful consideration of the elements of culture—namely, membership, socialization, identity, authority, interpersonal relations, and environment—this chapter is also usefully juxtaposed to the chapter by Rousseau on human resource management.

The chapters by Klein and Hall and by Schneider and Rentsch both consider the impact of the move toward greater service and of the shifting demographics of the labor force, especially toward greater diversity. But Klein and Hall indicate what might be some work innovations, while Schneider and Rentsch emphasize what must be done to create a culture that handles the new demographics. They are thus complementary.

But perhaps most interesting in chapter 10 are the requirements for creating a culture of interdependence, another word for networking. Many of the chapters have stressed this theme of interdependence, and we have seen that it can occur in many ways and at different levels. In his consideration of the global impact of technology, Tuttle argues that both staff and professional workers must work more closely with managers and production people—another kind of interdependency. Many of the chapters have stressed the importance of participation in or decentralization of decision making, which makes the problem of interdependence just that much more important. Schneider and Rentsch provide a way of proceeding to ensure that the organization is capable of having a culture that supports this new form of relationship.

All three chapters stress the importance of training as an effective part of any strategy for adjusting the firm to various kinds of environmental changes or for building the necessary culture or climate for the future. This echoes the idea of adding to the knowledge base of managers, as Carroll described it in chapter 5. Indeed, one might summarize by saying train, train, and then retrain.

8

Innovations in Human Resource Management: Strategies for the Future

Katherine J. Klein
Rosalie J. Hall

Successful organizations change their course—their products, their strategies, their standards and goals—in response to change and uncertainty in the organizational environment. This truism of modern management science (for example, Lawrence and Lorsch 1967) has guided us in our exploration of the future of the American workplace. To the extent that we can predict organizational and environmental changes occurring in the next two to three decades, we can more accurately anticipate the strategies that organizations may adopt to accommodate and excel in changed circumstances.

We have identified three sets of changes that we believe will shape the character and conduct of future organizations. These are: (1) demographic changes in the size and composition of the labor force, (2) technological advances in manufacturing and office automation, and (3) changes in the economic environment of the organization (that is, the shift to a service economy, increasing international competition, and changing labor-management relations).

For the organization, these three changes are fundamentally different in nature. Demographic and economic changes are environmental changes, beyond the control of a single organization. Technological change, on the other hand, is voluntarily introduced to the organization; the organization can and does control the extent and the timing of the technological change it experiences. Nevertheless, the broad effects of all three changes on the social system of the organization are quite similar; each set of changes necessitates modifications in the organization's human resource management or maintenance subsystem (for example, the organization's recruiting, selection, training, and reward systems; see Katz and Kahn 1978). In essence, the organization must strike a new balance between the environmental and technological inputs to the system, on the one hand, and the internal operation of that system, on the other (Goodman and Kurke 1982, Majchrzak and Klein 1987). Our chapter, then, is designed to preview the strategies that organizations may adopt to achieve this new balance.

In addition to the three sets of changes upon which we focus, a host of unpredictable events and developments could, we realize, play an even larger role in shaping workplace innovation. These include the overall state of the economy, the event of war, the onset of a severe energy crisis, major changes in social values or norms, significant breakthroughs in science, medicine, and other technical fields, and the development of new federal government policies and practices. We focus on the three changes mentioned above because we believe that they are more certain to occur and that we can therefore better predict their probable consequences.

We will review the nature and implications of changes in the demographics of the labor force, in technology, and in the economic environment of the firm. We conclude by summarizing the innovative human resource management strategies that we believe may be critical for the success of the organization of the future.

Demographic Changes

Fifteen million additional workers are expected to enter the labor force in the ten-year period from 1984 to 1995 (Fullerton 1985). At first glance, this might appear to be a continuation of the high growth trend seen in the 1960s and 1970s. However, the overall *rate* of growth will slow down considerably, accompanied by shifts in the age, sex, and racial composition of the work force. Three demographic changes or trends are most critical in shaping future organizations: (1) the sharp decline in the number of individuals entering the labor force after 1985, (2) the aging of the baby boom generation—that is, those individuals born between World War II and the early 1960s, and (3) the continuing increase in the number and percent of working women. See table 8–1 for an overview of the predicted demographic changes, their effects upon the organization, and the innovative strategies organizations may adopt in response.

The Decline in the Number of New Entrants into the Labor Force. The decline in the overall growth rate of the labor force is caused in large part by the drop in the number of young workers aged sixteen to twenty-four entering the labor force (Fullerton 1985). The total number of workers in this age group grew 3.6 percent from 1970 to 1980, but will *decline* 1.3 percent from 1980 to 1990 (Kutscher 1984). Workers aged sixteen to twenty-four will thus account for a much smaller percentage of the labor force than before. The effect of this decline in the number of new labor force members depends, clearly, on the state of the economy. Assuming a fairly robust economy, with substantial creation of new jobs, men and women in their late teens and early twenties should find it relatively easy to obtain entry-level jobs in the decades to come.

Table 8–1
Demographic Trends

Trend	Results	Innovations
Decline in new entrants to labor force	Less competition for entry-level jobs Fewer applicants to choose from for lower level jobs	More emphasis on training vs. selection of new employees, better starting wages, more concern for education—including business advocacy in public schools
Aging of the baby boom: Short term	Stalled careers, dissatisfaction with job, demand for more perquisites and new benefits	Job enlargement, worker participation, flextime sabbaticals, gain sharing, better long-term benefits
Long term	Age specific concerns, demands for new benefits and increased retirement options	Retirement counseling, long-term benefits, part-time employment for retiring employees
Women in the work force	New issues of concern to women	Day care, maternity and paternity leave, accommodation for dual careers, relocation programs
	Continued need to address pay and promotion equity problems	Training programs

Organizations, conversely, will find it more difficult to attract and retain new, young employees. In order to attract the employees they want, organizations may be forced to change the inducements that they offer starting employees. Offering better starting wages than the competition may give an organization the edge in recruiting new workers. (This strategy may, however, lead to dissatisfaction if current workers believe that the high starting wages are inequitable. Further, the strategy may reduce the overall salary range in the firm, making promotions more difficult or less desirable.) A cafeteria-style benefit plan (Lawler 1966) offering noncash benefits attractive to a younger age group, such as access to fitness facilities or organization-sponsored social affairs, may help woo youthful employees. Younger workers may also find that alternative work schedules (such as long workweeks with extended annual vacations, occasional work sabbaticals) act as inducements affecting their choice of organizations (Best 1981).

Because of increased competition among organizations for the "cream of the crop," organizations that have counted upon selecting only the top percentage of their applicants, or that have hired a large number of young employees with the intention of using the job to weed out those inappropriate for the job, may be forced to change their strategies. Businesses may find that they must de-emphasize selection of employees in the younger age group and instead emphasize training of new employees. Organizations that in the past have depended upon new, young workers as a way of updating the technical knowledge and skills of a group or department may have to put more effort into the continuing education of their current workers.

Rather than take the entire training burden upon themselves, businesses may take a stronger advocacy role in lobbying for improvements in the public educational system so that all entrants to the workforce possess basic skills in writing, reading, and math. (Recent public demands for educational accountability and solid backgrounds in "the basics" are congruent with employers' demands for better-educated workers.) Employers may also push for technical training programs (for example, training in computer programming) through joint programs with secondary schools and colleges.

The Aging of the Baby Boomers. The number of new entrants into the labor force swelled in the 1960s and 1970s as baby boomers flooded the market. Today, these baby boomers have been absorbed into the work force, but their relative numbers will continue to present problems and challenges to business for decades to come. By 1995, three-fourths of the workers in the labor force will be in their prime employment years (age twenty-five to fifty-four), compared with approximately 60 percent in this age category in 1975 (Fullerton 1985). We therefore expect to see a larger proportion of employees whose career goals include advancement and maintenance, as opposed to the exploration and establishment goals of younger workers (London and Stumpf 1982). That is, a large majority of the labor force will be at the stage in their work lives in which they desire and expect steady advancement in their chosen careers. Two consequences are most obvious: (1) increasing competition for advancement within the organization and, as a result, increasing numbers of individuals who have stalled in their rising career trajectories; and (2) a change in the nature of worker demands, reflecting the older age of the average employee in the workplace.

As a result of the first consequence, we envision that baby boom–age employees will make increasing demands for the job freedom, flexibility, responsibility, and salaries associated with low- and middle-managerial roles—with or without the managerial titles. While career progression has traditionally been conceptualized as movement up the organizational hierarchy, it may also include work-role changes that increase "job, career, and life satisfaction; feelings of psychological success and self-worth; feelings of competence, mastery, and achievement; [and/or] attainment of organizational rewards such as money, power, prestige, and status" (London and Stumpf 1982, 5). Organizations can therefore respond to employee demands for career progression with programs involving some combination of job enlargement/enrichment, worker participation, flextime, work sabbaticals, gain sharing, and employee ownership. If organizations fail to provide either these kinds of innovations or traditional opportunities for advancement, employees may respond by leaving the company in search of more promising career opportunities. The current growth of new, small businesses and of entrepreneurialism may already reflect this dynamic (see Smith's chapter in this book).

As a result of the increasing numbers of older employees' expressing age-specific concerns, organizations may find increased demand for improvements in such areas as health insurance and pension plans. These issues are likely to be of particular concern to baby boomers, aged thirty to fifty, when they face growing financial responsibilities for their families. As the baby boomers age beyond fifty years, a large percentage of the work force may agitate for changes in retirement policies, including, for example, the development of retirement counseling programs and options for continuing part-time employment of older workers. Indeed, this process has started already with the Congress's recent elimination of mandatory retirement for most occupational groups.

Women in the Work Force. Since the 1970s and 1980s, an increasing number of women have joined the labor force. Indeed, women accounted for more than three-fifths of the increase in the civilian labor force between 1973 and 1983 (U.S. Department of Labor 1984a). In the next decades, the presence of women will continue to grow and to exert greater influence in the workplace. In spite of this, women also continue to carry the major burden of domestic and child care chores (Nieva 1984). As a result, organizations that support comprehensive day care programs and liberal maternity and paternity leave policies (Galinsky, in press, U.S. Department of Labor 1980, 1984a) may be better able to attract and keep excellent women employees. Flextime and flexplace plans (Nollen 1979, 1982) may become more common as women (and hence their employers) juggle the dual role demands of work and family. Similarly, dual-career issues will make it ever more difficult for organizations to transfer employees at will, without consideration for the spouse's career (Galinsky, in press). Organizations may respond to this by providing relocation programs for the employee's spouse and family (Hall and Hall 1979).

For the first time ever, women compose more than half of the professional work force (Greer 1986). Though this trend is encouraging, it masks still present inequities. Women are underrepresented in upper-level management and in many of the more lucrative and prestigious professions. Almost 15 percent of working men hold managerial positions while only 7 percent of working women do (U.S. Department of Labor 1984a). Further, less than 1 percent of chief executive officers are women (Field 1982). These figures suggest that gaining access to upper-level positions is still more difficult for women. This concentration of women in the lower-level and lower-paying professions is reflected in the difference between the median weekly earnings of the male professional ($581) and of the female professional ($419) (Greer 1986).

If women's rise in the workplace (in terms of pay and position) fails to match men's, women may push for a legislative or judicial solution to the problem. Business may respond with special training programs for women managers or even with voluntary—or, perhaps, legally mandated—equal pay policies. This may in turn require innovation on the part of personnel researchers and practitioners as the ability to provide fair pay depends upon the development of techniques to analyze and assign values to dissimilar jobs.

Summary. Our discussion above strongly suggests that the most successful organizations of the future will be those that recognize and effectively address the subtle demographic shifts that will occur in the labor market over the next several decades. Virtually every aspect of the human resource or human maintenance subsystem is involved, including selection, training, pay, benefits, retirement, career planning, job design, and participative management plans and policies. Although few organizations will implement sweeping changes throughout these programs, many organizations will, we believe, explore possible changes so that they may more effectively attract new, young employees while simultaneously retaining their most talented older employees.

Technological Change

Technological change has already had a huge impact on the American workplace. It will continue to do so as the next decades bring still greater technological advances. Two technological developments are certain to play a critical role in shaping the future workplace. The first, programmable automation, will have its most direct effects upon the manufacturing sector—especially upon the jobs of blue collar production workers. The second, office automation, will affect the jobs of white collar office workers at all organizational levels. Table 8–2 details the predicted effects of these innovations upon organizations and suggests strategies that organizations may adopt in response to these changes.

Programmable Automation. In the next several decades, the use of programmable automation in U.S. factories will become the rule rather than the exception (Office of Technology Assessment 1984). Though the United States now lags behind Japan in the implementation of advanced computer-manufacturing automation (Lynn 1983), more and more U.S. firms are adopting these production technologies.

As a group, the technologies include: (*a*) *robots* (reprogrammable, multifunctional machines that manipulate material, parts, and tools through a programmed series of motions); (*b*) *computerized numerical control*, or CNC (devices that cut or form a piece of metal according to computer-programmed

Table 8–2
Technological Trends

Trend	Results	Innovations
Programmable automation	Automation displaces large numbers of semiskilled and unskilled workers	Career counseling programs, job retraining programs
	Job content changes for workers remaining in automated factories	Job enrichment, retraining, pay for knowledge, human factors, worker participation programs, safety programs
	"Flatter" organizations, change in supervisory tasks	
Office automation	Deskilling of jobs, less human contact, possible increased boredom and stress	Increased user participation in design and implementation of systems, human factors work, training, financial incentives programs, ergonomics
	Blurring of traditional distinctions between tasks of secretary and other office workers	Job and organizational redesign based upon new job analysis
	Increased options for flextime and flexplace	More use of flextime and flexplace, new selection criteria, development of management tools for communication, evaluation, and promotion of off-site workers

instructions); (*c*) *computer-assisted design*, or CAD (an electric drawing board for draftsmen and design engineers that allows the programmer to analyze and test the performance of the computerized representation of the product); (*d*) *computer-assisted manufacturing*, or CAM (a battery of CNC equipment in which numerous CNC machine tools are controlled by a central computer); and (*e*) *flexible manufacturing systems*, or FMS (systems that combine CAM capabilities with robots and other forms of automated materials handling to move material between workstations, all controlled by a central computer) (OTA 1984, 4; Gerwin 1982).

Specific estimates about the likely impact of programmable automation on employment vary. Hunt and Hunt (1983), for example, estimate that robots will displace 100,000–200,000 workers by 1990. The Office of Technology Assessment (1984) argues that programmable automation "is not likely to generate significant net national unemployment in the near term" (5). Ayres and Miller (1983), taking a longer-time perspective than either Hunt and Hunt or the Office of Technology Assessment, estimate that up to 4 million workers will be displaced by robots over the next twenty years.

Despite these disagreements, experts do agree that programmable automation will have its greatest impact on semiskilled and unskilled jobs in the metal-working industries. The demand for metal-working craft workers and operatives (for example, welders, production assemblers, production painters) will fall sharply (OTA 1984). Many of these displaced workers will have to find jobs outside the automating organization (OTA 1984). Their skills will simply no longer be needed by their organization or, for that matter, by any similar organization. Although experts (for example, Harris 1985) believe that automation will ultimately stimulate the economy and create new jobs (as a result of the lowered costs of manufactured goods), these new jobs are likely to differ greatly from the displaced workers' old jobs. Many such jobs will be in the service sector or will demand more education and technical skill than the worker needed in the past. Manufacturing firms may be forced—by their union contracts, federal or state legislation, and/or simply by their desire to maintain employee morale, community support, and a good public image for the firm—to bear at least part of the burden of counseling and retraining displaced workers for the new job market (Tornatzky, Hetzner, and Eveland 1984).

The human worker is still an essential part of the automated factory, however. Though robots are stronger than humans and are impervious to fatigue, boredom, or hazardous working conditions, they are easily "confused" by changing environments and they come nowhere near to possessing the sensory and problem-solving abilities of the human worker (Ayres 1984). The challenge for the manufacturing organization is thus to create effective human-automation teams (Gerwin 1982, OTA 1984, Majchrzak and Klein 1987, Parsons and Kearsley 1982, Shaiken 1985). The alternative is decreased productivity because of the waste of human potential, resistance to change, and possibly even costly deliberate sabotage by dissatisfied workers who find their deskilled jobs boring and stressful (Argote and Goodman 1984, Shaiken 1984).

Manufacturing firms may avert the potentially negative consequences of implementing advanced manufacturing technology in a number of ways. First, workers who stay in the organization may be retrained, possibly in the repair and running of the new automated machinery. To aid this process, organizations may want to adopt "pay for knowledge" plans (Jenkins and Gupta 1982) to motivate workers to take a continuing interest in updating their technical knowledge. Reassignment of the most routine and dangerous tasks to computerized equipment (Parsons and Kearsley 1982) will free the more varied and challenging tasks for human workers, an ideal condition for job enrichment. There will be an increased need for human factors applications both to create "user-friendly" manufacturing automation and to reduce the chances of human errors multiplied many times over by automated machinery. Worker participation in the implementation and management of the new equipment may make the transition to programmable automation easier (Argote and Goodman 1984, Gerwin 1982, Leonard-Barton and Kraus 1985, Tornatzky, Hetzner, and Eveland 1984). Training and education programs will also be necessary to teach operating techniques and safety precautions to those running the new equipment.

In addition, managerial and supervisory employees will find themselves running a "flatter" organization, as the numbers and categories of workers decrease (Gerwin 1982, Leonard-Barton and Kraus 1985). As a result, lower-level supervisors in particular may find that their jobs vanish or are changed radically. The organization will have to accommodate these employees' needs for security and new career options.

Office Automation. White collar workers compose an increasingly large portion of the American work force. Most white collar workers are employed in office settings where their principle task is the effective procurement, storage, retrieval, and communication of information (Guiliano 1982, OTA 1985). The tools used in office work have changed dramatically over the last century, progressing from the manual typewriter of the late nineteenth century to the microcomputer of the late twentieth. Because of the rising costs of office work and the organization's increased need for complex information (Olson and Lucas 1982), office automation (microelectronic information and communication technology) is increasingly viewed by many managers as a necessity, not a luxury. Automation will create both new problems and new possibilities for the office of the future.

The benefits of office automation to the work group or organization are a direct function of employees' willingness to use the systems effectively. Since use of the systems can sometimes result in deskilled jobs, decreased human contact, health hazards, and increased stress (Sauter et al. 1985), particularly for data entry and clerical employees, these employees may resist their implementation and use (OTA 1985). Organizations will have to respond with increased user participation in the design and implementation of systems (Driscoll 1982), job redesign, and improved human factors applications. Retraining programs (see, for example, Goldstein 1986) and financial incentive programs (for example, "pay for knowledge") will be necessary if employees are to make full use of complex and frequently updated equipment. Because of rapid technological improvements, the most effective training programs over the long run may be those that provide a broad knowledge base, rather than train employees in narrow aspects of a single system (OTA 1985).

Long-term effects of office automation include the blurring of distinctions between clerical and other office functions, as managers and professionals use microcomputers and spreadsheet or word-processing software to produce their own typed copy (Sokol 1986). In fact, this trend, as well as the current interest in more efficiently capturing and sharing data, means that clerical and data entry jobs are the positions most likely to be eliminated or changed drastically in the long term. In the short term, however, many organizations actually increase their personnel when automating, because of initial inefficiency and the need to create new parts of the organization with expertise in use, repair, and purchasing of office automation (OTA 1985). Thus, office automation will lead to changes in the occupational distribution of the workforce, which in turn force new job descriptions and a re-evaluation of organizational pay structures (for example, flatter organizations with reduced numbers of clerical staff and their first-line supervisors) (OTA 1985).

Office automation, especially electronic communication and networking capabilities, has the capacity to free the organization from some of the existing constraints of time and place (Olson 1983). Scheduling of work hours may become more flexible, and employees who previously had little communication because of geographical separation may now interact frequently (Hiltz 1984, Olson 1983). Telecommunications capacities make it easier for workers to do their jobs at a site remote from the office. The organization may benefit from reduced rent and utility costs, increased worker productivity, and decreased turnover and absenteeism (Pratt 1984). As workers become more independent of the organization, they may be increasingly hired on a piecework or contract basis, again cutting labor costs. Organizations will need to develop selection tools to identify workers who can maintain high levels of productivity and satisfaction outside of the office. Organizations will also need to develop methods that allow managers to communicate with, evaluate, and promote off-site employees.

Summary. As organizations implement new manufacturing and office technologies, they must, the discussion above suggests, simultaneously implement a variety of changes in their human or social "technologies." Four such changes stand out: (1) training and counseling of employees who lack the skills necessary to operate the new machinery, (2) job redesign to maximize the effectiveness of both humans and machines, (3) worker participation in the selection and implementation of the new technologies, and (4) redesign of the managerial structure to create flatter organizational hierarchies. A fifth change goes hand in hand with the implementation of both manufacturing and office technologies: the rise of the technology experts, those individuals who design, program, and maintain the new automated equipment (Silvestri, Lukasiewicz, and Einstein 1983). The importance of their unique skills and knowledge will make them increasingly powerful within the managerial hierarchy of both industrial and service firms.

Changes in the Economic Environment of the Firm

Our discussion of changes in the economic environment of the firm focuses on three predictable shifts—three shifts that are, indeed, already evident: (1) the shift from a manufacturing to a service economy, (2) increasing international competition, and (3) the changing nature of unions and labor-management relations. Table 8–3 contains a list of the economic changes, their effects upon the organization, and suggested organizational strategies for dealing with these changes.

The Shift from a Manufacturing to a Service Economy. The steady shift in American business from manufacturing to service is striking. Between 1950 and 1980, service sector jobs increased from fewer than half to approximately 80 percent of all U.S. jobs; by the end of the century, service employment may account for 95 percent of all jobs (Macarov 1983). Almost nine out of ten new jobs added to the economy in the period 1984–95 are expected to be in the service-producing industry (Personick 1985). As impressive as these figures are, they mask a great deal of confusion in the definition of *service sector*. A common definition distinguishes between people who create or change physical objects and those who do not (Macarov 1983). If this definition is operationalized at the company or industry level, however, it overlooks the fact that a large percentage of people employed in goods-producing industries actually hold service jobs (for example, secretarial, advertising, and janitorial work).

Table 8–3
Trends in the Economic Environment of the Firm

Trend	Results	Innovations
Shift from manufacturing to service economy	Businesses focus new attention on service delivery	Selection, training, and reward systems to improve service delivery
	Employee dissatisfaction with low pay and security of service work, possible unionization of service sector	Higher starting wages, career development programs
International competition	U.S. firms strive to enhance their ability to compete with their foreign counterparts	Flexible compensation and benefit plans (for example, gain sharing), interest in foreign innovations, cross-cultural skills and knowledge as selection criteria, improved methods of measurement and reward for employee effort, increased marketing and consumer research
Unions, labor management cooperation	Unions attempt to reverse their decline, recruitment of younger employees in the service sector, possible success in unionization drives	Lifetime employment, increased in-house training and retraining programs, profit sharing, day care, QWL programs, accrued pension benefits

In spite of these definitional difficulties, it is clear that the shift from manufacturing to service—whatever its precise magnitude—is changing the nature of the American workplace, especially for lower-skilled, nonmanagerial employees. That is, the shift from manufacturing to service work may present the nonmanagerial employee with two significant changes in the nature and circumstances of his or her work: (1) an increase in the importance of "people work"—dealing with customers and clients, not just co-workers and things—and (2) a decline in pay and security.

Insofar as the service and the delivery of that service are often indistinguishable (Schneider and Bowen 1984), businesses must do all they can to improve service delivery in order to attract and keep customers. As a result, service organizations may begin to select employees for their superiority in managing customer relations, may develop programs to train employees in these skills, and may reward employees for mastering them. Today, the technologies to do these things are still new and imperfect; they will only become more essential.

Similarly, we also envision that performance appraisal and career development in the services will become increasingly important and difficult. Evaluating productivity and performance in the service sector is notoriously difficult (Lawler 1983, Macarov 1983, Sink, Tuttle, and DeVries 1984). Further, many low-level service jobs are perceived as dead-end positions (Arnowitz 1986). In order to keep their best employees, service organizations may need to learn to assess performance better and to reward it with increments in prestige, responsibility, and pay.

This brings us to the second critical aspect of a shift from manufacturing to service work: pay cuts for low-skilled workers who have lost manufacturing jobs and must find new employment in the service sector. According to 1980 figures, the average gross weekly wage in the U.S. private sector, excluding supervisory and managerial employees and all agricultural employees, was $235 (Macarov 1983). Mining, construction, manufacturing, transportation, and public utilities nonmanagerial employees earned more than average, while employees in wholesale and retail trade, finance, insurance, real estate, and services earned less (Macarov 1983). These figures suggest that displaced nonmanagerial workers in the manufacturing sector may suffer a cut in pay when they take jobs in the service sector.

Currently, service organizations appear to have little difficulty in filling low- and entry-level positions, even if the job pays less than a comparable job in the manufacturing sector. It is possible to imagine, however, that service organizations will be forced to pay higher low-level and entry-level wages and salaries if more and more service organizations compete for employees, or if employees become dissatisfied with their wages in the service sector. This last possibility in turn raises the chance of increasing unionization of service employees, a point we discuss in greater detail below.

Increasing International Competition. International business competition has already had a major impact on American business, resulting in layoffs in the auto, steel, and shoe industries (to name but a few) and in a tremendous push for "excellence" and innovation in all industries. Unless the government passes substantial protectionist legislation, international competition is here to stay. As a result, American businesses are likely to take numerous actions to enhance their ability to compete with their foreign counterparts. Some are already in place. We expect, for example, to see continuing attempts on the part of American firms to lower U.S. wage costs—particularly by creating flexible compensation and benefit plans that link employee rewards to the profitability and productivity of the firm. Similarly, it seems likely that American businesses will continue to thirst for workplace innovations that appear to hold the key to the success of their foreign competitors; witness, for example, the American fascination with the Japanese quality circle just a few short years ago.

More novel strategies are sure to arise as well. Pilot projects in offshore data entry are currently under way—the advantages of low wages and a surplus of workers may outweigh the disadvantages of long-distance electronic data transfer (OTA 1985). We imagine that U.S. companies will increasingly attempt to select employees who, through their formal education or previous work experience, are knowledgeable about foreign countries and who may therefore improve the company's operations in, and sales and service to, foreign customers. To compete better both in the United States and abroad, American firms are also likely to press for more accurate measures of, and stronger rewards and sanctions for, both the quantity and quality of employee effort. Finally, American firms will devote increasing attention to marketing and consumer research in order to accommodate customer demand better. Underlying all of these possible changes is one fairly obvious rule: As international competition erodes the confidence and complacency of many American firms, so American firms will continue to challenge any such complacency on the part of their employees.

The Changing Nature of Unions and Labor-Management Relations. With union membership as a percent of the total American labor force at its lowest point in fifty years, many observers have been sounding the death knell of the American labor movement. Recent evidence suggests, however, that labor leaders have heard that death knell and are struggling now to revive the patient (AFL-CIO 1985).

Many of the trends we have discussed have already hurt the labor movement; union declines stem in part from problems in the manufacturing sector as a result of technological changes, the growth of the service sector, and foreign competition in the smokestack industries. To adjust to these changes, unions have been forced to accept wage concessions while fighting with some success for lifetime job guarantees, employee-retraining programs, increased worker

influence in shaping company policies and practices, and even employee ownership (Rosen, Klein, and Young 1985) and/or profit sharing. At the same time,
many unions are now striving to reach out to new groups of workers—particularly to clerical and low-level service workers (Greenhouse 1985). Further,
to attract younger, often female workers, unions are focusing more and more
on issues beyond pay and job security, including quality of work life, child
care, employee education and training, and—reflecting the high mobility of
today's workers—accrued pension plans (Greenhouse 1985).

Union success in these areas, or even the simple threat of union success,
may force American businesses to innovate—whether to carry out the union
contract or to anticipate employee desires and thereby avoid unionization of
the firm. The alternative possibility is that the labor movement will continue
in its slow and steady decline. In such a case, unions will pose less of an immediate threat to American firms. Still, no firm can be so utterly confident
or oblivious as to disregard concerns for employee satisfaction.

Summary. The economic changes outlined above will bring changes in employee
selection, training, performance appraisal, and compensation systems as
organizations maneuver to capture the competitive edge. In an increasingly complex and competitive environment, organizations will be forced to build new
rigor into their maintenance subsystems so that they may select particularly talented employees, train them further, and then reward them for their performance.

Conclusions

Changes in the demographics of the labor force, in manufacturing and office
automation, and in the economic environment of the firm are likely to engender
a variety of workplace innovations over the course of the next twenty years.
Despite the diversity of the changes, the resulting innovations fall into five fairly
neat categories: (1) quality of work life (QWL), job redesign, and sociotechnical
innovations, (2) innovations in financial reward systems, (3) new employee
benefits and policies, (4) innovative selection and performance appraisal practices, and (5) innovative developments in employee training, counseling, and
education.

The quality of work life, job redesign, and sociotechnical innovations sub-
sume a variety of techniques, including job enlargement/enrichment, worker
participation programs, flexplace, and flextime. The goal of these techniques
is to use workers' intimate knowledge of their own jobs to remove productivity
inhibitors and to make the workplace more intrinsically rewarding. By increasing
the involvement of employees, such QWL programs may aid in attracting and
retaining qualified employees, increase worker productivity, and/or decrease
employer costs. Thus, these innovations are valid responses to all three of

the general changes that we have discussed: demographic changes, automation, and a changing economic environment.

Innovations in financial reward systems include improvements in starting wages, pay-for-knowledge plans, profit-sharing plans, employee ownership plans, accrued pension plans, and improved health, insurance, and retirement benefits. Like QWL innovations, financial reward innovations also help ease workers' transitions to the challenges of a changing work force and an increasingly competitive (and technological) organizational environment. Because change involves a certain amount of individual stress and strain, workers may be reluctant to change. Financial reward innovations are likely to communicate to employees that management is willing to invest not only in new technology, but also in human resources. This vote of confidence may make the difference in retaining valuable employees when the organization faces stress and change.

New employee benefits and policies include corporate child care programs, maternity and paternity leave, relocation programs for dual-career couples, delays in mandatory retirement, part-time work for older workers, worker sabbaticals, and related programs. These innovations are particularly appropriate responses to changes in the demographics of the labor force. The organizational investments that these programs require will be offset by the increased ability of the organization to attract and retain workers—members of a new work force that will be older and more predominantly female than today's.

If employers are to invest more in workers, it is especially important for them to select the best possible workers. We have not yet completely developed the selection techniques and criteria for choosing good service workers, off-site workers, or workers knowledgeable about foreign countries. There is also room for improvement in performance appraisal techniques for these workers. Unlike the preceding set of innovations, the selection and performance appraisal innovations reflect employer, not employee, needs.

Finally, innovations in employee training, counseling, and education are particularly needed in response to increased automation—both because of the need for employees to work with the new automation, and because increasing numbers of jobs will involve working primarily with information. Thus, we need to develop techniques for retraining and counseling displaced workers and for training new entrants to the labor force (possibly in tandem with public education). The changing demographics of the labor force may also require training for female managers and increased attention to retirement counseling.

We find four aspects of this list and of our entire review particularly surprising and intriguing. First, we are struck by the continued utility of traditional human resource management techniques such as selection, performance appraisal, and training. These are hardly "sexy" innovations, touted in the popular business press. (By contrast, the first three sets of innovations are on the current cutting edge of business practice.) Yet the success of the workplace organization of the future may depend to a great extent on their application to both old and new challenges.

Second, we are struck by how little is known about maximizing the effectiveness of the innovations discussed above. How should a pay-for-knowledge plan be designed and implemented? What are its long-term consequences? We might ask the same questions about worker participation systems, flexplace plans, retirement policies, technical-training programs, performance appraisal systems—indeed, about all of the innovations we have described. Thus, we see a tremendous need for systematic, longitudinal, and multisite evaluation of maintenance subsystem strategies.

Third, although many of our suggestions may seem commonsensical, even simplistic, there is evidence that organizations find it difficult, for a variety of reasons, to change their internal structure and processes in response to new technologies and environmental contingencies (Child, Ganter, and Kieser 1987). This may be one reason why many of the innovations we describe above are now only in limited use in American businesses, even though they would benefit companies today and even though the innovations have been promoted in the literature for years.

Finally, we are struck by the potential for a conflict to arise between *organizational* and *employee* goals and needs. Indeed, this may be little more than an age-old labor-management struggle. Over and over again in our review, we implicitly or explicitly posed two conditionals: "If organizations want to maximize productivity and profitability, they will . . ." and "If organizations want to maximize employee satisfaction, they will . . ." Many theories of organizational behavior assume that the two conditionals lead to the same place, that what is good for employees is good for business. We hope this is true, but as businesses face increasing competition and as employees demand increasing financial, practical, and psychological benefits for their work, it is possible to imagine not harmony between organizational and employee demands but a collision course.

9
Technology, Organization of the Future, and Nonmanagement Roles

Thomas C. Tuttle

Introduction

"The paradox is that when introducing advanced technology calling for less labor per unit produced, people become more important and their competence more desirable" (Berth Jonsson, in Jonsson et al. 1984, 6).

This quote from the head of organization development for Volvo AB, one of the world's leading edge organizations, provides an appropriate framework for this chapter. What is the organization of the future? Of course no one is really sure. Obviously there will be many "organizations of the future," perhaps very different from each other. Nevertheless, we can speculate on some of the common elements that will characterize these organizations— that is the purpose of this book. This chapter will discuss one view of those themes and their implications for the working lives of nonmanagement employees.

The Berth Jonsson statement addresses several themes that will probably characterize the organization of the future. One is a reduction of labor input per unit of production. This is likely to be accomplished by an increase in automation. This automation will occur not only in the production process, but also in the support areas. However, this resulting decrease in the number of employees has an interesting effect. The remaining people become more critical to the total operation. Their competence becomes a more essential ingredient for the competitive success of the organization. In essence, this is the message of this chapter.

The chapter has two major sections. The first attempts to describe the organization of the future with respect to strategy, structure, technology, and human resource management. The second part of the chapter will describe the implications of these changes for various nonmanagement roles—staff, professional/technical, production, and support.

Glimpses of the Organization of the Future

Strategy

The competitive strategy of a firm is a combination of the ends it seeks (goals) and the means it selects to achieve those ends (policies) (Porter 1980). Competitive strategies are shaped by factors both internal and external to the organization. In his introductory chapter to this book, Hage discusses some of the major external forces that will shape the strategies of the organization of the future. Hage addresses issues such as the globalization of markets and organizations, shorter product life cycles, increased market segmentation and product differentiation, increasing concern about the educational ability of American workers, and demographic shifts that will produce labor shortages. Survival in this era of new competition will require the development and implementation of strategies that lead to a sustainable competitive advantage.

What will be the key elements of these strategies? The essence of strategy development is an attempt to differentiate one organization from another. Despite this, similarities in the environments faced by organizations will lead to some general commonalities among successful strategies. From this writer's perspective these will be increased organizational flexibility, increased focus on core values as a basis for guiding policy, product and process innovation, cost reduction, and improved quality.

Increasing Organizational Flexibility.

> Surprisingly to many, in the last decade even our share of world exports of high technology products has declined from 25 to 20 percent. And the U.S. share of world trade in such services as insurance, finance, aviation, shipping and engineering also has declined from 25 to 20 percent. . . . In order to seize the competitive edge, we must maximize the flexibility and adaptability of American workers and managers (Richard Foxen, in NASA 1984, 3–4).

Increased competition, technological development, and shorter product life cycles all suggest that organizations must be able to respond more quickly to changes in the future than they have in the past. These conditions will require that organizations operate differently. These differences will be seen in structure, the integration of information systems across functional boundaries, decentralized decision making, fewer job classifications and multiskilled work forces, more effective communication among functional groups, strategic thinking at all organizational levels, and team problem-solving activities.

Adherence to Core Values.
As organizations face the need to change more rapidly, they also have a greater need for stability. This "dynamic stability," or consistency in the face of rapid change, comes from clear articulation and adherence

to a set of core values. This value-driven approach takes many forms. Peters and Waterman (1982) provide many examples of firms that are "hands-on-value driven." The core values may be articulated in the form of a corporate philosophy:

> Success is people working together. Preston's most important asset is people, not tractors, trailers, terminals, or management systems. The following quotation from the German philosopher, Goethe, summarizes our regard for people, "Treat people as though they were what they ought to be and you help them become what they are capable of being." This means that Preston People must be regarded as partners rather than as adversaries.
>
> The person doing the job knows more about it than anyone else. It is the responsibility of managers to ask for suggestions, to listen to possible solutions to specific problems, and to help implement productive change. Each employee has unlimited possibilities. Good managers have the ability to recognize and unleash the potential for better performance. Managers have no more important responsibility than to develop our people and continually create a better, more productive environment. At Preston improvement is always possible and is continually sought.
>
> Every Preston employee deserves to be treated with respect. Each group of employees must understand what is important for its success and how it contributes to the progress of the Company. Coordinators are expected to hold regular meetings which will accomplish this objective. Employees are encouraged to ask any questions which will give them better information about their jobs, benefits, the Company, or the performance of their groups. The better informed each employee is about his job and how it relates to other jobs, the greater will be the opportunities for making the organization more effective.
>
> It is the responsibility of those in management to regard each employee as an effective performer until specific results indicate where there are areas for improvement. To achieve this refinement, managers first pinpoint the performance area, develop a baseline, and work with the employee to establish and reach a goal for improvement. As soon as progression is recorded, appropriate reinforcement is given.
>
> Managers are to be fair, firm, and positive in correcting substandard performance and inappropriate behavior. Discipline such as firing or time off without pay is employed only as a last resort for flagrant violations of ethical standards of work rules which have been clearly communicated. In all areas where correction is needed, managers must first counsel the subordinate about his actions and obtain a commitment for constructive change. The manager must ask what he can do to help the employee bring about the needed change. If the worker perceives an obstacle to improvement, this hindrance should be addressed. Warning letters are used only after the individual has been clearly informed of the problem, and then has been given sufficient time and assistance to correct it.

Adopted with permission from Preston Corporation.

Although managers observe and rectify errors, it is just as important that they give credit when a job is being done properly. No healthy work environment should have more negative comments than positive ones. The obligation of managers and supervisors is to create an atmosphere wherein employees constantly gain more knowledge and are able to participate in setting challenging goals to achieve outstanding results.

Customers. Our survival and success depend on how well we consistently serve our customers. Each job has an impact on the timeliness, quality, and cost effectiveness of what is expected to respect and have concern for customer needs. Once a commitment is made to a customer or another employee, it must be fulfilled on time.

Our dealings with our customers and each other are to be conducted in a professional and respectful manner at all times. This means that each person must strive to be a better listener than a talker. A professional is one who never stops learning from others, so he is always able to perform his job better for the benefit of Preston and our customers.

No matter how excited a customer is about his problem, it is our obligation to remain calm at all times. Another person's problem is always important to him, so we must always treat it as such. Once the issue has been identified we must pinpoint the steps that are to be taken to correct it in a timely manner. If we are unable to accomplish our objectives in the time frame that has been established, we must call the customer and set a new timetable so he knows what progress is being made. After the problem has been solved, those responsible for its occurrence should understand what took place and what can be done in the future to prevent the problem from recurring. Acknowledgments of superior service from customers should be communicated immediately to those employees who are able to achieve outstanding results. Each person should never forget that when he talks to a customer, he is a vital part of our sales effort during each conversation. It always should be our objective to make the best impression on our customers whenever we have the opportunity. The respect that Preston earns from its customers is determined by the actions of each employee.

Satisfied customers are the best advertising that Preston can have. Although errors will occur, our goal is to achieve 100 percent customer satisfaction. It is our objective to constantly minimize the frequency of customer complaints. At the same time there can be no excuse for the same problem recurring when it is in our control to prevent this from happening. Dissatisfaction with Preston only benefits the competition. Dedicated customer awareness will enable Preston to enjoy sound growth in partnership with satisfied customers. At Preston customer satisfaction is the number one priority.

Other organizations may state guiding principles, and still others may explicitly state core values. Not only do the core values help steer the organization through the turbulence of environmental change, they also serve to unite a diverse work force. The common values, consistently communicated, built into management control systems, and used as signposts to guide decisions and actions serve to build a common organizational culture.

Product and Process Innovation. Responding to the new rules of competition requires that an organization creatively adapt through innovation to customer needs. Product innovation is the most visible evidence of the innovative organization. However, process innovation is equally important in sustaining competitive advantage. Creating a climate that encourages innovation requires dedicated management attention. It also places demands and expectations on nonmanagement employees. "Business as usual" is no longer acceptable. Nonmanagement employees are expected to be a source of new ideas that will fuel the innovation process.

Cost. A key element of competitive strategy is the organization's position regarding its cost and pricing structure in the marketplace. In some product lines, cost is the major determinant of competitive success. However, more educated consumers are increasingly considering other factors in addition to initial cost in product selection (for example, quality, delivery time, design, and so forth). Nevertheless, global competition will continue to drive a strong concern for cost reduction in virtually every industrial and service sector.

Quality. Another product of the forces shaping the environment for the organization of the future is a renewed interest in quality. The essence of this quality revolution is a greater focus on products and services that "meet the needs of the customer." Definitions of *quality* are changing from conformity to the designer's specifications to a concern with making sure the product specifications meet the customer's specifications.

Within the production process, a concern with "process quality" has become a major focus. Process quality is concerned with building quality into the product as opposed to inspection and rework of a poor product. Hayes and Wheelwright (1984) point out that before you can build quality in, you must first "think it in." These authors list five practices necessary to thinking in of quality. These are:

1. Carefully preplanning during the product design stage, and involving engineering, production, quality assurance, and marketing

2. Training workers so that they are capable of delivering high quality, and developing expectations of high quality in them

3. Developing a working environment in which people are encouraged to surface, discuss, and resolve quality issues, not hide them

4. Working with suppliers to assure defect-free parts, and accepting only perfect parts

5. Purging your thinking of the concept of acceptable quality level (AQL) and instead accepting the concept of continuous improvement—no defect is acceptable

Organizations that fully institutionalize these concepts find that quality increases and costs decrease. Hayes and Wheelwright quote a Japanese manager as saying:

> If you eliminate the production of defective items, things become much simpler and less costly to manage. You don't need as many inspectors as before. You don't need to have production workers doing rework, or systems that manage the detection and flow of rework through the process. Waste goes down. Inventory goes down. But morale goes up. Everybody feels proud when you produce only perfect products (1984, 363).

When organizations adopt quality as a competitive strategy, they are committing to a major organizational culture shift. Nothing less will be sufficient to meet the new competition.

Structure

A second major organizational trend is a shift in organizational structures. Figure 9–1 depicts the shift that is taking place in many organizations.

Naisbitt refers to this trend: "Computers and the whittling away of middle management are toppling hierarchies, flattening the pyramid. At Apple Computer, for example, fifteen people report to CEO John Sculley" (Naisbitt and Aburdene 1985).

FROM THIS . . . . TO THIS

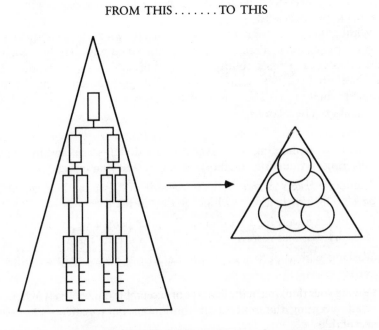

Figure 9–1. Shift in Organization Structure

Replacing the pyramid are decentralized, product-oriented divisions, or profit centers. Within these divisions, team structures are common. Names given to such new organization types vary from W.L. Gore's "lattice," to 3M's biological organization, to Magna International's "organic" organizational structure. However, in many cases the objectives are similar. These objectives are manageable organization size, flexibility, and low management cost, which are reflected in few layers and few managers relative to the number of "production" employees.

One of the United States' most successful firms at continuous innovation is 3M. As cited by Naisbitt and Aburdene, their commitment to decentralization is legendary. A firm with approximately 87,000 employees has a "biological" structure characterized by

- Medium plant size of 115 people
- Five of ninety plants have more than 1,000 people
- Plants are located in small-town America.

Although there are many variations of this theme with respect to organizational structure, the direction of movement seems inescapable. The rash of corporate restructurings occurring in the 1980s carries with it downsizing and a reduction of layers of management.

The moves toward restructuring are driven by strategic considerations. Foremost among them appear to be cost/profitability considerations. Either as a result of corporate takeover or as a defense against takeover, moves are made to increase profitability or stock value by cutting costs. A second motivation is to increase organizational flexibility and the capacity to react more quickly to environmental demands, including changing customer needs. From this author's experience, both of these strategies can lead to leaner and flatter organizational structures. Most restructurings are probably driven somewhat by both goals. However, in terms of the effect on the organization, there is a difference depending on which of these motives is primary.

When cost reduction is primary, and it is implemented in a top-down autocratic fashion, it is likely to have negative consequences on flexibility, innovation, quality, and employee commitment. When flexibility and customer responsiveness are primary, innovation, quality, and employee commitment are likely to be enhanced. However, cost reductions will probably occur at a slower rate. Therefore the competitive environment and the organizational culture will probably determine the approach taken to restructuring. Too often, these decisions are made in a crisis mode, which leads to cost reduction strategies becoming primary. Organizations are then forced to attempt to recreate a culture that is more conducive to performance improvement.

By necessity and design, flatter organizational structures will push decision making to lower levels. However, as Lawler (1986) argues, this in itself is insufficient to create high-performing organizations. In addition to moving decison-making authority to lower levels, successful "high-involvement management"

(Lawler 1986) also requires that rewards, knowledge, and information be moved down concurrently.

Such an organizational design based on decentralized and more autonmous work groups places a greater demand on communication and information flow. Information must flow to the levels at which decisions are made. In addition, decision making must become more collaborative. Information technology, properly designed, can facilitate these communication and decision requirements. However, person-to-person communication linkages will always remain vital.

Technology

In his opening chapter, Hage presents an innovative conception of technology. He views technology as a subset of the broader category of knowledge. The more typical notion of technology Hage refers to as "machine" and "method." However, he accurately points out that these cannot be totally divorced from the other categories of knowledge—that is, the theories or models and the skills of people.

The importance of this broad conception of knowledge as opposed to the typical narrow conception of technology is illustrated by the example depicted in figure 9–2.

In the first column of this diagram we can trace the steps required to produce a letter using the old electric typewriter technology. Column two, "Without Culture Change," uses a potentially improved technology but the same method and same model—that is, handwritten manuscript and mail delivery. As a result, the new technology leads to little improvement, only the elimination of the retype step. Column three begins to reap the benefits of the new technology, and column four shows even greater benefit. In column three we see a new model, the originator keys in the document. This also requires new skills, skills of keyboarding. Column four moves further toward a new model in that the document is transmitted electronically. This new model involves new machines (for example, a modem), new methods (for example, direct data communication), and new skills (for example, use of communication software and hardware). However, the process depicted in column four is the most efficient by far. In order to achieve these increased performance gains more than new technology was required. Also required was a new way of thinking about document creation (a new model) and new skills. In essence, to reap the benefits of new machines a new culture is required.

This rather simple example illustrates very clearly the difficulties associated with efforts to reap the promise of new technology. It also helps explain where failures can occur of new technology to live up to the promises made by vendors.

This section makes no attempt to forecast specific types of technological gains in the organizations of the future. Rather, it attempts to describe this

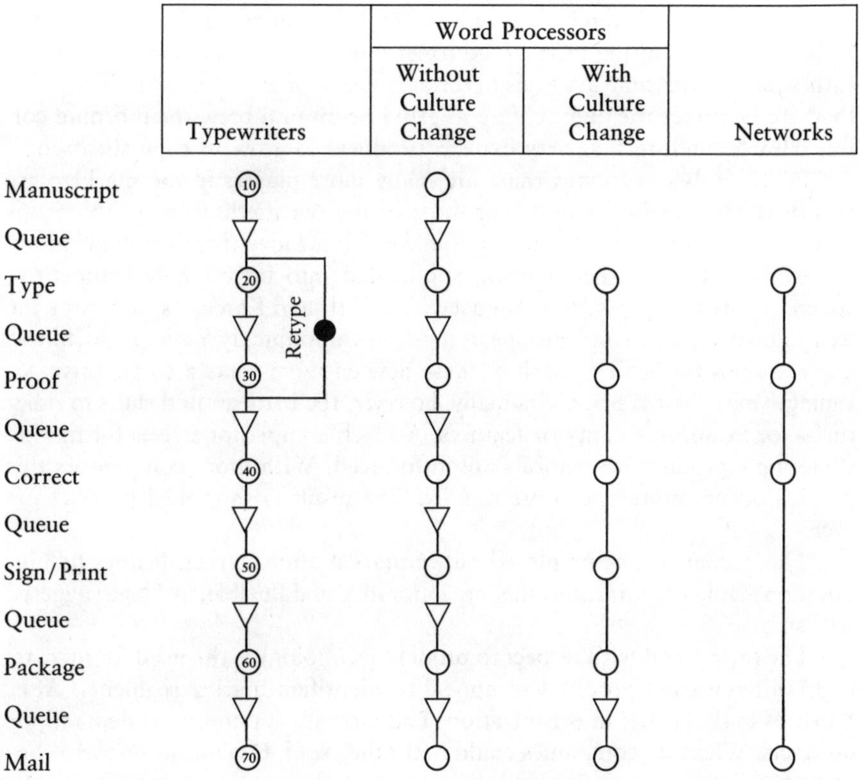

| | | Word Processors | | |
	Typewriters	Without Culture Change	With Culture Change	Networks

Manuscript

Queue

Type

Queue

Proof

Queue

Correct

Queue

Sign/Print

Queue

Package

Queue

Mail

Source: Dhin (1987).

Figure 9–2. Training-aided Culture Change—An Example

author's view of some major directions or purposes of this new technology and the implications of these trends for the nonmanagement employee. The section will be split into two major sections that focus separately on product and process technology. Within these, some key developments will be addressed.

Product Technology. Product technology refers to the characteristics of the final product that is delivered to the customer. With respect to product technology three trends are readily apparent: (1) product technology is becoming more sophisticated, (2) product life cycles are being reduced, and (3) increased differentiation of products is required in order to appeal to an increasingly diverse market. From automobiles to toys to office equipment to weapon systems to food processors, our products are becoming more technologically complex. To some degree this increased sophistication is driven by the technologies themselves. That is, the technology exists, therefore it should be put to use.

In other cases it is driven by consumer or customer demand. For example, the combination of shifting tastes to gourmet food and a concern in a two-wage-earner family with time use leads to the acceptance of an automatic coffeemaker that can be preset the night before to grind beans and brew the morning coffee. Clearly, high-tech society expects products to grow in sophistication.

In the global economy, there are many more players in the marketplace than was the case in the past. For most of the twentieth century Americans had a choice among three major automakers, but today there are many more. A shrinking U.S. market is being subdivided into increasingly competitive spheres by new imports from Yugoslavia, Brazil, and Korea, as well as by the well-known Japanese and European models. Undoubtedly Soviet and Chinese autos are not far behind. Each of these new entrants seeks a competitive advantage. Initially it is price. Gradually, however, the battleground shifts to other turf—for example, quality or features. As each competitor strives for market share, new product innovations are introduced. With more competitors this process occurs more and more rapidly. The result is shortened product life cycles.

This scenario is being played out in market after market. It does fuel innovation. Only organizations that are innovative and flexible, as Hage suggests, will survive.

The third trend with respect to product technology is the need for increasingly differentiated products to appeal to identified market segments. After World War II, American organizations had virtually an unlimited demand for products. Whatever companies could make they sold. Organizations were concerned with increasing output to keep up with demand. Today, and into the foreseeable future, this situation does not exist. The Japanese are moving into a similar period of stability, following rapid economic growth. In a period of stable markets, competition is greater. Organizations cannot sell all that they make unless it has consumer appeal. As a result, we hear of organizations today describing themselves as "market driven."

Using Hage's ideas, the models, technologies, methods, and skills of a market-driven organization must be quite different from those of a production-driven organization. The market-driven organization must be much more sensitive to the signals it receives from the environment. Instead of a few marketing people with their "ears to the ground," every employee must become a marketing person. The organization must decentralize functions, be able to integrate information from diverse functional units, and act quickly on that information to produce new products and services.

Process Technology. The most far-reaching effects of new technology on nonmanagement employees will result from changes in process technology. The forces driving product technology changes have considerable implications for the technology required to produce these products.

One view of how these processes will change is provided by a National Science Foundation report (Solberg et al. 1985). These analysts concluded that production technology in manufacturing organizations will be characterized by

- Dramatically reduced cycle times from order to delivery

- Flexibility—the range of capabilities of hardware will be expanded and set-up times will become negligible in order to make small batches economical

- Transition to more machine intelligence—however, this must move beyond simply capturing human expertise in expert systems to systems built on rational process models and physical laws

- Integration of technologies—advances in narrow fields of technology are wasted if bottlenecks occur at the interfaces

The authors of this NSF report (Solberg et al. 1985) argue that these changes are being driven by manufacturers' requirements for increased quality, lower costs, and reduced flow times. These strategic variables, combined with product technology and image in the marketplace, are the basic ingredients of competitive advantage. Thus, what is happening in process technology is that organizations are attempting to use production processes as a strategic tool.

Significant changes are being made in production technology in manufacturing. However, the so-called indirect or overhead functions are also being affected by new technology. Since for many organizations the greatest labor costs are in the so-called white collar areas, these areas are increasingly becoming targets for automation. Examples of one firm's efforts to modernize production technology in these areas can be seen in the list of proposed projects in figure 9–3.

Management Systems

The final aspect of the organization of the future to be discussed will be management systems. This is a broad category that encompasses human resource management systems, management control systems like performance measurement, budgeting, accounting, and planning systems. It is through management systems that organizational strategy, vision, and core values become institutionalized.

In the past these management systems have often been viewed as separate systems, designed by professionals or technical specialists to help the organization control various facets of the operation. In the organization of the future these management systems will be viewed as strategic tools to help the organization develop and sustain a competitive advantage. This approach to the design of management systems requires that business strategy, core values, and operating principles be defined in advance. Next, this approach requires that organizations define the types of behaviors (for example, risk taking, decisiveness, collaborative

SUPPORT	MODERNIZATION	AFFECTED SALARY WORKFORCE (%)	AFFECTED SALARY WORKFORCE (%)	MODERNIZATION	SUPPORT
MATERIALS	• AUTOMATED MATERIALS REQUIREMENT AND PROCUREMENT	4	2	• COMPUTER-INTEGRATED MANUFACTURING	IMOD
HUMAN RES	• COMPUTER GRAPHICS AUTOMATION	2	1	• COMPUTER-AIDED FACILITIES DESIGN	FACILITIES
LOGISTICS	• TECHNICAL PUBLICATIONS AUTOMATION	1	6	• CAD CAM	IMOD MFG ENGRG
MFG CONTROL FINANCE	• COMPUTER-AIDED ESTIMATION AND PRICING	3	2	• CONSOLIDATED HUMAN RESOURCES DATA BASE	HUMAN RES
LOGISTICS HUMAN RES	• COMPUTER-BASED TRAINING	1	3	• COMPUTER-INTEGRATED ENGINEERING	ENGRG
IMOD	• COMPUTER-AIDED CONFIGURATION MANAGEMENT	2	1	• PLANT WORK ORDERS AND SPARES INVENTORY CONTROL	FACILITIES
IMOD	• ARTIFICIAL-INTELLIGENCE-BASED BIDS AND PROPOSALS	1	2	• CENTRALIZED BUDGETS AND CONTROL SYSTEM	FINANCE
FACILITIES IMOD	• CAPITAL RESOURCE ALLOCATION AND CONTROL	1	3	• EMPLOYEE BADGE BASED AUTOMATION	IMOD FINANCE HUMAN RES
MFG CONTROL MFG ENGRG	• MANUFACTURING INFORMATION SYSTEMS	6	3	• COMPUTER-AIDED QUALITY ASSURANCE	IMOD QUALITY
HUMAN RES	• COMPUTER-AIDED SECURITY ADMINISTRATION	1	10 / 55	• OTHER SYSTEMS (TO BE IDENTIFIED)	TBD

(Left and right SUPPORT columns are labeled vertically "INFORMATION SYSTEMS SUPPORT")

Source: Dhin (1987).

Figure 9–3. A List of Projects for Office Administration

decision making, and so on) required to achieve the strategy. Finally, the management systems must be developed to support and sustain these behaviors, as well as provide sufficient organizational control.

For nonmanagement employees, the human resource management systems will have the grestest impact. Therefore, this discussion will focus on the changes that can be expected in human resource management systems.

Employee Selection. Driven by the paradox described by Jonsson (1984), organizations will begin to place greater and greater emphasis on employee selection processes. As job security and employment security become part of the organizational policy, the selection decision becomes a more critical one. Therefore, applicants for full-time, permanent employment can expect to undergo a more rigorous screening process.

Employment Security. The strategic objectives of quality, flexibility, and reduced cycle times require a committed work force. Commitment is a two-way street. Organizations cannot expect employees to be committed to the organization unless those organizations exhibit a commitment to the employees. Therefore, employment security will increasingly be an issue in the organization of the future. The auto industry bargaining of 1987 foreshadows things to come.

The way this issue is likely to be resolved is that a very small core group of employees will receive employment security guarantees. In addition it is likely that public policy changes will be enacted to ease the transition for displaced employees. Employment security protection will enable the core employees to make suggestions for improvements, even suggestions that could eliminate their own jobs, since they know they will be retained and moved to another position.

Compensation Systems. Future reward systems will be consistent with the move to employment security. They will be implemented by various forms of variable compensation. A significant portion of the pay for core employees will be in the form of a bonus tied to the productivity or financial results of the organization.

In his prescription for restoring the competitive power of the United States, Lester Thurow (1985) addresses the need to modify reward systems:

> The place to start is by altering the present structure of salaries and wages. Instead of receiving straight wages or salaries with all of the residual profits allocated to the capitalists, part of each worker's or manager's income should come in the form of a bonus based upon increases in value added per hour of work . . . (bonuses should) account for, let's say one third of total labor income. These bonuses become an important of everyone's—blue collar workers, management—annual income and thus everyone shares a common interest in higher productivity and success.

Not only will reward systems provide for variable compensation, but they will become more performance based. Advances in information systems will permit better accountability for individuals and groups. Pressure for performance will be strong, and this will be driven in part by the fact that there is a closer link between pay and performance for individuals, groups, and the total organization.

Employee Development. Driven by the need for flexibility, organizations will require individuals who are multiskilled and who can be retained. The ability to learn will be a selection criterion. Once employed, individuals will spend a considerable amount of work time in training.

The Impact of Trends on Nonmanagement Roles

In this section we will consider how the trends that will, at least in part, define the organizations of the future will also affect nonmanagement employees. To permit some specificity in this analysis, we will consider different categories of nonmanagement employees. Four categories will be discussed:

1. Staff, which includes individuals who deal with external environmental issues (for example, public relations, finance, real estate). Also included in the staff category are individuals in "corporate" staff roles concerned with creating the organizational context for production or service delivery (for example, human resources, administration, information systems, accounting).

2. Professional/technical, which includes professional/technical employees who are in direct product or service development or delivery (for example, design engineers, R & D scientists, sales and marketing employees, customer service engineering, quality control, manufacturing engineering, draftsmen, laboratory technicians).

3. Production, which includes people in those roles traditionally referred to as "blue collar" or "hourly employees" who are in direct production or service delivery positions (for instance, machine operators, assemblers, bank tellers, shipping/receiving specialists, claims examiners).

4. Support, which includes individuals in direct production or clerical support to product or service delivery, product development, or staff functions (for example, maintenance, clerical, customer service).

Impact on Staff Roles

1. *Fewer staff.* The role of staff groups in the organization of the future will be quite different from the typical roles today. A major driving force for the differences is that staff organizations will be leaner than today. Individuals remaining in staff functions will be under more pressure to demonstrate their contribution to the performance of the organization.

2. *Strategic view.* Staff professionals will be drawn more tightly into the business strategy of the organization. Whether their focus is on external relationships or on building or monitoring internal management control systems, they will be expected to ensure that these activities reflect the strategic focus of the organization. For example, human resource staff will be concerned with ensuring that people who "get ahead" (in terms of pay, promotion, and so forth) in the organization are those whose performance is characterized by quality, cost improvement, and innovation—three important strategic performance dimensions.

3. *Customer-supplier viewpoint.* Staff people exist in organizations in part to ensure that the production organization has what it needs to carry out its activities successfully. Thus, production managers are "customers" of the staff professionals. In traditional organizations, this relationship is often reversed in practice. Staff people, coming from "headquarters," sometimes treat operating managers as their suppliers (of data and reports) rather than as their internal

customers. In this manner, staff functions may actively interfere with the production process rather than facilitate it as they should. Increasingly, staff professionals must adopt the idea that their measure of performance is in terms of the impact their actions, decisions, and policies have on the operating groups.

4. *Staff as consultants/trainers.* As the need for flexibility and cost reduction flatten organization pyramids and move decision making and accountability to lower levels, many staff employees will become essentially internal consultants to operating groups. The role of consultant/trainer as opposed to monitor/evaluator requires new skills. It requires a new perspective, as was mentioned earlier. But for the staff members to carry out that new role, technical skills within the discipline are not sufficient. These staff members must also be able to deliver that knowledge effectively to "customers" in ways that meet the internal customers' needs. This requires listening skills, presentation skills, writing skills, and the ability to establish empathy with the customer.

5. *Continuous learning.* Staff professionals must maintain state-of-the-art knowledge in their rapidly changing disciplines. As the eyes and ears of the organization within their areas of expertise, these individuals must stay abreast of changing technology, environmental forces, government policies, actions by competitors, and a wide range of external issues.

6. *Staff as a source of product development information.* Particularly, as a result of their attention to the external environment, staff professionals have data that are important for the product development process. This requires that they understand their responsibilities in this regard and that they have the information system or communication mechanisms to provide relevant input to this process. In traditional organizations there are often barriers to the flow of information across functional boundaries (for instance, human resources to marketing, or public relations to R & D). In the organization of the future, these "walls" must be broken down to allow the free flow of relevant information in a timely manner. Because of competitive pressures, short product life cycles, differentiated customer groups, and so on, extensive market intelligence networks are required. Staff professionals have information that is relevant to this process and must be tapped.

Impact on Professional/Technical Roles

Many of the effects on professional/technical employees will be similar to those on staff professionals. With respect to the need for strategic thinking, continuous learning, and developing consulting skills there are strong similarities. Driven by decentralization and gain-sharing schemes, professional/technical employees will see their fate increasingly tied to the performance of other groups that they can influence but not control. There are several effects that are especially relevant to this group.

1. *Developing organization loyalty that supersedes technical discipline loyalty.* Driven by more emphasis on employment stability and competitive pressures, professional/technical employees will move less frequently from firm to firm. Partly as a result of this type of mobility (probably most visible in the aerospace and electronics industries), technical employees often develop a stronger loyalty to their technical discipline than to their employers. As human resource management practices designed to develop employee commitment become more prevalent, technical employees would be expected to move less frequently and to subordinate discipline loyalty to organizational loyalty.

2. *Closer interaction with other functional areas.* Whether concerned with product development or process innovation, technical employees in the organization of the future will not be able to isolate themselves from individuals in other functions. This will be driven by decentralization of technical functions and greater accountability to operating managers. In other words, design engineers will be forced to interact more closely with manufacturing people who will build the product and with marketing or sales people who will sell the product. This will require professional/technical professionals to develop the interpersonal skills that will allow them to work effectively in interdisciplinary teams. These skills include listening skills, speaking skills, and the ability to view the world from other perspectives (such as marketing or manufacturing). In addition, the pressure to operate within the strategic focus will place greater emphasis on the need to design products with consideration of cost, quality, and timeliness, not necessarily emphasizing the ultimate in technical sophistication.

Impact on Production Roles

The organization of the future will have a strong impact on the production employees. As the quote from Berth Jonsson at the beginning of this chapter implied, there will be fewer production workers, as we now know them in traditional organizations. However, the remaining ones will be more critical to the operation's success. Let us consider some of the ways production workers will be affected.

1. *Understanding how business strategy and core values relate to production jobs.* As fewer production workers assume more responsibility for the production process, it is essential that they begin to think like managers. That is, they must understand the strategic implications of their actions. With more and more automation moving into the production process, the production worker's ability to make real-time decisions and corrections to a production process becomes more important. For safety reasons and for reasons of cost and quality, the more the operator can make correct decisions regarding production activities, the better the quality and the lower the cost.

2. *Accepting more responsibility for process improvements.* Coupled with the greater role in production process decision making is the expectation that production employees will be a major source of ideas for process improvement. Flatter organizational structures will give production workers more autonomy. Since they know their jobs better than anyone else, they are in the best position to suggest ways to improve the process.

3. *Using structured mechanisms for problem solving.* The importance of production employees in suggesting process improvements will be recognized by formal training in problem-solving methods. Techniques such as cause and effect diagrams, statistical process control methods, data gathering and analysis methods, and group process techniques will be stressed.

4. *More cross-training and broader job classifications.* Production employees will be expected to learn a wider range of job skills and tasks. The requirements for flexibility and quick response times for customer orders require a cross-trained work force.

In addition to cross-training, production employees will spend increasing amounts of time being trained just to stay abreast of new process technology. They will have to become extremely skilled at performing complicated machine setups in shorter and shorter times. In addition, production employees will have to be able to understand and in some cases debug software problems in robotic or flexibile machine environments.

Their interactions with professional/technical employees will be more frequent, and the nature of the relationship will change. As was mentioned earlier, the technical employee must become a consultant to the production employee. However, the production employee as a customer must accurately communicate his or her requirements to the "consultant." Thus both parties must learn new skills and a new relationship.

Impact on Support Roles

This category includes both production support and clerical employees. In the organization of the future as compared with traditional organizations, increased automation will lead to a larger number of production support employees. Hardware and software maintenance employees will be very critical. However, information technology will probably lead to a considerable decrease in the number of clerical employees. Thus we predict a shift in the support area. The overall number, unlike other categories of nonmanagement employees, may not decline to a great degree. However, the composition of this group will change.

1. *Customer-supplier viewpoint.* All support employees will be required to adopt the view that they exist to serve the requirements of their internal customers. As such they will be required to communicate more frequently with their "customers" and better understand their needs.

2. *Frequent training.* Support employees will be required to maintain current skills and keep abreast of new technology and systems. Their job classifications will broaden as they are required to learn to operate and maintain a wider range of hardware and software. Change will become a way of life.

3. *Greater accountability.* The capabilities of automated systems will enable management to monitor the performance of support employees more closely. Automated equipment will permit individual performance monitoring. The potential exists for a reduction in autonomy and more pressure for timely performance.

4. *Involvement in problem solving.* Support employees, especially those in production support, will increasingly be involved in team problem-solving activities. This will require support employees to learn problem-solving techniques and to develop skills required for working effectively in groups. In efforts to improve process technology, support employees have important knowledge that must be included.

Clerical employees, who will increasingly become operators of automated information systems, will be required to assist in improving business processes. They will be required to learn and use techniques for conducting process flow analyses as a way of streamlining processes, reducing redundant activity, and preparing additional processes for automation.

Conclusion

The organization of the future will operate in a tumultuous environment. It will face a vast and rapidly changing world economy. Competition will be intensified. Traditional organizational strategies, structures, technologies, and human resource systems will give way to very different organizational forms.

The nonmanagement employees who will operate successfully in this environment will be stimulated, challenged, and rewarded. Organizations that can successfully unlock this human potential and combine it with the technical resources associated with new technologies will be the competitive successes.

The critical linchpin is strategy. Organizations will be forced to improve dramatically the process of strategy development and especially strategy implementation. To navigate through the demands that the organization of the future will face will require a form of dynamic stability that exceeds what most organizations can envision today. As we stated, dynamic stability is possible with a strategy that emerges from clearly articulated visions and values. Only with such clear direction will organizations be able to guide and develop their culturally heterogeneous, nonmanagement work forces and move through continuous improvement toward competitive success.

10
Managing Climates and Cultures: A Futures Perspective

Benjamin Schneider
Joan Rentsch

T
o manage is to grapple effectively. Managers must cope with literally tens of thousands of issues, and the issues are sometimes slippery, sometimes hard, frequently in conflict, and almost always difficult to predict. The prediction problem, in particular, must occupy an increasingly large proportion of managers' time as change occurs with increased rapidity. From strategic product planning to strategic human resource management, anticipation of the future permits managers to develop strategies to cope with the future when it arrives.

Correct anticipation of the future is critical because the web of issues requiring management attention is very great indeed. As Kilmann (1985) says, there is no quick fix; all the problems require attention. Management tries to anticipate the future successfully in order to establish conditions in the organization to cope with the future. However, since *all* the conditions necessary to grapple with future problems can never be specified, management needs to establish a way of thinking among organizational members such that even when a future arrives for which conditions are *unspecified*, they will react in appropriate ways. In Katz and Kahn's terms:

> The organizational need for actions of an innovative, relatively spontaneous sort is inevitable and unending. No organizational plan can foresee all contingencies within its own operations, can anticipate with accuracy all environmental changes, or can control perfectly all human variability. . . . An organization that depends solely on its blueprints of prescribed behaviors is a very fragile system (1978, 403–4).

Katz and Kahn are suggesting that human systems need some glue, some central themes, to guide behavior. In the absence of these guiding themes, members do not know *when, where,* or *how* to direct their energies. Organizational

We want to thank Jerry Hage, Rosalie Hall, Katherine Klein, Janice Roullier, and Art Brief for their helpful comments on earlier versions of this chapter.

climate and organizational culture provide this thematic coherence to the behavior of organizational members.

Although climate and culture will be defined below, it is useful to note here that they are complementary terms that refer to usually unwritten guidelines for behavior in organizations. These guidelines indicate what is important in and to the organization; they indicate to members the imperatives of the organization. The concern in this chapter, however, extends beyond the definition of climate and culture to (1) the creation and maintenance of climate and culture, and to (2) the application of climate and culture concepts to the management of some issues that effective organizations will have to confront in the future.

In summary, a brief overview of the climate and culture literatures is presented first. Then a framework that specifies six facets of organizational behavior that contribute to the creation and maintenance of climate and culture is described. Finally, the framework for the creation and maintenance of climate and culture is applied to managing three environmental changes with which managers of organizations of the future will have to cope (increased service orientation, demographic diversity, and organizational interdependence).

Organizational Climate and Culture

Researchers have studied organizational climate since the 1950s (Argyris 1957). In the thirty years of research on the topic, *climate* has generally referred to incumbent perceptions of what is important in the organization, be it service (Schneider and Bowen 1985), creativity (Litwin and Stringer 1968), and/or safety (Zohar 1980). Researchers have typically tried to specify organizational policies, practices, and procedures (hereafter *routines*) that, through rewards, support, and expectations (hereafter *rewards*) indicate to people in organizations the kinds of goals that are important and the means (behaviors) by which the goals are to be accomplished. The network of routines and rewards are said to create a sense of imperative, which in turn guides behavior. It is this sense of imperative that is *climate*.

Climate researchers often attach an abstract label or meaning (for example, "service climate" or "innovative climate") to routines, rewards, and behaviors that they observe. These researchers assume that the meaing they attach to these routines and rewards is the same meaning that organizational members attach to it.

While climate researchers attach meaning to organizational routines, rewards, and behaviors, culture researchers are more likely to learn from organizational members the meanings they attach to these routines, rewards, and behaviors (Siehl and Martin 1984). Culture researchers are especially interested in the norms surrounding the behaviors on which the meanings are based and in the underlying values that the norms connote (Louis 1985).

For example, climate researchers might define an organization's climate as "friendly" based on observations, interviews, and/or surveys that indicate strong formal and informal rewards and supports for helpful and cooperative behaviors. Culture researchers might observe the same behaviors being rewarded and supported, but they would ask the members what meaning they attach to the behaviors themselves and to the fact that these behaviors are rewarded and supported. In addition, they would attempt to identify the etiology of these organizational routines and rewards—that is, the history of them (Schein 1985).

In the past five years the construct of *culture* has become popular, and in spite of sparse research, although a lot of writing (see Frost et al. 1985), it has become a more accepted term than *climate*. *Culture* refers to the values that lie beneath the organization's routines (Schein 1985), the norms that surround and/or underpin the organization's rewards for behavior, and the meanings members share about what these norms and values connote.

Climate and culture are perhaps most meaningful when used in conjunction. In a real sense climate is the manifestation of culture. That is, climate is communicated to members through routines and through the behaviors that actually get rewarded. Culture, on the other hand, is communicated in part through history, and it is history that provides the explanation for the norms and values that underlie routines and that underlie the reasons why certain behaviors are rewarded. Culture answers the question, "Why do things happen the way they do? Climate answers the question, What happens around here? Together, climate and culture offer organization members a guide for behaving and a link to the roots of the reasons for their behavior.

Thus, people who study culture may argue that it is the web of myths and stories about founders and critical organizational events (fires, mergers, new buildings, and so forth) that serve as metaphors for the organization's values and norms (Krefting and Frost 1985). When these norms and values are shared (culture) through rootedness in the organization's history *and* when the organization's routines and rewards (climate) reflect these norms and values, then climate and culture suggest to members similar themes. Climate will do this through overt routines and rewards, while culture will do this through shared meaning, a sharing of a common history, and a common set of explanations for why things happen the way they do.

In summary, climate refers to the ways organizations operationalize the themes that characterize everyday behavior—the routines of organizations and the behaviors that get rewarded, supported, and expected by organizations (the "what happens around here"). Culture refers to the history and norms and values that members believe underlie climate (the "why do things happen the way they do") and the meanings organizational members share about the organization's imperative.

Clearly climate and culture go hand in hand. Yet climate (the "what happens around here") is more immediately amenable to management than is culture.

To oversimplify, to manage climate is to manage routines (policies, practices, and procedures) and to manage rewards (to reward, support, and expect the routines).

Culture (the "why do things happen the way they do") is more difficult to manage because it involves values and the interpretation of these values. For example, if an organization's management is attempting to promote new values (for example, a service value to replace an efficiency value), the organizational routines and rewards (climate) may be managed to reflect the new values. But the message being sent through the routines and rewards will become clear to each organizational member only over a long period of time. The underlying organizational values for the routines and rewards may be accepted by some organizational members and integrated into their own unique set of values. Even if it is assumed that interaction among organizational members will yield shared interpretations (Schneider and Reichers 1983) management cannot be confident about how quickly this sharing will occur. Nor can management be overly confident that organizational members' shared interpretations will be the same as management's interpretations. Management must provide its interpretations to organizational members, as well as develop routines and rewards that accurately and consistently represent these interpretations. Presumably a new shared culture will emerge through members' repeated exposure to these routines and rewards, accompanied by interpersonal interaction and communication of management's interpretations.

Although it is tricky, we assume here that culture can be managed. One approach to managing culture is briefly described. There are three components to this approach.

First, the climate (rewards and routines) must be managed consistently across all levels and functions of the organization to reflect and promote the desired organizational values. Second, a messenger, or interpreter, must explicate the values underlying the climate. The function of this person (or persons) is to clarify the new organizational values and future culture. Typically, the organization's founder fills this role (Schein 1985), but in organizations where the founder is no longer a member, the role must be filled by another. The person in this role must accept the organizational values and must also understand that values are reflected by routines and rewards. Since the "interpreter" must communicate the values and perhaps the routines and rewards to organizational members, he or she must be seen as credible and trustworthy. Typically persons perceived to be credible tend to have status, power, and success. Thus, the "interpreter" should have status, power, and success in the organization to increase the probability that the message communicated will be accepted (Aronson 1984).

Third, organizational members must be able to understand and be willing to accept the values that are being espoused by the organization. According to Schneider's (in press) Attraction-Selection-Attrition model, different organizations will probably have people in them with different values. If the new values being communicated are incompatible with members' values then those members will leave the organization, and if the new values are compatible with their values, they will stay.

This threefold approach to managing culture is really an oversimplification of how it may be managed, but it is clear that managing culture requires a huge investment of energy over long periods of time. Therefore, because of space limitations the framework to be presented in this chapter is primarily relevant to climate, and the specific details of how organizational values are transmitted to organizational members through climate are *not* addressed. However, the framework does suggest how to develop a consistent climate, which is the first step in managing culture. It will become obvious that developing and maintaining a consistent climate is also a complex management problem.

In the next section, a framework that can be used to manage climate is presented. That discussion will be followed by a brief description of three kinds of conditions that organizations of the future may anticipate. Finally, it will be shown how the framework can be applied to create climates (and eventually cultures) that are applicable to these future organizational conditions.

Managing Climate and Culture: A Framework

If climate and culture are to be effectively managed, the question is *what* to manage—that is, what facets of organizational life should be the focus of management attention. A few frameworks have been proposed to answer this question. Peters and Waterman (1982), for example, adopted McKinsey's "7-S" framework: Structure, Strategy, Skills, Staff, Style, and Systems. Schoorman and Schneider (in press), on the other hand, adapted Katz and Kahn's (1978) subsystems model of organizational functioning. The Katz and Kahn framework, like Peters and Waterman's, specifies various facets of organizational functioning requiring management attention (production, maintenance, support, adaptive, and managerial subsystems). Both frameworks have a wholistic thematic orientation to organizational "effectiveness," although Schoorman and Schneider have shown how Katz and Kahn's framework can be adapted for use to assess specific themes (for example, service; Moeller and Schneider 1986) or sales (Moeller et al., in press).

Schein's (1985) conceptualization of culture puts the burden on corporate leadership, especially the founders' vision(s) of the organization. Of special importance to Schein is the idea of leader-member, leader-group, and intergroup relationships in organizations, since what happens interpersonally in groups is the source of culture.

The major goal in developing the present framework was to identify behaviors in organizations that can be managed through specific actions. A second goal was to present a model that could be targeted on the creation of particular *kinds* of climate and culture. The goal was to specify aspects of organizational life that, when managed, would serve to communicate to members the organization's imperatives.

Obviously, any number of models of organizational functioning could have been chosen (for example, Galbraith 1973, Perrow 1970, Thompson 1967). The choice was a framework adapted from Katz and Kahn (1978) and used by Schneider (1986). This particular framework emphasizes not only organizational routines and rewards, but also the *kind of people* in an organization, the psychological *attachment of people* to an organization, and the *interpersonal behavior* in an organization. In short, it captures the psychology of behavior in organizations through a focus on six facets of organizational life. What is important here is the idea that the imperatives of organizations dictate the specific focus of the facets.

According to this framework every organization needs to manage six issues in order to create and strengthen a desired climate and culture (Katz and Kahn 1978, Schneider 1986). When all six issues are focused on the same imperatives or themes, then those themes will become shared among organizational members. The six issues are:

1. Membership issues
2. Socialization issues
3. Identity issues
4. Authority issues
5. Interpersonal issues
6. Environmental issues

Membership Issues. It is the people behaving in and interpreting organizations who constitute an organization's climate and culture. Since people differ dramatically in their predispositions to behave in certain ways and to interpret their world in certain ways, all organizations need to be concerned with the kinds of members they attract, select, and retain. Evidence has been accumulating for years to show that different kinds of people are attracted to and are selected and retained by particular kinds of organizations (Schneider, in press).

In general, people and organizations tend to make choices that are appropriate matches. For example, assertive sales types tend to go to stock brokerage houses, not YMCAs; socially and interpersonally oriented people tend to do the reverse (Campbell and Hansen 1981), that is, they join agencies that do not demand aggressive behavior. When individuals in organizations have made inappropriate choices turnover occurs. A result of the natural attraction, selection, and attrition cycle that occurs in organizations is that a relatively homogeneous membership in specific organizations is created (Schneider, in press).

Socialization Issues. Appropriate attraction (recruitment) and selection can provide organizations with the members who "fit" an organization's climate and culture. That is, individuals whose values and interpersonal behaviors are consistent with the climate and culture will be attracted to, and selected and retained by the organization. However, some newcomers to the organization may learn and accept the values reflected in the climate and culture after entering the organization. When newcomers enter an organization, both formal and informal socialization experiences are critical to this learning process.

Informal socialization refers to what newcomers are told by supervisors and co-workers and what they experience happening to them and around them. When people are new to a setting they try to acquire information to make sense out of what they hear, see, and experience (Louis 1980). This makes the early experiences of newcomers regarding routines and rewards, as well as the learning of norms, potentially overdeterministic of their sense of the organization's imperatives.

Training is the most prevalent form of formal socialization. Training provides organizations with an early opportunity to influence *how* newcomers will do their work and how *well* they will do it. Thus, the company's surface commitment to particular kinds of work outcomes (for example, quality versus quantity) is made clear to newcomers in training. Goldstein (1986), however, states that the two most frequently overlooked problems with training programs concern (1) a lack of a comprehensive needs analysis as the basis for training, and (2) insufficient attention to the transfer of training to the job.

When training programs are not congruent with the prevailing climate and culture of the organization, problems arise. In brief, failure to conduct an appropriate needs analysis may yield incomplete training; important knowledge, skills, and abilities may not be taught because they may not have been identified. Training time and effort may thus be wasted because training will not be relevant for the real requirements of the job.

Failure of training programs may also result from a failure to consider the situation *surrounding* the job. That is, the training may in fact be targeted on job requirements, but newcomers entering the job from training may find that what they learned in training is not rewarded, supported, or expected (that is, training will not transfer to the job). In short, the training may be denigrated by supervisors and/or co-workers who say something like, "Forget everything they taught you—I'll show you how it's really done." When the transfer situation is incongruent with training, training may provide only a surface impression or even an inaccurate impression of organizational climate and culture (for example, Marx 1982).

Identity Issues. How people come to feel a part of their organization—how they come to identify with the organization's goals and values—also constitutes organizational climate and culture. In organizational behavior, the issue of identification and commitment has a rich theory and data base (see Mowday, Porter, and Steers 1982). In general an increased sense of identity is correlated with improved job satisfaction, improved extrarole performance (going beyond the job description; see Bateman and Organ 1983) and lower turnover (Kaufman 1960).

However, the antecedents of identity are not clear. There is evidence that stronger organizational identification is related to shared goals and values, rewards for continued participation, a perception that multiple commitments can be actualized in the organization (for example, commitment to a profession as well as to the organization), and enhanced self-esteem from organizational membership (Kaufman 1960, Mowday, Porter, and Steers 1982, Reichers 1985). Identity probably begins with a good match of persons to organizations. If this is true then organizations need to state clearly their goals and values. This will facilitate recruiting, selecting, socializing, and retaining people who identify with those goals and values.

Authority Issues. Authority issues are all those policies, practices, and procedures (routines) that provide guidelines for life in most organizations. The question is, What are the end goals that organizational authority structure are designed to achieve? All of the traditional functions of management (planning, organizing, controlling) can be thought of as authority issues, and no one would argue that organizations can exist without them. The point is that organizations need to ask themselves *how* to plan for *what*, *how* to organize for *what*, *how* to control for *what*. The *what* here refers to the imperatives of the organization, the goals management wants to emphasize. The *how* here refers to authority: planning autocratically versus participatively (McGregor 1960), organizing in competing groups versus cooperating groups (French and Bell 1978), and controlling through fear versus democracy (Lewin, Lippitt, and White 1939).

The dichotomies just presented regarding authority styles can be misinterpreted to suggest that managers abandon their authority. This is not an appropriate interpretation. In McGregor's terms:

> Abdication is not a workable alternative to authoritarianism. We have learned there is no direct correlation between employee satisfaction and productivity. We recognize today that "industrial democracy" cannot consist in permitting everyone to decide everything, that industrial health does not flow automatically from the elimination of dissatisfaction, disagreement, or even open conflict. Peace is not synonymous with organizational health; socially responsive management is not coextensive with permissive management (1960, 46–47).

Employees interpret organizational routines and authority structures to determine what is important to the organization in terms of goals and people. Perhaps managers assume that they communicate with employees only through memoranda and newsletters. A climate approach, however, emphasizes the idea that routines and rewards are also important communication media.

Interpersonal Issues. The interpersonal interactions that occur within an organization (especially regarding authority issues as noted above) communicate to members how people are viewed by the organization. One can think of a chain of interactions starting with upper-level personnel interacting with people the next level down, down to the lower levels in the organization. How the upper-level people treat those who work under them will influence how these second-level people treat the people who work under them, and so on (Smith 1982). Obviously, then, managers must consider managing the interpersonal relationships within the organization as part of their job.

It is thought that members come to share their perceptions through interpersonal interaction in the organization. They also come to share their perceptions, their interpretations of their observations, and the attributions they make about the organization (Schneider and Reichers 1983, Schein 1985). Of course, members in organizations that are designed to suppress interpersonal interaction (for example, assembly line jobs in noisy environments) will still share their views with each other, but not on company time and their views will probably not be congruent with mangement's stated goals and objectives. Members of such organizations may feel alienated from the organization and lack identity with the organization and its efforts to be effective (Hackman and Oldham 1980).

The sociotechnical systems perspective on organizational behavior (see Miller 1976) reveals the critical role the opportunity for interpersonal interaction plays in worker behavior and affect. Yet it is clear that management decisions to seek efficiency in organizations can ignore interpersonal issues even where, as in service organizations, the interpersonal facets of work are central to long-term effectiveness (Bowen and Schneider 1985).

Environmental Issues. Schein (1980, 233) asks the following questions regarding the larger environment of organizations:

> How does an organization cope within its environment? How does it obtain information and process it validly? What mechanisms exist for translating information, particularly about alterations in the environment, into changed operations? Are the internal operations flexible enough to cope with change? How can the organization's capacity to cope be improved?

Managers do not manage the environment so much as they cope with it, as Schein notes. So, in comparison with the other five issues, issues over which management may have some control, the environment is not controllable. However, managers can manage the *effects* of environmental changes. That is, managers can manage *to* the environment changes and can anticipate and prepare for these changes. Management has little ability to manage *what* the environment will be, but organizations can be managed in light of the environment (Pfeffer and Salancik 1978).

When an organization can anticipate environmental changes it can manage *to* these changes by paying attention to the other five issues outlined above: membership, socialization, identity, authority, and interpersonal. By managing in these five areas concurrently, organizations can create an appropriate climate and culture for the future the environment presents.

Managing in Environments of the Future

Managers who can anticipate changes in the environment can prepare for these changes so that managing the organization after the change will be more efficient and effective than if the change had not been anticipated. The problem is the *identification* and *anticipation* of the future. What are some likely futures for organizations? Future organizational changes may center around (1) new technologies (for example, computers, programmable automation), (2) increased dependence upon teams and task forces, (3) demands for increased social and political responsiveness (for example, comparable worth), (4) change in the location of workers (for example, a return of the so-called cottage industry, increased geographical dispersion), (5) increased service orientation, (6) greater demographic diversity among organizational members (for example, more women, older workers, changes in racial composition of the work force), and (7) greater organizational interdependence (for instance combinations, internationalization, joint ventures).

Though all of these changes may be important for future organizations, only three of them will be discussed here: increased service orientation, demographic diversity, and organizational interdependence. The question addressed is, How can climate and culture be managed to facilitate organizational effectiveness if these changes occur? Prior to answering the question, let us briefly review the three predicted environmental changes.

Increased Service Orientation. As work moves increasingly away from the manufacturing of goods toward the production of information and service, some basic differences between manufacturing and service organizations become salient. The differences can be summarized with respect to participation of the consumer in producing the service (for example, using an automatic teller machine), the simultaneous nature of production and consumption (a visit to a golf tournament, for instance), and the relative intangibility of services (they cannot be inventoried; see Czepiel, Solomon, and Suprenant 1985, Maister 1982). Finally, the *process* by which service is delivered to customers frequently is the service. This means that people who deliver the service become very important.

To complicate matters, some organizations may be moving toward a manufacturing/service duality in which organizations may have customers within the organization. For example, staff functions (for example, personnel) frequently service other parts of the organization. To facilitate organizational effectiveness, high-quality service should be offered to internal consumers as well as to external customers. This situation may occur more frequently as organizations increasingly acquire supplier organizations, forming a "consumer-servicer" relationship within the combined organization.

Thus, as the number and variety of service organizations increase, the role of employees in determining both customer and other employee satisfaction will also increase. Since employees are likely to treat customers and each other no better than they are themselves treated, the challenge for service organizations is to manage employees as if they were themselves valued customers (Norman 1984, Schneider and Bowen 1985).

Increased Demographic Diversity. The demographic changes in future organizations may be a product of several factors: (1) In future organizations women and blacks are more likely to hold higher positions in organizations (Fullerton 1985). (2) It is also likely that there will be greater diversity of race and nationality among organizational members. Fullerton (1985), for example, reports that blacks, because of an increase in birthrates in the last few decades, can be expected to account for 20 percent of the growth in the future labor force. (3) The working population will have an older average age because of the aging of the baby boomers. (4) More highly specialized education of employees will lead to demographic diversity within organizations. (5) Finally, a more subtle diversity of the work force's age, sex, race, and education may become salient. Kohn and Schooler (1983) have shown how the history of black culture and the release of blacks from serfdom affects them with respect to such diverse issues as intellectual functioning, orientation to authority, and moral value systems.

While this latter issue may seem somewhat farfetched for organizations of the future, reality suggests that people with different cultural heritages will move into different levels of the organizations of the future. For example, the Vietnamese influx to the United States in the late 1970s will probably be reflected in the rise of persons of this culture to managerial roles at the turn of the century. Clearly the role of the cultural heritage of people will continue to be a factor in their behavior at work.

In the future, then, organizations must learn to manage the demographic diversity they will confront. Demographic changes will have to be accommodated through explicit routines and rewards that create a theme of fairness and an appreciation for individual differences in the climate and culture of a demographically diverse organization. For example, in the area of pay, some organizations allocate to each employee a sum of money that each employee can choose to receive as he or she desires. Some desire it all in salary, while others choose salary plus benefits, and, within the latter selection, high variability in percentages exist (Kopelman 1986, Lawler 1981). In principle there is no reason why all kinds of rewards cannot be available differentially as a function of desires. Leadership, for example, already has been conceptualized in an individual differences model through the vertical dyadic linkage idea. In this model leaders behave toward each subordinate in accord with the subordinate's attributes (Dansereau, Graen, and Haga 1975).

The point here is that traditional models of managing have implicitly homogenized the work force, resulting in the artificially "equal" treatment of all. In the future, given the increased demographic diversity of the workplace, it will be time to seek models of managing that acknowledge diversity.

Organizational Interdependence. The themes of fairness and appreciation of differences may also be useful in coping with increased organizational interdependence. Examples of organizational interdependence include mergers and acquisitions, internationalization of organizations, joint ventures, and consortia of competitors working together in the university setting (see chapter 3 in this book).

These interdependencies involve two or more organizational (and perhaps national) cultures' interacting. Research in the merger and acquisition literature highlights the difficulties encountered when two organizational cultures join (for instance, Marks and Mirvis, undated, Sales and Mirvis 1984). Perhaps an appreciation of individual differences and cultural differences would lead to more efficient and effective organizational interactions. These organizations may also desire a climate and culture for effective communication and conflict resolution.

Creating this climate and culture will be a difficult task for interdependent organizations if a major assumption of organizational sociologists, that organizations desire to maintain autonomy, holds (Hage 1980). According to the above premises, this value for autonomy will need to be replaced by a value for cooperation and teamwork if the outcome of organizational interdependence is to be effectiveness.

Summary. In summary, future organizations will have to diagnose the kinds of climates and cultures that need to be promoted—that is, the kinds of climates and cultures that are likely, given their specific environmental conditions, to facilitate organizational effectiveness. Service organizations will have to foster a climate and culture in which service excellence is valued. Organizations with demographically diverse membership will have to develop a climate and culture in which fairness and individual differences are appreciated. Finally, increased organizational interdependence will require that organizations promote a climate and culture with a theme of cooperation, communication, and cultural appreciation.

Managing Climates and Cultures for Change

To demonstrate how the framework for understanding climate and culture outlined earlier can be useful, each of the five facets of climate and culture (membership, socialization, identity, authority, and interpersonal) will be reviewed. Given the three anticipated environmental changes, this review will involve explaining how each facet (for example, membership) can be managed to create the conditions (for instance, climate for service) that are necessary to cope with the new environment. The following pages are summarized in table 10–1.

Membership Issues. Membership issues concern the attraction, selection, and retention of organizational members. Simply stated, service organizations need

Table 10–1
Managing Climates and Cultures for Change

	Future Organizational Features		
Issues	*Service Orientation*	*Demographic Diversity*	*Organizational Interdependence*
Membership	Recruit and select people who value service, are socially sensitive	Recruit and select people who value individual differences, are open to new values and attitudes	Recruit and select people who value diversity, have communication and interpersonal skills
Socialization	Train service skills Reward service role models	Train in diverse groups Reward respect for differences and cultural exchange	Train and reward communication skills and cultural appreciation
Identity	Employees' ideas for service Symbols of membership	Ads promoting fairness and diversity Participation in decision making by diverse persons	Treat acquired personnel as equal Advertise gain of acquired personnel
Authority	Plan, control, and organize for service Service-oriented routines	Design jobs to promote interaction Plan for child care or retirement	Discussion groups (intergroup routines)
Interpersonal	Reward effective service-oriented relationships	Reward effective interpersonal relationships	Reward effective conflict resolution skills
Environmental	Capitalize on employee knowledge of environment	Know demographics of labor force	Learn culture of other organization

to attract service-oriented people. Difficulty arises when organizations and individuals are simultaneously attracting and selecting (evaluating) each other (Porter, Lawler, and Hackman 1975). Each may make selection decisions based on limited or faulty information because of two sources of conflict. One source of conflict comes from individuals' efforts to attract the organization and the organization's need to select individuals. The second source of conflict stems from organizations' attempts to attract individuals, and the individual's need to select an organization (Porter, Lawler, and Hackman 1975). Given these tensions, individuals and organizations sometimes make erroneous choices. The organization can deal with the tension by using selection systems that help it choose people who fit the organization and reject those who do not.

Most selection systems have some kind of informal nondirective (unfocused) interview and, if they use some more formal procedures, paper and pencil tests of cognitive competence. Service organizations, however, will need a formal procedure for assessing the interpersonal competence and service orientation of applicants. Such a system answers this question: When faced with problems requiring good service and the creation of a positive service experience for consumers, how will employees respond? Techniques now exist for developing work simulations that can be used to find persons with service-oriented skills and competencies (Schneider and Schmitt 1986).

Membership issues may also affect the climate and culture of the demographically diverse organization. When people of both genders, many races and nationalities, and specialized education are attracted to and selected by organizations, climate and culture should have themes for fairness and the appreciation of individual differences. Because organization members will be more diverse, the organization will benefit from recruiting, selecting, and retaining employees who value diversity, are open to conflicting ideas and attitudes, and are comfortable with ambiguity (Moses and Lyness, in press).

A similar membership issue exists in interdependent organizations. Members should appreciate cultural diversity, be competent at communication, and be interpersonally competent in conflict situations. Conflict resolution and communication skills would be essential for people working in these organizations, especially for managers. Members could be selected for these values and skills.

In summary, membership issues are critical for ensuring a desired climate and culture. This is true because it is the people who behave and interpret behavior in organizations who create and transmit climate and culture. Thus, organizations must invest heavily in determining the kinds of members they accept and retain (Schneider, in press).

Socialization Issues. Organizations have two major opportunities to socialize new members, the formal and the informal. For example, for a service organization to provide quality service, the skills required for the delivery of quality service must be taught during training (formal). However, to ensure transfer of training, newcomers must also encounter role models and supervisors in the job setting who reward what is learned in training (informal).

Similarly, in an organization with demographically diverse members, if newcomers observe that some organizational members are treated unfairly because of their demographic differences, then the newcomers may reach the conclusion that unfairness is accepted in the organization. A "class" system may develop in the organization, and what Etzioni (1975) calls "organizational elites" (deriving from position power) or, more relevant to demographic diversity, "nonorganizational elites" (deriving from other personal attributes) may emerge.

In an organization that interacts frequently with other organizations, newcomers may also observe cultural differences in the way their own organization interacts with other organizations. Newcomers will learn, in these observations, whether an appreciation of cultural differences and effective cooperation and communication are important to their organization.

The issues regarding training and the creation of climate and culture can be outlined as follows. In a service organization, are service skills as well as technical skills (operating the cash register, the computer, and so on) taught, or is the emphasis only on the technical skills? In a demographically diverse organization, are managers taught to deal with individuals and their individual differences (Dansereau, Graen, and Haga 1975), or is this issue ignored? In an international organization, are the cultures of the other nations discussed in training, and are the skills necessary for working with members of those cultures taught? In organizations that are active in making acquisitions, are communication and conflict resolution skills taught? Are techniques for managing the tension between autonomy and cooperation taught?

Furthermore, interdependent organizations involved in an acquisition may face special socialization problems. The socialization of the acquired personnel may require more attention than that of the typical newcomers. Newcomers to an organization are never "blank slates" (Van Maanen 1976) who have no expectations or values prior to entering the organization. In fact, prior beliefs, expectations, and values may be especially important for "newcomers" from an acquired organization. As a group they are going from one culture (that of the acquired organization before the acquisition) to a new, established culture (that of the acquiring organization). It may be more difficult for them, as individuals, to accept the climate and culture of the acquiring organization because as a group they will be interpreting events together and reinforcing their own shared meanings from their original organization. Their socialization process may be facilitated by:

- Ensuring that the acquired persons have complete *formal* information about the policies, practices, and procedures of the new organization (pay, fringe, benefits, vacations, ordering supplies, arranging for travel, reporting hierarchies, and so on)

- Ensuring that the acquired persons have opportunities to obtain *informal* information about the kinds of behavior that is rewarded, supported, and expected, as well as about the myths and stories that underpin shared meaning—so the new persons can *share*

Clearly the combination of formal and informal socialization can be a powerful form of communication.

Identity Issues. After people are hired and socialized, organizations must manage identity by promoting a sense of belonging. Some ways of doing this in a service organization, for example, include:

- Involving employees in the design and development of new services (Schneider and Bowen 1984)
- Advertising quality service
- Using symbols of membership such as buttons, coffee mugs, or even uniforms (Van Maanen 1976)

Organizations need to reward and support continuously the attachment of employees to the organization. In a service organization this may be particularly important because attachment is such an influential *marketing* issue. When employees identify with their organization's service value, then *consumers* will be more likely to have "brand loyalty" (Schneider and Bowen 1985).

The above methods can also be used to promote a sense of belonging in demographically diverse organizations. In addition, demographic diversity can become a source of identity through:

- Use of diversity in persons from the organization as models in advertisements of the company's products and services
- Creating systems for maximum participation by diverse persons in all decision-making circumstances as a way of capitalizing on the diversity in perspectives (for example, Rice 1969)

Identity issues can be extraordinarily important for the interdependent organization. For example, following an acquisition, acquired personnel often experience a sense of lost identity (Levinson 1970). Marks and Mirvis (undated) speak of losing a loved one. A merger or acquisition can be traumatic, particularly for those who identified strongly with their original organization.

To promote a climate and culture for cooperation and communication following an acquisition, attention needs to be focused on the acquired personnel, especially with regard to creating a sense of identity with the new organization.

Efforts should be made to help them cope with their sense of loss and to help them to feel part of their new organization. Some ways of doing this include:

- Taking care to treat the newly acquired personnel as people and not as numbers (that is, management should learn their names, treat them as equal to the acquiring personnel, place them in responsible jobs)
- Marketing, both internally and externally, the benefits associated with bringing the acquired personnel into the combined organization

Authority Issues. These issues concern the traditional management functions that guide organizational activities. Again, management must ask Planning for *what*? Organizing for *what*? Controlling for *what*? The answers to all of these questions should focus on the same *what*, or organizational goals. Some research has shown that when service organizations establish rules and procedures to promote a goal of bureaucratic efficiency instead of service, service employees tend to be dissatisfied, frustrated, and likely to leave (Parkington and Schneider 1979). In addition, when organizational routines and rewards create an "efficiency ethic" rather than a "service ethic," consumers experience poor service (Schneider and Bowen 1985).

Thus, in a service organization if the answers to the above questions are directed toward superior service quality, then the organization is on the way to creating a service climate. If the answers are, planning to reduce costs, organizing to increase efficiency, and controlling human variability, then high-quality service is not a likely outcome (Norman 1984).

In a demographically diverse organization, if the questions are answered with "an appreciation of individual differences to enhance cooperation and understanding among employees," then the organization may be fostering a climate or culture that values individual differences. For example, jobs can be organized to promote interaction among diverse employees, and planning can center around not only strategic external issues, but also such internal functioning as facilities for child care and the retirement problems of older workers, and, in general, directly confront demographic diversity as salient issues in the management of the firm.

In interdependent organizations, a value for cultural appreciation may be the outcome if the answers to the questions are directed toward a discussion and confrontation of organizational cultural differences, communication, and cooperation. Discussion and confrontation here mean explicit consideration by management in its planning, organizing, and controlling of ways to forge a *common* set of routines and rewards out of the diverse climates and cultures that come together in internationalization, joint ventures, and/or the combinations associated with mergers and acquisitions. This is especially difficult given the paucity of models on which to depend for guidelines, but at a minimum, data suggest that issues of autonomy, power, job security, identity, varying interpretations, and intergroup conflict will require attention (Berney 1985, Rentsch 1985).

Interpersonal Issues. High-contact service organizations are dominated by interpersonal interaction. To be effective, these organizations need to attract, select, and retain interpersonally oriented people, and these people need to be formally and informally socialized to be interpersonally sensitive and responsive. Part of their organizational identity will be their attraction to other persons in the organization, and the organization's structures should facilitate interpersonal interaction.

In other words, a central management responsibility in service organizations is the management of interpersonal relationships. Interpersonal relationships require effective management in every facet of organizational life—selection, training, planning, and so on. To the extent that interpersonal issues are at the forefront of management's concerns in a service organization, the service organization is more likely to be effective.

More specifically, at the boundary of service organizations, the relationship between server and served is an interpersonal transaction (Maister 1982). The quality of that transaction will depend upon everything the organization does to reward, support, and expect effective interpersonal relationships. The "messages" members receive about the importance of excellent service come to them through interpersonal interactions with trainers, co-workers, and supervisors. The chain of internal interpersonal relationships begins within the organization but extends beyond its boundaries to the consumer. It seems safe to hypothesize that the quality of the link between service providers and consumers can be no stronger than the quality of other organizational interpersonal links.

Since the culture of organizations depends upon sharing norms, values, and meanings, it is obvious that the nature of interpersonal relationships is key. In demographically diverse organizations and in organizations that have many interdependencies, the degree to which culture is shared will be a function of the extent to which interpersonal interaction is facilitated—that is, how interaction between different groups is routinized and rewarded.

Beer (1980) notes that stages of interpersonal learning are best described in terms of *depth*. By *depth* he means the centrality of the issues discussed to the core of a person's self-concept. At the least threatening level are discussions of task issues (goals, policies), then process issues (role expectations, decision making), then personal and interpersonal issues (leadership style, trust), and then competence issues (credibility, personal effectiveness). When *all* of these issues have been explored by persons in an organization, then interpersonal and organizational effectiveness will be facilitated.

The interpersonal issues in culturally diverse and interdependent organizations, because of their salience, will be especially difficult to manage. This will be true because such organizations will force people to confront dissimilarity when their usual impulse is to seek similarity (Festinger 1954).

Of course, the study of interpersonal issues at work has received considerable attention, but much of that work has focused either on leadership (see Bass 1981) or on group effectiveness (see Hackman 1987). The management of interpersonal conflict and the understanding of intergroup relationships (see Miller 1976), as well as an understanding of the role of interpersonal relationships in the formation of climate (Schneider and Reichers 1983) and culture (Schein 1985), is more recent. These more recent writings emphasize both the potentially positive and the potentially negative consequences of interpersonal and intergroup conflict. However, most seem to agree that conflict (that is, power) in organizations is a fact of life, that it is only one facet of life in organizations, and that it can be managed in ways that meet individual, intergroup, and organizational needs (see Bolman and Deal 1984).

Summary and Conclusion

In summary, five issues that organizations must manage in order to create particular kinds of climate and culture were applied to three possible characteristics of future organizations. It is not a simple task to create a desired and strong climate and culture. First, the nature of the environment must be accurately anticipated or determined. Then each of the five facets—membership, socialization, identity, authority, and interpersonal relations—must be managed to express climate and culture. Climate and culture, then, are a result of a network of interacting systems.

Managers must realize the interacting nature of the five facets, because managing one facet will often automatically involve managing another facet. For example, managing socialization involves managing identity and interpersonal issues. Socialization also reflects authority issues. Identity issues become salient during the socialization process because newcomers are learning what it means to be a member of the organization, the kinds of commitments that can be fulfilled by being a member of the organization, and so on. Interpersonal issues are relevant during socialization because newcomers tend to seek information from their supervisors and co-workers (informal socialization). If training is a part of the socialization process (formal socialization), the newcomers will interact with the training instructors. These interpersonal relationships during the early socialization stages will send long-lasting messages to the newcomers and to the other employees. Authority issues are reflected in how socialization occurs (formal or informal), who is responsible for it, and when (or if) it occurs.

Managers cannot forget the interconnectedness of the five issues. Inconsistent and conflicting messages may be sent to employees if managers concentrate on only one facet of the system. The organization that sends inconsistent messages breeds ambiguity, frustration, and perhaps hostility. If management wishes to foster a particular climate or culture, it must be aware of and consistently manage the five issues across all situations.

To complicate matters, some organizations will desire multiple climates. That is, some organizations will wish to emphasize several themes in the organization. For example, the demographically diverse organization may also be a service organization. There will be a theme in the climate and culture for quality service and there may also be another theme that addresses demographic diversity. Many "messages" will be sent in the organization, and ensuring that the members interpret the messages and apply them in the manner desired by the organization is a complex task.

Clearly, managing climate and culture requires that managers grapple with slippery, interconnected, and intricate issues. The difficulty of managing these five issues is further complicated by the need to anticipate correctly the organization's future. Since climate and culture exist in all organizations, managers are wise to manage climate and culture in such a way that the organization can deal effectively. The major point of this chapter is that this is a very complex task, for, in Kilmann's (1985) terms, there is no quick fix.

IV
Motivation and Human Resource Management

The problems of motivation have already emerged in part III, especially in chapter 8 where Klein and Hall consider the effects of deskilling and greater boredom and stress. That reward or compensation issues have emerged in previous chapters also speaks to the issue of motivation, especially if one assumes that training is a highly motivating force.

Just as chapter 3 reviewed some organizational forms, and chapter 5 looked at the problem of the previous kinds of organizational forms, chapter 11 by Gary Latham examines the past, present, and future of motivation. Unlike the authors of chapters 2 and 3, who perceived that enormous changes will occur, Latham believes that the problems of motivation remain largely the same and that there are no easy solutions.

Latham does perceive some changes in the standard mechanisms of maintaining or enhancing motivation. He does believe that goal setting will be manifested in a clearly defined mission, thus echoing chapter 10. He also believes that another significant change is the reduced importance of authority as a motivation; this parallels the discussions of greater unit autonomy. Finally, he argues that training and job security are greater motivators, thus picking up on some of the same ideas that Tuttle mentioned in chapter 9.

Klein and Hall observed at the end of their chapter that the conflict between individual and organizational goals is as great as ever, and may be getting greater. This theme is pursued in chapter 12, in which Joseph Lengermann suggests that the assumption made by many analysts that the future will see many happy workers is seriously flawed. He cites a number of reasons why the workers' goals may be in conflict with organizational goals, the basic dilemma that makes motivation troublesome and that leads to attempts to control worker behavior. If motivation were not problematic, then there would be no reason to control the behavior of the workers.

That Lengermann may indeed be right about the conflict between individual and collective goals is suggested in one of the case studies reported in chapter 11. Although the manager believed very much in the technical systems approach, it appears that the organization had too little structure and too little relationship between reward and performance. It is interesting to contrast this case study with the situation in Silicon Valley (see chapter 7). Clearly, different organizational structures—or their absence—appeal to different people and presumably in different parts of the country. Again, we are led to the idea that contingency theory is the only way to speculate about the futures.

Chapters 11 and 12 appear to differ on the relative importance of monetary rewards. The study of Silicon Valley in chapter 7 suggested that monetary rewards were very important, but there is a considerable amount of evidence that it is more important to some than to others. Managers concerned about the motivation of their employees also need to worry about defining and reaching their individual goals. One can imagine that in the future there may be even greater differentiation among individual goals than there has been in the past, which may make the fit with organizational needs even greater.

Because of the stress in part III on the need for training and its applicability in changing organizations, the real question may be how much training is itself a reward. Both Latham and Lengermann suggest that it may be, and if this is the case, human resource management becomes all the more important.

Because human capital is growing more important, as chapters 1, 5, 6, 8, and 10 suggest, the last chapter focuses on the issue of how to manage human resources. In it, Denise Rousseau provides a number of useful questions that again set limits on what might be perceived as simple solutions. In particular, she discusses the problem of overtraining or of underuse of human capital, an especially interesting idea, given the focus on training as a solution to many adaptive problems faced by organizations and the assumption that training is motivating.

Rousseau also adds to the discussion of the changes taking place in the labor force by observing that many firms are changing their employment practices and that this in turn has made human resource management issues more complicated. She also suggests that Lengermann's cautionary tale about workers may be more applicable to some of the "new" workers or employment strategies, such as greater reliance on part-time help, temporary employment, and home-based workers. Do these employees have job security, or are they likely to be accultured to the kinds of values discussed in chapter 10?

Rousseau's discussion of the psychological contract nicely complements the analysis of the establishment of culture by Schneider and Rentsch. One way of thinking about cultures is as a kind of contract, and as unions and other formal agreements gradually disappear—assuming that they do—then these kinds of contracts may become especially important. Not everyone does believe that unions will disappear. Klein and Hall observe in chapter 8 that unions may change their strategies, and fight for job security and move into new areas.

Chapter 1 suggested that in the future organizations will have to stress innovation. Rousseau picks up on this theme and considers what the strategic considerations in human resource management are in relation to this idea.

Comparing her formulation with that of Schneider and Rentsch, one finds some overlap, but differences as well.

These last three chapters discuss yet another important aspect of any strategy for firm survival. Many of the chapters in the first two parts of this book emphasized market position, competitiveness, and strategies for coping. But if human capital (and its mobilization) increasingly becomes the most important element in production, then motivation and human resource management become perhaps the key components of any successful strategy. Correspondingly, human resource managers should become as important as, if not more so, than marketing and financial managers.

11
Employee Motivation: Yesterday, Today, and Tomorrow

Gary P. Latham

> The primary goal of good management is to show average people how to do the work of superior people.
>
> —John D. Rockefeller

As the source of this quotation might indicate, *motivation* is a word often associated with big business. Moreover, the organizational scientists who study this subject are usually employed or consulted by large corporations. Associating motivation with business, however, blurs one's recognition of a force that has a profound influence on the internal workings of organizations of all kinds, from the United Nations to the corner store.

To consider the subject of motivation is, in the end, to ask ourselves the meaning of human beings, and why they do the things they do. In that form, however, such questions are often phrased improperly, and thus the answers are faltering and inconclusive. This is because the question of why is less scientific than it is philosophic. It is infinitely regressive. Behind every "Why?" lurks another "Why?" The question of how is less philosophic than it is scientific; it can be observed, measured, and recorded.

As can be discerned from the title, the focus of this chapter is on where we have been, where we are now, and where we are likely to be tomorrow in terms of how people grapple with the subject of employee motivation. In writing this chapter, I was stimulated by the following questions: Have the themes underlying motivation changed over time? Have the concerns of employees changed? Have the principles regarding motivation changed with time? Do researchers think of motivation differently today from the way they did yesterday? If the answer to any of these questions is no, are the answers likely to be different tomorrow?

I would like to thank several colleagues for their helpful insights, given while I was preparing this chapter: Wendell French, Louis W. Fry, Dale Henning, Phil Kienast, Bud Knudson, Bud Saxberg, Bill Scott, and Charles Summer.

In reviewing the motivation literature, two contradictory themes have prevailed throughout this century—namely, first, that one cannot motivate others; one can only create the conditions that will allow people to motivate themselves. This is done by focusing on the way jobs are designed. The second theme is that by focusing on the individual—that is, on the person's behavior, needs, drives, and goals—one can indeed motivate that individual. These two themes are explained from the vantage points of yesterday and today. The emphasis is on examining how these different methodologies can or cannot be effective in influencing the choice, effort, or persistence of people, rather than on looking at the philosophical views of the people who espouse these methodologies and at the philosophical views of those who were or were not motivated.

In the section entitled "Yesterday," parallels are drawn between what was and what is being done. In the section entitled "Today," two case studies are presented in which the two respective approaches to motivation were used in two organizational settings with very different outcomes. In the section entitled "Tomorrow," what is likely to remain constant and what is likely to change in the way motivation is studied and applied is discussed.

Yesterday

Job Design

In the first two decades of the twentieth century, motivation was the subject of intensive study by industrial engineers. Foremost among them was Frederick Taylor (1911), who promoted the idea of scientific management. This approach to motivation is best remembered for its methodology—namely, time and motion study, in pursuit of "the one best way" to accomplish a task. Thus the primary dependent variable of interest to industrial engineers was worker efficiency. Time and motion study was used to remove the ignorance of employers as to the proper *time* in which work of various kinds should be completed (Taylor 1911).

Three assumptions are implicit in this approach. First, the concept of individual differences can be ignored. People are people, just as a Model T is a Model T. Second, the way to motivate people to be efficient is to focus on the work itself. Third, the employee is motivated primarily by the carrot of pay and advancement and by the stick of discipline and job insecurity. The first two principles have survived in various guises to the present day.

With regard to ignoring individual differences, a visit to many corporations will reveal an emphasis on variations of work design in which the underlying principle is that participative decision making is highly valued by most, if not all, employees. The belief of the upper management in these companies is that the satisfaction of this need for participation in decision making will lead to greater efficiency in terms of an increase in employee attendance, a decrease in employee grievances, an increase in product quality, and a decrease in organizational costs. Most recently, Sashkin (1986) has argued that fostering participative decision making among employees is an ethical imperative on the part of managers.

A primary change in the thinking of those who believe that one's work is the key to motivation is the way in which they now believe a job should be designed. Scientific management advocated breaking down tasks into their smallest components so that the job could be done in a uniform repetitive manner. Today the emphasis has shifted to designing jobs that require workers to be multiskilled to the point where each can assist in the work of others (Emery 1985). This is a far cry from the practice of simplifying tasks to the point where even a skilled job meant the monotonous repetition, day after day, of the same overlearned tasks.

A second significant shift in the thinking of researchers in this area concerns the degree to which the job itself motivates people to perform at their best. The scientific management school viewed the employee as a timorous specimen, terrified of taking a chance of being deprived of a living. At the same time the employees were viewed as forever wanting as much money and property as they could possibly acquire. Thus, the worker was seen as motivated by the pull of pay and advancement and by the push of discipline and job insecurity.

Considering the influx at the time that scientific management was being formulated of near penniless immigrants to North America who could not speak English, this focus on the security needs of the workers may have been correct. Even today it would be foolish to underestimate the effectiveness of these devices. Money might not be everything—otherwise movie stars would be the happiest people on earth—but there is no evidence that the mass of humanity has ceased to have a strong desire for the comfort and possessions that money will buy (Lawler 1971, Locke et al. 1980). But today's sociotechnical advocates downplay the importance of money in favor of designing jobs that allow people to take into account and develop their multiple skills.

The implicit theory of sociotechnical advocates is that motivation is the sum of a person's aspirations, values, self-esteem, and sensibilities. It is a person's own property, to be given or withheld depending on how he or she feels about a job. Consequently, the stimulus for motivation is not viewed as something "outside" but within the body. Thus, one cannot motivate others; one can only concentrate on creating and maintaining a psychological climate that enables people to motivate themselves.

One way to create an effective psychological climate is to make pay a nonissue for employees. This is done by paying them at or above the prevailing industry standard. Pay is not contingent upon performance because if the job is designed correctly there is no need to do so. Everyone will be motivated to do his or her best. Thus a focus on the individual rather than on the design of the job is unnecessary; people are people. The way to motivate people is to design jobs that will enable them to motivate themselves.

Focusing on the Individual

From the 1930s to the present day, motivation has been largely the province of psychologists. The early research focused primarily on arousal states. The dominant work in that period was Hull's (1943) drive theory. *Drive* was defined as an energizing influence that determines the intensity of behavior. All behavior was to be explainable in terms of drive reduction. For instance, I am thirsty, I get a drink of water, and this reduces the drive for liquids. Drives can be distinguished as primary or secondary. Primary drives include thirst, hunger, pain, and sex. They are built into the response structure of the organism. Secondary drives are learned or acquired through their pairing with primary drives.

Innovative experiments, however, ended research on drive reduction theory. Olds and Milner (1954) found that electrical stimulation increased the frequency with which a behavior is repeated. By implanting electrodes in the hypothalamus of rats and then running electrical current through it, these researchers found that rats repeated those actions that were immediately preceded by the electrical stimulation. In a subsequent study, Olds (1958) found that sexual intromission served as a reinforcer for rats even though they were not allowed to ejaculate. Drive or need reduction, with its emphasis on satisfaction, obviously could not explain this behavior.

This is little evidence that industry was aware of, let alone influenced by, Hull's theory. However, another theory of arousal (Mitchell 1982) has been taught religiously in business schools since the 1950s. Its legacy to industry is akin to Freud's to psychiatry. In fact, the two theories are similar in that they present an interesting paradox: both were widely accepted even though there was little research to support either of them. This arousal theory, proposed by Maslow, is known as need hierarchy. It was described in a heuristic or speculative article in 1943, the time when Hull and his colleagues were conducting their carefully crafted experiments. The acceptance of the need hierarchy was so widespread that it was not until the mid-1960s that empirical studies were conducted to test its predictions.

In brief, Maslow (1943) stated that people have five needs that they strive to satisfy, namely, physiological, security, affiliation, self-esteem, and self-actualization needs. Once a lower need is satisfied (for example, physiological), the person automatically focuses on ways of fulfilling the next higher need (for example, security). This emphasis on fulfilling lower-order needs before attending to higher needs is not incongruous with Frederick Taylor's observations that newly landed immigrant workers were very concerned with making money and obtaining property. Like Hull, Maslow explained behavior in terms of deprivation and gratification of needs. Maslow argued that the gratification of a lower order need submerged it and activated the next higher need in the hierarchy.

The problems with Maslow's theory are at least twofold. First, empirical research did not provide support for the postulate that human needs are classified into five distinct categories or that these categories are structured in a specific hierarchy (Wahba and Bridwell 1973). Second, the theory defied application. It would appear that management should focus on pay, hours of work, the physical work setting, and the sociability of the work group so that the employee will automatically focus on self-actualization. Certainly a government that espouses this theory should advocate a minimum wage for its citizens so that the needs for food and security are satisfied and higher-order needs automatically addressed, resulting in citizens' becoming productive. But how is self-actualization observed and measured? Does it differ for different people? Does the need hierarchy itself vary for different people? How exactly can a job be designed so that it allows an individual to gratify the lower needs out of existence? Answers to these questions, based on data, have not been forthcoming. This theory, like others before it, suffered because it failed to take into account individual differences. One attempt to circumvent this problem has been Hackman and Oldham's (1980) theory of job enrichment. They found that an enriched job is one that provides variety, autonomy, and feedback, but only for those people who appreciate these facets.

An approach to motivation that is based on scientific studies is advocated by Skinner. It was an outgrowth of, and a reaction to, Hull's drive theory. Rather than focus on internal drive states, Skinner advocated focusing on a person's observable behavior. His research is among the most dominant influences on North American psychology (Heyduk and Fenigstein 1984).

Skinner (1953) showed how behavior is a function of its consequences. If the immediate consequence is positive, the frequency with which the behavior is repeated is increased; if the immediate consequence is aversive, the frequency with which the behavior is repeated is decreased. Such consequences (for example, providing task variety, giving praise, allowing a person to participate in the decision-making process) are called either reinforcers or punishers (Skinner 1953).

The word *motivation* was shunned by Skinner and his followers because it implied an internal need state or a cognitive process. Neither were given an explanatory status in Skinner's research. The sole focus was on behavior and on the stimulus conditions *outside* the body that affected it (Estes 1958). This work took into account individual differences by showing that what is reinforcing for one individual (for instance, sex, praise, participative decision making) might be punishing for another.

Of interest to industry was the finding that the frequency of a behavior could be changed by altering the schedule of reinforcement (Latham and Dossett 1986). Contrary to common sense, a reinforcer presented on a variable or intermittent schedule results in a faster and more persistent response rate than does a reinforcer administered on a continuous schedule. In one study (Heron and Skinner 1937) a rat received a food pellet each time a bar was pressed. Gradually, this continuous schedule was stretched and stretched to a variable ratio schedule such that the rat expended more calories than it was taking in and consequently died. Such experiments may explain how "job burnout" can occur from too much motivation's resulting from too little reinforcement. Early in their career, executives may receive constant attention and praise. Gradually, as they receive less and less, they work harder and harder in the organization until they suffer mental and physical exhaustion.

Skinner's work has been criticized (for example, Locke 1977, Mitchell 1979) for failing to take into account cognitive processes as an explanation for how reinforcers and punishers shape behavior. Empirical research has shown that cognitive influences can weaken, distort, or nullify the effects of reinforcers and punishers.

For example, Kaufman, Baron, and Kopp (1966) conducted a study in which one group was correctly informed about how its performance would be rewarded, whereas two other groups were told incorrectly that their behavior would be reinforced either every minute (fixed interval schedule) or after they had performed on the average 150 responses (variable ratio schedule).

The data showed that a person's beliefs about the prevailing schedule of reinforcement outweighed the influence of the actual experienced consequences. Although everyone was rewarded on the same schedule, those who thought they were being reinforced once every minute produced a very low response rate (mean = 6); those who thought they were being reinforced on the variable ratio schedule maintained an exceedingly high response rate (mean = 259); while those who were correctly informed that their behavior would be rewarded on the average once every minute displayed an intermediate response rate. Thus, identical environmental consequences can have different behavioral effects, depending on one's cognitions.

Skinner's work led to the development of cognitive theories of motivation. The most popular theory in the scientific community in the 1960s was Vroom's (1964) expectancy theory. In brief, the theory stated that one's expectancy or belief that one's effort would result in a given behavior or level of performance, multiplied by one's belief that one's performance would lead to a given outcome, multiplied by the value that one attaches to that outcome, affected choice. Perhaps because of its mathematical assumptions, this theory had little or no effect on industry. In the 1970s its mathematical assumptions were questioned by scientists (for example, Schmidt 1973), and the theory was gradually put aside. A second cognitive theory, however, developed during the same time period, is to this day embraced by cognitive psychologists and by many of the followers of Skinner (for instance, Bandura 1977, Kanfer 1980). This theory is goal setting (Locke 1968, Locke and Latham 1984a). It is considered a milestone in industrial-organizational psychology (Dunnette 1976).

Goal-setting theory states that it is goals that mediate the effects of variables such as praise, participative decision making, and monetary incentives. The underlying assumption of the theory is that a person's cognitions are a primary variable that explain behavior. Of interest to management is the finding that specific, difficult goals result in higher performance than do abstract or easy goals. Moreover, given that a goal is accepted, the higher the goal, the higher the performance. Reinforcers and punishers affect goal commitment (Kanfer 1980). Reviews of the literature have shown that goal-setting theory is among the most scientifically valid and useful theories in organizational science today (Miner 1980, Pinder 1984). Its widespread applicability and use in organizational settings has been reviewed elsewhere (Latham and Yukl 1975, Latham and Locke 1979, Locke and Latham 1984b).

Today

Have the themes underlying motivation changed over time? The answer is no. From the employer's perspective, the concern with quantity and quality of work performed in a timely fashion by the employee remains the same. From the researcher's perspective, there are still two camps, with little communication between them. The human resource philosophy of organizations reflects, in many instances, the philosophy of the consultants the managers employ. One camp still maintains that one can motivate others through the setting of goals and the reinforcement of behavior that leads to goal attainment. The other camp remains adamant that one person cannot motivate another; employers can only create conditions under which employees will motivate themselves. Both camps, however, would probably agree with Hebb, who stated, "Motivation refers . . . to the energizing of behavior, and especially to the sources of energy in a particular set of responses that keep them temporarily dominant over others and account for continuity and direction of behavior" (Hebb 1961). This viewpoint has important implications for the subject of motivation. Employers might consider the employee as an energy storage system capable of a wide variety of responses. Changing the nature of the job frequently, providing more breaks in routine, and furnishing more cues for secondary drives, such as curiosity and exploration, might prove highly effective. The two camps, however, would disagree on how this can best be brought about.

Have the principles regarding motivation changed with time? The answer is yes. The scholars who advocate a focus on the job and the work setting have eschewed scientific management principles and argue instead for job complexity rather than job simplification. The ignoring of individual differences, however, remains strong. These advocates appear grounded more strongly in philosophy and rational discourse than in science or empirical data. Where data are collected, the focus on the individual is usually limited to job satisfaction, a variable distinctly different from motivation (for example, effort, choice, persistence). In addition to employee job satisfaction, organizational measures are often collected, such as attitude surveys and measures of organizational efficiency (for instance, costs).

For those who believe that one can motivate the individual, measurement is taken at the level of the individual using either behavioral or outcome measures derived from the behavior. These scholars have undergone a more significant shift in their thinking than have those who focus on the work setting. No longer is there the interest in the former camp on drive reduction. No longer is there an interest in need states—at least as they were operationalized in the 1940s. Few people believe that reinforcers can be used effectively without taking into account cognition. The current focus is on goal setting (that is, cognitive intentions) and ways of obtaining goal commitment. The importance of Skinner's work is that it demonstrated the importance of making a reinforcer, such as praise, specific to (that is, contingent upon) and relatively immediately after a desired behavior (for example, attaining the goal) occurs.

It is the issues of individual differences and of the importance of empirically derived data that strongly divide these two camps. One camp argues that an enriched job is good for almost anyone and therefore should be made available unconditionally to everyone. The second camp argues that what is reinforcing to one person (for example, task variety) may be punishing to another. The only way to find out, this second camp argues, is to observe and record whether behavior desired by management increases or decreases as a result of administering a specific consequence to an employee. Once a consequence is identified as a reinforcer or punisher, it should be made conditional, immediately, upon the demonstration of a desired behavior.

The focus on the individual is currently leading to an advocacy of self-management in the workplace, an advocacy that is philosophically compatible with those who focus on the job and the workplace as the key to employee motivation. Self-management involves goal setting, self-monitoring, and the self-administration of self-selected reinforcers and punishers (Kanfer 1980, Frayne and Latham 1987).

Have the concerns of employees changed? The answer is probably yes. The disinclination of many people to enter the government bureaucracy may well be the result of a policy that interprets rewards largely in terms of security and gradual promotion within a rigid hierarchy. Perhaps one reason some people do not become active in religious organizations is that the promise of salvation in a hereafter does not seem as challenging to them as an opportunity to be of service to others in the here and now. But all that is being said here is that there is a need to take into account individual differences. People are still entering the government; people are still seeking work in religious organizations. What is a goal for one person may not be a goal for another. What is a reinforcer for one person may not be a reinforcer for another. Only the principles of goal setting and reinforcement are applicable across people and across time. This is because *specific* as opposed to general goals provide *structure* by making *clear* what is *expected* of the individual. Specific goals make clear the desired *end results*. Reinforcers and punishers provide *consequences* of action. Positive or aversive consequences of attaining or failing to attain the goal provide meaning for one's action. Goal commitment generally leads to the development of strategies to attain it, and thus the seeking of *feedback* that is in a form that enables one to monitor easily the gap between one's *behavior* and one's goal. Thus *measurement* of one's progress toward the goal becomes valued. And *goal specificity* provides an objective means of rewarding a person or removing that person from the organization. The latter is done when it is clear that there is lack of goal commitment or that there is goal incongruity between the employee and the employing organization.

The following two case studies in which the author has been involved are presented to demonstrate the importance of taking into account individual differences in the study of motivation as well as the importance of goals, behavioral consequences, feedback, and measurement of goal progress.

Millview's Focus on Job Design

This plant, Millview, a wood products mill of approximately four hundred people was a start-up operation in the late 1970s. Employees from across the country were recruited for their technical expertise. A decision was made to have the company operate nonunion. An internationally known consultant in sociotechnical systems was hired to help in the design of this organization in the start-up phase. A clear mission statement was developed by upper management. The purpose of the mission was not only to communicate the values of the new organization, but it was also to prepare people for action. The underlying theme of this mission was employee involvement through participation in decision making. The slogan "the thinking man's mill" was enthusiastically adopted by top management. This enthusiasm was critical because of the important role top management plays in the climate for integrating the human resources philosophy with strategic planning and management. As the Conference Board of Canada (Nininger 1982) has stressed, the personal style and approach of the chief executive officer plays an important role in establishing and maintaining the desired climate in the human resource function of the organization.

Recognizing that satisfaction and a desire for excellence should inherently be in conflict, group discussions were held with the newly hired employees on what was wrong in the mills from which they came, and what needed to be done to prevent these wrongs from occurring in their new mill. Implicit in the discussions was the belief that dissatisfaction is a source of motivation in that it can lead to a desire to change that which is a source of discomfort. Explicit in these discussions was the need for employees to offer their ideas and to challenge the thinking of others, including their bosses. Bosses discussed ways to bring ideas together and to stimulate their own thinking and that of those with whom they worked. Safety was emphasized. Employees were not asked to risk their lives in the mill; they were asked to "risk" sharing their thoughts and feelings. The adage "work smarter rather than harder" meant that people should commit their mental rather than their physical energies.

The request by the mill manager for a commitment by employees of mental rather than physical energy to the job was a recognition of the diminished acceptance of authority as a basis for action, especially among people born in the 1950s and 1960s. Most people, the mill manager believed, no longer did things because someone with position power said to do so. This change in employee thinking required a change in thinking among bosses from a focus on command to a focus on consensus. Thus, a unity principle was advocated whereby value was placed on fully involving employees in decision making so that they felt in unity with, and ownership for, their work.

Financial rewards were not tied to performance. Instead, a commitment was made to make and keep employees among the highest paid in the industry. The same commitment was made with regard to benefits.

Today the mill is in the black, while many other segments of the industry are in the red. The mill benefits from state-of-the-art technology and from employees who have pride in that technology. Ironically, the only blot on the mill is in the area of human resources. Only the mill manager remains committed to the human resource principles on which the mill was founded. The employees, including his top managers, are divided with regard to these principles. What went wrong?

First, many employees were attracted to the new mill only by the wages, the benefits, and the excitement of a start-up organization. They did not come because of the mill's vaguely worded philosophy. Once the mill was no longer in a start-up mode, they made clear their disdain for employee participation. They mocked the concept whenever they personally were not consulted on the tiniest of matters. As my colleague Bud Saxberg (personal communication) has noted, some people want a structured environment. They want a defined base for what is expected of them in their job. Then they can choose either to put forth a minimum level of effort or to commit themselves to the participation process. Lack of structure creates a "fuzzy base" from which to negotiate one's social contracts. Structure was especially needed by the employees at Millview to use as an excuse to explain why they wouldn't do what they didn't want to do anyway.

To illustrate this point, the philosophy of the mill was multicraft. That is, any person could and would do any job for which he or she was trained. The reason for this philosophy was twofold. First, it ensured the employees task variety. It made the work itself challenging. It allowed the employees to grow and develop new skills. It would increase their marketability outside the mill should they ever desire to move to another part of the country. In short, a person would be taught any job in the mill over time that he or she had a desire to learn rather than be dead-ended within a craft line. The second reason for this philosophy was that it was an essential underpinning of job security, the philosophy that no one would be laid off. With the philosophy of multicraft, a minimum number of people could be hired with high wages to run the mill through any economic cycle.

In addition to the structure discussed earlier, Millview employees wanted a supportive environment. They wanted to know that management would not look for opportunities to get rid of them; but these same employees did not want multicraft. The electricians and mechanics resented it when one of them crossed craft lines. The pride of the paper machine employees was hurt when people from the pulp mill performed paper mill jobs—well. People who left the paper machine for "training" elsewhere in the mill were viewed by peers who remained on the paper machine as failures.

A second problem that occurred was that this perceived lack of structure led to an employee attack on the integrity of the mill manager. "What does Pat want?" became a euphemism for "don't trust Pat." The more Pat said he wanted their input, the more this distrust grew. And when a decision was made that failed to placate a given employee interest group, the cynicism toward employee participation grew. And as this cynicism grew, the mill manager and employees began to avoid one another. Management by wandering around (Peters and Waterman 1982) became management by avoidance.

Third, data were not collected at the level of the individual. Thus rewards could not be tied to performance. Performance appraisals were seldom, if ever, conducted. Those that were done had little or no consequence for anyone regardless of whether the appraisal was a positive or negative one (Napier and Latham forthcoming). This was fine with the employees. Rewards (for instance, pay, promotion, status), they argued, should be tied to seniority.

The group data that were fed back to the employees were frequently in a form that the employees did not understand. What they knew was that they were technically very good; that is the reason they were repeatedly given as to why they were hired. What they now heard was that their performance, based on customer feedback, was no longer satisfactory. The value of the data was, consequently, denigrated. Only through repeated contacts of managers and hourly employees with customers is the mill beginning to hear what is being said.

Fourth, the management style of the mill manager was a problem. He was selected because of his social, as well as his technical, skills. On the technical side of the equation the mill manager had a Ph.D. in engineering. On the social side of the socio-technical equation he came from a plant where he was respected for his leadership skills by both his peers and union officers. His words and actions showed that human resource considerations were an integral part of strategic and operational planning. He used formal and informal methods of organizational communication to relate his views on human resources. But, as noted earlier, he did not follow an established process of reviewing the performance of the individual employee or relating performance in the management of human resources to the reward system. Nor did he manage the organization succession planning process effectively. These three factors have been identified by the Canada Conference Board as critical to the role of the chief executive officer for motivating an organization's human resources. Instead, the mill manager clung to the belief of the inherent worth of every employee. People were promoted on the basis of seniority. Managers were allowed to speak openly of their disdain for the sociotechnical process. No one was replaced. The mill manager *knew* that in time employees would see the value of a sociotechnical system. After five years, he is still waiting.

Sixth, the mill manager, like other sociotechnical advocates, was guilty of overlooking the fundamental principle of sociotechnical systems, which is that employees should participate in the design of the work environment that is optimal for them. Like missionaries who attempted to convert people in Moslem countries to Christianity, many sociotechnical people *know* what constitutes the optimal work environment for everyone. Often they are right; sometimes they are wrong. In this case, no one listened to the employees' cry for a traditional mill. No one is listening today.

Woodlands's Focus on the Individual

Woodlands (a wood products mill) is a unionized facility of approximately 1,600 people. In the mid-1970s, the company's plants in this regional section scored the lowest on the company attitude survey (see figure 11–1). There were wildcat strikes, legal strikes, and repeated threats of strikes. Morale among management was low. Finger pointing was the norm in explaining who didn't do what and why. Consequently, the newly appointed region vice president conducted interviews with hourly employees, union leaders, and management personnel. Comments typical of hourly employees and union officers are shown in table 11–1. Comments typical of managers included a reference to a lack of structure of philosophy to guide them in their day-to-day actions.

The region vice president decided that a human resource philosophy was needed that would become a "region way of life" for improving the performance of the individual in ways that were acceptable to both the employee and the employing institution. In short, he directed attention to ways of aligning the goals of the individual with the goals of the region. The resulting philosophy

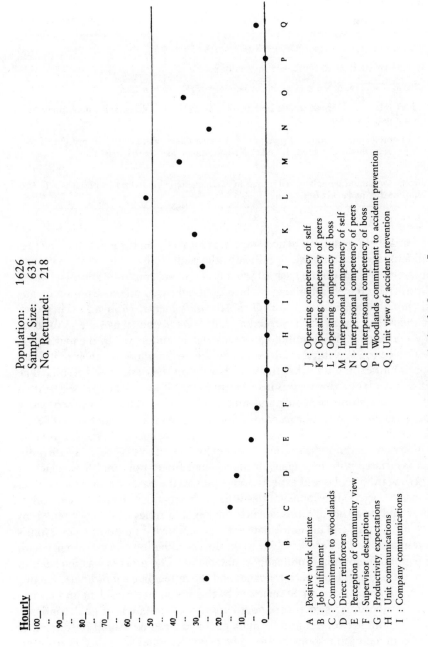

Population: 1626
Sample Size: 631
No. Returned: 218

A : Positive work climate
B : Job fulfillment
C : Commitment to woodlands
D : Direct reinforcers
E : Perception of community view
F : Supervisor description
G : Productivity expectations
H : Unit communications
I : Company communications

J : Operating competency of self
K : Operating competency of peers
L : Operating competency of boss
M : Interpersonal competency of self
N : Interpersonal competency of peers
O : Interpersonal competency of boss
P : Woodlands commitment to accident prevention
Q : Unit view of accident prevention

Figure 11–1. Attitude Survey, I

Table 11–1
Job Satisfaction

Comments of Hourly Employees

- Woodlands treats us like machines instead of people.
- Give us a supervisor we can talk to. *A member of the Human Race.*
- I don't think the foreman should be a two-bit, lying, back stabber, and I don't think he should play favoritism.
- (Take note)—When a foreman puts one of his men down or ridicules him in front of the whole crew, this is not good. It makes for bad morale among the crew, thus a decrease in productivity.
- Supervisor should be able to tell a man he is doing something wrong without treating him like dirt under his feet.

was a series of measurable action steps based directly on the input of employees at all levels in the company. Specifically, the philosophy addressed job design, employee selection on the basis of job requirements, employee appraisal based on those requirements, training of the individual based on those requirements, and employee motivation to fulfill those requirements. Motivation, however, was the undercurrent of the preceding four. The action steps were as follows:

Job Design: This terminology was used in a unique way by the new region vice president. He wanted employees to be able to communicate their individual responsibilities in a way that focused sharply on the desired end results. The traditional job description was insufficient in that it was, at best, a well-written elaborate definition of major and minor job duties. What he wanted was a concise statement of major responsibilities *and* the measures that would be applied to define whether the responsibilities were being discharged. Based on his interviews and his observations, he concluded that this would alleviate problems associated with management morale and finger pointing. It was lack of clarity regarding roles and expectations that was the basis for ongoing conflict among managers. If responsibilities were clearly defined, he reasoned, confusion would be avoided. Consequently, he began a series of group discussions involving himself and his immediate managers aimed at pinpointing everyone's job responsibilities. This was done to ensure coordination and consistency with the region's mission and philosophy statements. The process was repeated in group settings involving each manager and the immediate subordinate. Finally, the overall process was again reviewed by the region vice president and his immediate subordinates to ensure goal congruency and lack of goal conflict.

For example, several middle managers had been measured on outcomes not within their job responsibilities. The export sales manager had been evaluated on ship-loading costs. Other managers were being evaluated on vaguely worded goals that were not measurable (for example, maximizing the use of the region allocation process). There had been goal conflicts between managers (for example, the goal of "minimizing logging costs" resulted in higher transportation and log handling costs). A series of employee involvement groups highlighted and resolved problems associated with (*a*) truck foremen who didn't know the purpose of their job, (*b*) the financial group whose members couldn't agree on major priorities, and (*c*) individuals who viewed themselves as having little or no responsibility for items that were in fact a major part of their job (for instance, plant security, worker's compensation claims).

Job Analyses: Job analyses were conducted with hourly employees, supervisors, and managers to identify behaviors that are critical to the effectiveness of people in a given position. For example, the critical incident technique (Flanagan 1954) was used to identify behaviors that define the effectiveness of first-line supervisors (Latham, Fay, and Saari 1979). This focus on behavior reflected employee desire that effectiveness be measured on factors over which the individual has control as opposed to economic measures such as costs that are affected by myriad factors (Latham 1986). The behaviors were those that directly affected the performance outcomes indicated in the job design. An example is given in table 11–2.

Selection: On the basis of the behavioral analysis, situational interviews (Latham et al. 1980, Latham and Saari 1984, Latham and Finnegan 1987) were developed and validated against the effectiveness measures. That is, what people said in an interview was statistically correlated with what people actually did on the job.

Table 11–2
Behavioral Index

Employee Rates Foreman	Almost Never				Almost Always
Interaction with subordinates:					
Explains why a given job or procedure needs to be done.	0	1	2	3	4
Safety:					
Explains thoroughly to (for example, shows) a new employee how to do the job safely.	0	1	2	3	4
Work Habits:					
Delegates work (does not have to do everything himself).	0	1	2	3	4
Organizational Commitment:					
Proposes new ways of cutting costs, doing jobs more effectively, and producing the best possible product.	0	1	2	3	4

A unique aspect of the situational interview is that the questions are designed by job incumbents to identify the behavioral intentions of the applicant. The job incumbents then develop a scoring guide to assist them in scoring the interviewee's answers. Thus, one interviewer asks the questions, and two or more interviewers score the answer using a scoring guide that is not shown to the applicant. An example of a situational interview question is shown in figure 11–2.

An advantage to this approach to interviewing is that the questions are based on a job analysis. As a result, the applicant gets a preview of what is involved in the job. All applicants are asked the same questions and are evaluated against the same behavioral bench marks. Thus, bias and favoritism are minimized. These types of questions can be used to identify the person's motivation for such things as coming to work, team playing, and the desire to do a good job for its own sake.

Performance Feedback: The performance appraisal directly reflected the results of the job analysis. It defined effectiveness in terms of observable behavior on the part of the individual employee. True to the philosophy of participation in decision making, the instrument was developed by the people for the people.

In addition to emphasizing behavioral feedback, the region vice president attacked the accounting system. Included in the philosophy statement was the principle that feedback must be something the individual who controls an

Your spouse and three teenage children are sick in bed with a cold. There are no family or friends available to stay with them. Your shift starts in three hours. What would you do in this situation?

Answer: _____

_____

_____

_____

Interviewer's scoring guide:

1	3	5
My family would come first; I would stay home.	I would phone my boss and explain my situation.	I would come to work; they only have colds.

Figure 11–2. Example of a Situational Interview Question

operation can understand and respond to in a timely fashion. Accounting data did not meet this principle. People were polled on the information that was truly critical for managing their jobs and on the frequency with which the information was needed. With the region vice president's influence, the requested changes in feedback and frequency were made in a timely fashion.

Training: Leadership training was given for hourly employees, union executives, and managerial employees. The training (Latham and Saari, 1979) emphasized ways of focusing on an individual's behavior rather than personality, making praise specific and immediate, and emphasizing what people need to *do* to do things right. As Fran Tarkenton (1986) commented, Bud Grant, the football coach of the Vikings, knew how to get people "up" for a game. He would tell a player just what he wanted without making the person feel intimidated. He did this by giving clear, crisp directions as to what he wanted a player to *do* (that is, behavior) in the game; he followed up with clear, crisp feedback afterward on what he wanted a player to start doing, stop doing, or continue doing.

The results achieved at Woodlands over a five-year period have been impressive. In terms of man-hours per unit of production, the woods operation went from 1.46 to 1.34, the raw materials unit went from .20 to .15, and lumber went from 3.36 to 2.74. Work stoppages in terms of total hours lost over the five-year period went from 28,281 to 0. Hours worked per grievance went from 7,436 to 10,950. Voluntary turnover went from 10.6 percent to 5.6 percent. However, discharges increased from 1.0 percent to 1.7 percent. Absenteeism went from 3.9 percent to 2.7 percent. The attitude survey taken five years later is shown in figure 11–3. The subordinate evaluations of supervisors went from 2.9 to 3.2; the manager's evaluations of these same supervisors went from 2.8 to 3.5 on a 4-point scale.

Motivation: In addition to feedback and goal setting, money was made a direct consequence of the individual's performance. Innovative ways were found to make work fun by administering money on Skinner's variable ratio reinforcement schedules (Latham and Dossett 1986, Saari and Latham 1982). The result was high productivity levels.

Why was Woodlands successful relative to Millview? First, the human resource practices were based on what employees stated constituted effectiveness rather than on the new region vice president's personal philosophy or on the philosophy of a social scientist. Thus, employee involvement in the decision-making process truly affected the decision outcomes. Second, the focus was on the individual. Behavior consistent with the human resource philosophy was clearly articulated. Third, behavior consistent with this philosophy became the criteria for promotion, demotion, transfers, and termination. Thus, performance was reviewed, feedback was given, and rewards were administered contingent upon performance. There were consequences for doing well, and there were consequences for doing poorly in one's job. Fourth, goals were set in relation to

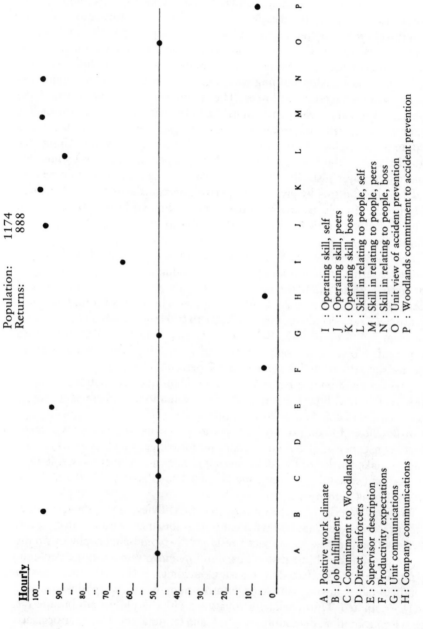

Population: 1174
Returns: 888

A : Positive work climate
B : Job fulfillment
C : Commitment to Woodlands
D : Direct reinforcers
E : Supervisor description
F : Productivity expectations
G : Unit communications
H : Company communications

I : Operating skill, self
J : Operating skill, peers
K : Operating skill, boss
L : Skill in relating to people, self
M : Skill in relating to people, peers
N : Skill in relating to people, boss
O : Unit view of accident prevention
P : Woodlands commitment to accident prevention

Figure 11–3. **Attitude Survey, II**

performance feedback. The goals were set progressively higher so that satisfaction with one's performance was discouraged. The focus on behavior and goals in relation to one's behavior made it difficult to ask, "What does Pete really want?" In addition, the focus on one's own behavior helped make people take responsibility for events rather than look for excuses in the environment. Fifth, the underlying philosophy of the region vice president was straightforward: "That which gets measured gets done." The individual was measured on performance. Sixth, the interrelationship of the action steps taken to implement the human resource philosophy (for example, selection, appraisal, training) was understood by the employee as defining the "region way of life" rather than a series of knee-jerk reactions to human resource problems.

Tomorrow

The motivational principles of goal setting and reinforcement will remain. The focus on job design will remain. Employee participation will remain. The difference between today and tomorrow is that the focus on employee motivation will include the macro organizational level in addition to micro levels, which have to do with the individual and the job.

At the macro level, goal setting will be evident in the form of a clearly defined mission. The purpose of the mission will be twofold. First, it will serve as a beacon for the type of individual who should join the organization. Validated selection techniques will be used more often to increase the probability that the employer and employee will make a correct choice. Second, the mission statement will be worded in such a way as to stimulate and unite people. In short, mission statements will be created to energize employees. This will be done by instilling in people a sense of purpose. Rather than relying on what Katz and Kahn (1978) called legal compliance, instrumentality, and job identification as sources of employee motivation, organizations will emphasize finding ways of getting people to identify with the very existence of the organization. Motivation will occur through each person's sense of achieving organizational goals.

An example of the power of a mission statement to motivate people is communism. Nowhere has this economic system worked well. And yet "redistribute wealth to the needy" has inspired people in Third World Countries far more than has the capitalistic slogan, "an individual's hard work will lead to his or her wealth."

In addition to searching for ways to minimize role conflict at the microlevel, organizations will analyze systems and structures at the macro level to identify and ensure goal congruency. These goals will be articulated in terms that are measurable. The goals will in essence consist of the action steps or strategies for achieving the organization mission.

Feedback ssytems will exist at the organizational level as well as at the level of the individual employee. Teamwork and working for the common good will be explicitly defined and rewarded. Thus, evidence that a unit's cost was sacrificed to maximize the total profit of the organization will be highlighted and rewarded. To ensure timely and accurate feedback that is meaningful to the receiver, accounting and technical services will be rewarded for aligning themselves with the needs of the internal customer, namely, operations. The feedback will allow individuals and the organization as a whole to see how they are functioning compared to their avowed mission, and to take whatever corrective steps are necessary. It will allow them to see what they look like when the organization's philosophy is operative. Thus, feedback from superiors, peers, subordinates, customers, and legislators will be solicited.

There will be an emphasis on structure to facilitate stability. Simon (1976) has argued that there is a biological limit to the human ability to cope with change. Hence the desire of people at Millview to escape from the "chaos" that they perceived was a result of management's abandoning responsible authority in favor of employee participation. Employee participation in job analyses and goal setting will contribute to employee stability in that "what is expected" will be defined a priori by the employees themselves.

The design and redesign of jobs to help achieve the mission will be based on both socio-technical considerations. The socio aspects will be based on the wisdom of job holders rather than social philosophers. Thus, the blind adherence to participation as an ideology among social scientists may disappear. Employee involvement will continue in regard to determining clear expectations as to departmental and individual goals, as well as the behaviors necessary to achieve those goals which in turn will enable the organization to fulfill its mission.

Arguments about whether leaders can directly motivate their subordinates or should provide job conditions under which subordinates will motivate themselves will fade away once it is recognized that both are possible. Ways will be found to make it easier for employees to perform high-quality work because doing high-quality work is more intrinsically reinforcing than performing low-quality work. However, people will also realize that intrinsic reinforcement by itself is not always sufficient (Bandura 1977). Work can become difficult, frustrating and tiring. Intrinsic reinforcement derived from one's performance cannot be counted on to maintain high motivation levels. Extrinsic reinforcement controlled and delivered from others enhances intrinsic reinforcement (Bandura 1977). For example, a person may take pride in the quality of work performed (intrinsic reinforcement), but a compliment from the boss (extrinsic reinforcement) may make this feeling even stronger. And the research of both Hull and Skinner shows that extrinsic reinforcement can make a task intrinsically reinforcing through association. As Miller (1984) noted, if meeting a deadline is repeatedly followed by extrinsic reinforcement, it may eventually feel good to meet a deadline, even in the absence of extrinsic reinforcement, because of the past association.

At the staffing level, employees will be taught the principles of goal setting and reinforcement so that self-management will become a well-developed skill. There is aleady abundant evidence of the success of this technique in the areas of alcoholism and drug abuse (Kanfer 1980); it has also been used effectively to increase employee attendance (Frayne and Latham 1987).

One of the most pervasive forces on the face of the earth in the last twenty years may be the diminished acceptance of authority as the basis for action. People don't do things anymore just because someone tells them to. Hence, as was mentioned earlier, there will be an emphasis on finding ways to get people to identify with the goals of the organization. In addition, there will be a reawakening among leaders of what Barnard (1938) called "the zone of indifference." Authority does not reside in the source of authority but in the acceptance of authority by the employees. Individuals have a "zone of indifference" within which orders will be accepted without question. This zone of indifference is affected primarily by the employees' perception that instruction is consistent with the organization's goals. Thus, employee-supervisor integrity will be defined in terms of observable behavior that leads to its measurement. There will be major consequences for engaging or failing to engage in these behaviors.

There will be an increase in reliance on technical specialists. Managers will thus of necessity share their power with these specialists. Managers will be trained in leadership behaviors that maintain cohesion in the work group. With an increase in technology and an increase in employee specialists, employees will be given the authority to do the job with little supervision. They will be encouraged to think about their work in terms of purpose (what), process (how), and product (outcome). This increase in time for and expectation of thinking about one's job will result in the generation of ideas on better ways to do (behavior) one's work.

Interest in compensation and incentive systems will be revived. This will be especially true in labor contracts. The underlying theme will be to give employees a sense of ownership in the company. The existence of two-income families make the likelihood of this occurring especially great. With two sources of incomes, the individual can afford to have an income fluctuate with company profits. Breakthroughs, however, will be needed in finding ways to ensure that employees see that what they do affects the financial rewards that they receive. Without a close relationship between performance and pay, employees may at best identify with the job rather than with the organization and become highly mobile.

In addition to money, the reinforcers of tomorrow are likely to include training and stability. Mergers, acquisitions, bankruptcies, and technological advance have already resulted in a high level of instability in employment. The delayering of management has meant that middle managers, in addition to hourly employees, are being laid off. *Motivation* in some organizations has become a code word for "fewer people doing more and doing it better" than has been the case in the past. Thus motivation means loss of work. An effective incentive for someone joining the organization tomorrow will be training. An effective reward for desired behavior will be training. Training will help ensure loyalty to the organization because it is a signal that the organization is investing in its human resources to keep them from becoming obsolete. Stability in employment will give the employee a reason to believe that newly acquired skills will be used effectively.

Finally, the issue of how to deal with people who want minimum involvement with their work will be dealt with through job design and assignment to those jobs. Do we truly want everyone to be motivated to work? Some people see work only as a paycheck. They want to devote their energy not to their work but to other interests such as child rearing. Do we want to channel the energy of such people into their work at the expense of such endeavors? Society might be the poorer for it if we do.

12

Compatibility between People Needs and Organization Needs: Projections and Cautions on Quality of Work Issues in the Future Organization

Joseph J. Lengermann

This chapter explores the probable impact of the new rules of competition, which are featured throughout this book, on prospects for quality of work in the future organization. More specifically, it explores the validity of a currently popular theme that the future organization will differ considerably from that of today in that it will be built more typically around "people needs" and will rely more directly on employees' "commitment" as motivation for achieving high quality and productivity. It emphasizes a number of cautions, drawn from a variety of literatures sympathetic to such an ideal, against any easy realization of this expectation. And it suggests several conclusions and strategies that emphasize the likelihood of a variety of future organizational models, the likelihood of continued conflicts surrounding selection among these models, and the need for good management in constructing the form most appropriate to the specifics of any particular organization.

The Articulation and Popularity of the Theme

The recent Naisbitt and Aburdene book *(Reinventing the Corporation,* 1985) represents perhaps the most explicit articulation of a theme that has become increasingly popular in both management and worker literature. This theme argues that there is now a "new compatibility between organization needs and people needs" and that "work organizations not only can but should be reorganized for mutual benefit to take advantage of this compatibility" (Naisbitt and Aburdene 1985). It is an optimistic theme of writers that feeds a comparable hunger among audiences. It generates a popular optimism precisely because it promises to resolve simultaneously the anxieties stemming from several conflicting concerns. It speaks, first of all, to a widespread concern over the need to improve organizational productivity, efficiency, and product quality in order to match the increasingly competitive levels of foreign groups, especially the

Japanese. Second, this theme speaks to widespread concern and frustration over the levels of worker effort, the levels of worker satisfaction, and the appropriateness of worker motivational schemes (the poor match between the values of new workers and traditional hierarchical forms of organizational control). Third, it speaks to the concern and frustration in academic and in popular literature over the American inability to manage effectively the innovation and high-tech change rates required in today's worldwide postindustrial economy. In so doing, this theme incorporates in one way or another the values and the ideas of a variety of different audiences.

No wonder then that there has been an enthusiastic response to Naisbitt and Aburdene's scenario for management to move away from traditional bureaucratic organization-worker relationships to one based on this new compatibility of people needs and organization needs. In one sweep this scenario is expected to relieve anxieties and fulfill values by its promises to increase productivity; improve quality; lower unit costs; encourage innovation; satisfy the workers' need for challenge, growth, variety, and involvement; prevent workers from being rewarded simply for showing up; help beat the Japanese and other foreign competition, and restore the United States to Number One. Readers can respond positively to a confidently stated message that the nation's various problems and anxieties stem from a unified undercurrent of change that can now be sufficiently recognized and understood, so as to allow American managers to respond with a fortuitous new synthesis that resolves numerous issues that appeared in the old synthesis to be separate, contradictory, and unresolvable. This is a more detailed specification at the organization level of the sweeping themes of Bell (1973), Toffler (1981), and Naisbitt (1982), who described the "megatrends" culminating in the "postindustrial society," the "Third Wave," and the "information society." Whereas those earlier books challenged us to understand their themes of change and suggested very general guidelines by which we might adjust to them, this newer book by Naisbitt and Aburdene offers an optimistic synthesis based on the new compatibility between people needs and organization needs, exhorts us to follow a series of prescriptions for worker-organization relationships, and reassures us with anecdotal success stories.

However, while the old synthesis clearly is giving way to the new, and while we can take hope and excitement from its vision, the vision may yet be flawed, and certainly the specifics of the new synthesis are still being shaped—and being shaped at an uneven pace in an atmosphere of uncertainty and conflict, with more than a single group to orchestrate its progress. To ignore the possibility and need for this new synthesis is shortsighted management. To ignore the unevenness, conflict, and contingencies involved in the shaping of this new synthesis is naive management.

Grounds for Taking This Optimistic Theme Seriously

Are there grounds for taking this theme seriously? For thinking of it as any different from the earlier unfulfilled premises and promises of the human relationists? Proponents would argue yes on both counts. As was indicated earlier, improvement in the organization-worker relationship is seen as the key to significant increases in worker motivation and subsequently to a number of important outcomes for the worker (quality of work, fulfillment), the organization (innovation, quality, productivity), and the country (dynamic national economy, stronger international standing). In turn, the optimism about this key, about being able to bring about this improvement in organization-worker relationships, is based on four interrelated factors:

1. Recognition that current organization-worker relationships are inappropriate and that worker motivation is very low
2. Perception that workers value fulfillment through work and want (need) to be motivated and to work harder than presently
3. Assessment that the kind of work organizations now need to have done is precisely the kind of work that allows and needs the worker values and motivations that current workers need to have actualized
4. Recognition that there is a new economic necessity and set of rules of competition that give "economic impetus for change"

The first factor, while widely described, can be seen most acutely in the findings reported by Yankelovitch and Immerwahr (1983) on worker attitudes and motivation. These findings include the following: (*a*) half of those interviewed said they worked just hard enough to avoid getting fired, (*b*) 75 percent said they could be significantly more effective on the job, but (*c*) don't work harder because they don't get paid any more for working harder and managers provide little incentive to work harder, despite the fact that (*d*) more than 50 percent said they have an inner need to do the very best job regardless of pay, and that (*e*) 88 percent want to work hard and do the best they can on the job. These points suggest that there is an unnecessarily poor fit between organizational motivational schemes and workers' readiness for hard work, and that, furthermore, there is here a potential source for great improvement in organizations' effectiveness and efficiency.

In reference to the second factor (workers' values), Yankelovitch (1979, 1981) has been making much of the "new breed" work values for some time, and Clark Kerr (1979) has referred to this transformation in attitudes about work as the fourth great revolution in the history of the American workplace. Rather than perceiving a loss of work ethic (as many managers have complained), these analysts perceive a "crisis of aesthetics"—people not only want jobs but they want good jobs. They look for self-fulfillment in their jobs. The 1983 Public Agenda Foundation report (Yankelovitch and Immerwahr 1983) lists the top ten qualities people want in a job today:

1. Work with people who treat me with respect
2. Interesting work
3. Recognition for good work
4. Chance to develop skills
5. Working for people who listen if you have ideas about how to do things
6. Chance to think for myself rather than just carry out instruction
7. Seeing the end results of my work
8. Working for efficient managers
9. A job that is not too easy
10. Feeling well informed about what is going on

These top ten items are all self-fulfillment items. Job security, high pay, and good benefits appear only within the next five choices. Workers are seen as wanting to make their company successful while also wanting greater psychic ownership in it. These values are linked to the increasingly higher proportions of workers who are college educated and to the "coming shortage" of young workers because of shrinking cohort sizes. Thus, two of Naisbitt and Aburdene's "ten considerations" are (1) the best people want ownership—psychic and literal—in a company, and the best companies are providing it; and (2) the best and brightest people will gravitate toward those corporations that foster personal growth.

The third factor seen as a basis for optimism about major improvements in the organization-worker relationship and worker motivation is the assessment of changes in the nature of today's work itself. More and more work involves considerable information exchange and processing. Increasingly, products and solutions are being customized. Naisbitt and Aburdene's most basic trend and principle behind "Reinventing the Corporation" is precisely "the shift in strategic resource from financial capital in the industrial society to human capital in the information society." And other of their ten considerations include as buzzwords quality, intuition, creativity, and entrepreneurship. In short, the type of work being required can best be done by motivated workers committed to the organization under conditions where supervision has given way to self-management and where independence, self-confidence, and competence are seen as critical assets.

The fourth factor, which stems from the third, is that of economic necessity. Tapping the internal motivaton of workers has become an economic necessity because it provides the competitive edge essential to producing today's products in today's competitive world. Naisbitt and Aburdene especially stress this point. The humanistic values of worker commitment and motivation have been around for some time, but today's "confluence of changing values and economic necessity" provides the real impetus for change.

What these four factors add up to is an optimism that relationships between management and workers should be and can be changed in a major way. Organizational structure and mangement style will be characterized by these changes:

- Authoritarian management yielding to a networking, people style of management
- The rigidity and regimentation of the industrial economy being replaced by the flexibility and fluidity of the information economy
- The workstyles of self-employed entrepreneurs being copied into large corporate contexts
- Self-management on a large scale

Such a prediction and prescription of how work and organizations will be organized in the future is clearly consistent with the themes of "autonomy/ entrepreneurship" and "productivity through people," which are described by Peters and Waterman (1982) as two of their eight attributes of "excellent" companies. And Naisbitt and Aburdene (1985) ask impatiently, "Why are we still running our offices in the old industrial mode (where people get paid for showing up) when we should be reinventing the work place to take advantage of the natural alignment that exists between the corporation's economic needs and the new worker's values? . . . And the new forces such as the coming seller's market, the whittling away of middle management, and the new definition of human resources as the company's competitive edge are reinforcing that economic imperative." These factors, therefore, add up to very powerful and very attractive reasons for taking the risks involved in reinventing the corporation and in reinventing work along lines sensitive to this new compatitibility between people needs and organization needs.

Cautions against Great Expectations

This compatibility and these changes are attractive to many of us. We see any number of "success stories" being written, at least of the public relations type, of changes in specific organizations along these lines. Almost always these changes are presented as models that enlightened managers of other organizations will inevitably follow. Managers do some soul-searching with regard to this popularly portrayed wave of change, set in motion in-house discussions of how to achieve comparably successful changes, or even "order" their organization to adopt decentralized decision making and other such new organizational virtues. But it remains very unlikely that organizations will bring these changes about on any wide scale, or even that some of the exemplary changes will become more permanent and pervasive than anecdotal experiments in the most innovative companies. Yankelovitch himself (1985) has on occasion made much of the fact that when major executives are presented with the findings about worker values and motivation mentioned earlier, they react with no surprise or disagreement with the workers' harshly negative assessment of the motivation/reward system, but also with no sense that such systems need be or will be changed. Both management and workers have a number of reasons for examining the prospects for such changes carefully before undertaking them and for avoiding expectations of quick and easy successes. In this section we explore some of the cautions that both management and workers need to keep in mind. These cautions stem from a variety of perspectives that share some interest in such change but also provide experiences and research that suggests the need either to modify the vision itself or to qualify the optimistic predictions about its realization. These perspectives include those of humanist organizational psychologists, contingency perspective organizational theorists, Theory Z and Japanese model proponents, reinforcement theorists, occupational sociologists, and researchers of work values.

Cautions from Humanist Organizational Psychologists

An important caution stems from a recognition that humanist social psychologists have for years been calling for job redesign and motivational schemes that are very similar to what is being prescribed as so appropriate today and so capable of fulfilling the needs of both organization and worker. This model—built on the assumption that motivated workers can be integrated with the goals of their organizations through their opportunity to exercise and fulfill their multilevel needs through work activity—was essentially what was being proposed by Maslow (1954), McGregor (1960), Argyris (1965), and Herzberg (1968), to mention a few of the most prominent theorists. Most of the "top ten" qualities people are reportedly looking for in their work today (Yankelovitch and Immerwahr 1983) were previously included, for instance, in the list of job characteristics featured in Hackman and Oldham's (1975) Job Diagnostic Survey (JCI), which has been widely used as a basis for job redesign approaches. How might this literature help us interpret the optimistic compatibility projections of today?

This social psychological literature on satisfaction, motivation, and organizational development through job redesign has built a solid, research-based, cumulative record of information and specification of how and when these ideals could be successfully implemented. The research maintained a commitment to the validity of these approaches but also came to document the difficulty of successful implementations—the need to do it carefully and thoroughly. Most of the points stressed in this literature are directly relevant to a judgment about the current theme of compatibility and about the projected changes in organizational design and quality of work, about which some have become so optimistic and enthusiastic. For example:

- A total system approach is important, so redesign decisions become very complex (managerial, situational, and environmental differences are combined with crucial individual differences such as experience, cognitive complexity, needs, values, valences, perceptions of equity)

- Positive benefits of these programs are often moderated by lack of challenge and by accomplishment needs among some employees, with reactions of stress, anxiety, and erratic performance, and of turnover, and difficulty in getting groups of workers to experience positive perceptions of core job characteristics

- Anticipation by managers of problems leads to many small compromises, so changes made are actually not very substantial (the "small change effect" discussed by Hackman and Oldham 1980)

- If substantial changes are begun, resultant stresses lead to chipping away, to the "vanishing effect phenomenon" (Hackman and Oldham 1980) or to "regression under pressure" (Lawler 1983)

- Managers too often attempt to make changes through prepackaged programs, which won't work in behavioral science areas; "redesign of work is much more a way of managing than it is a prepackaged fix for satisfaction and motivation problems" (Hackman and Oldham 1980)

In view of this sensitivity to complexity and interdependence, it is not surprising to find someone like Lawler (1983) cautious about the prospects for "high-involvement" organizations and Hackman and Oldham (1980) leaning toward the more pessimistic, mechanistic "Route Two" in their projections of two possible future scenarios for work redesign in the 1980s. Route Two (fitting people to jobs) contrasts sharply with the vision of compatibility discussed earlier. It would maximize first for technological and economic efficiency and then help people adapt. It would be characterized by (1) dominance of technical and engineering considerations (more productivity and pay, less discretion and challenge); (2) close monitoring and control by managers, with the help of sophisticated information systems (a bigger gap between those who control and others, between managers/professionals and others); (3) desired on-job behavior elicited by sophisticated use of extrinsic rewards (for example, behavior modification); and (4) organizationally sponsored programs to help people adapt and cope (for instance, employee assistance programs—note that much of this is often questionably assessed as being "people oriented"). Hackman and Oldham believe the U.S. managers are likely to keep moving down this Route Two with some vigor because (1) they are more familiar with Route Two; (2) they cannot yet measure all the costs and benefits relevant to Route One; (3) behavioral science always has lost out to hard engineering and traditional economic beliefs about organizational efficiency; and (4) Route Two is more consistent with the styles and values of both managers and employees. As Hackman and Oldham (1980) put it, "Learning how to function within a Route One organization could be a long and not terribly pleasant process and it is unclear how many would be willing to tolerate the upset and anxiety of the change process long enough to get a sense of what work in a Route One organization might have to offer."

Clearly, therefore, the humanistic social psychologists, who would in principle be more supportive than any group of the compatibility between people needs and organization needs, provide a lot of reasons to be cautious about Naisbitt's and others' projections for rapid significant change or realization of their vision.

Cautions from Contingency Perspective Organizational Theorists

A more critical assessment of the compatibility projections might come from the "contingency" approach to organizational theory. It has to be skeptical of claims that effectively deny contingencies and stress almost total homogeneity of work process needs, people needs, and appropriate organizational structure. The two basic contingencies stressed in this approach are technology and environment. Despite a general agreement that these two factors are increasingly being characterized by "Information Society" or "Third Wave" developments that make organic organizational structure ever more appropriate, this approach also stresses that the technology and environment characteristics are sometimes such that mechanistic rather than organic organizational models are called for in such organizations or in some sections of organizations. Moreover, mechanistic models in such circumstances are expected to lead to higher levels of productivity, efficiency, and even satisfaction. This approach stresses that the nature of the basic contingencies in specific organizations and organizational units needs to be examined *empirically,* that these are likely to vary considerably, and that organic organizational models "work" only where the appropriate contingencies actually exist (Hage 1980, Shortell and Kaluzny 1983).

Cautions from Proponents of Theory Z and the Japanese Model

Optimistic compatibility models such as that of Naisbitt and Aburdene frequently suggest borrowing aspects of Japanese organization and work motivational schemes. But Theory Z proponents, such as Ouchi (1981), who propose a model of organization that borrows from Japanese as well as from American experience, are likely to find fault with the willingness of "compatibility enthusiasts" to bypass some of their critical assumptions. Ouchi, for instance, would want to pay more atteniton to the extent and characteristics of the new organizational culture, and stress that unless essential control properties of hierarchy are replaced by appropriate "clan" mechanisms, new organizational forms are not likely to be successful. He emphasizes that appropriate organizational philosophies and cultures that are "socially responsive" and capable of integrating a basic commitment to individual values with a highly collective nonindividual pattern of interaction are quite hard to develop in the United States. Studies of workplace democracy and worker ownership have found that these conditions are very difficult to maintain in the United States because American workers are rather weak on cooperative ideology and political consciousness, which are important in making such projects successful. Moreover, even where such programs are established, American workers still tend to see their cooperation more as a way of accumulating capital rather than of assuring stable employment, good working conditions, decent wages, and control over the workplace (Sirianni 1984).

Another indication that control through the corporate culture does away neither with control nor with conflict can be seen in Kantor's (1982) description of the role of modern middle managers in more entrepreneurial rather than bureacuratic firms. She emphasizes the greater opportunity and need for skills of persuasion, creativity, and initiative in building influence for both oneself and one's unit; she also points out that power issues become more important and apparent and that the very looseness of the authority structure serves as a control on individual action. People constantly need to seek legitimation, to form coalitions, to generate persuasive information, and to count on others for support, so that "in an ironic sense, freedom and control in organizations are roughly equilateral."

Also, it is important to note that the recent American characterization of Japanese management models, which used to be so positive in its emphasis on mutual organizational commitment and loyalty, has taken on a decidedly negative tone. From worker and management perspectives alike we see more and more criticism of that system's emphasis on conformity, pressure, excessive work priority, and fear. Kotkin and Kishimoto (1986) have dubbed this aspect of the Japanese motivational scheme "Theory F." In Kotkin and Kishimoto (1986), but also in studies by Cole (1971) and Sengoku (1985), we see quotations from Japanese workers who are questioning the benefits of their hard work and commitment once expected extrinsic rewards like pay and promotion are no longer as rapidly forthcoming as they were under conditions of a more favorable age cohort structure. And we see increased interest in the existence of an extensive "other" Japan of small, competitive companies where work conditions, wages, routine, security, and authority are almost on sweat-shop levels, but workers continue to work hard because their work ethic is based not on commitment-type management approaches but on the special Japanese cultural traditions of a harsh feudal past. What is at issue here is not simply whether or not authors like Naisbitt and Aburdene (1985) are accurately describing the Japanese system; more important is the possibility that their emphasis on an American version of an integrative "organizational culture" and "core values," for which they turn to Japanese practice for examples, might contain a comparable unacceptable dose of paternalism or authoritarianism that would be antithetical to the individualistic self-actualization values featured in their appeal.

Cautions from Reinforcement Theories

Although the emphasis in the vision of compatibility between people needs and organization needs seems to be on motivation through the fulfillment of self-actualization, there are sporadic references to the linking of desirable behavior to more external rewards, and even to the harsh treatment of participants who do not produce or believe in the organizational core values. Because these references appear sporadically, one is not sure whether to view them as reassuringly realistic or sinisterly elitist. Process theories of motivation, whether psychological or sociological in nature, would in any case find the Naisbitt and Aburdene type of optimistic vision unrealistic (*a*) because of its need theory based "self-actualizing model" of people, and (*b*) because of its insufficient attention to the importance of perception and expectation.

Reinforcement theorists would question whether those top-ten self-actualizing quality of work items desired by workers (Yankelovitch and Immerwahr 1983) are in fact the goals that determine their work behavior. As argued by Tausky and Parke (1976), demonstrating the need for self-actualization is not sufficient; it is also necessary to demonstrate the consequences for on-the-job effort. As argued by Fein (1976), money, benefits, and job security are in fact among the most important rewards that affect work effort—provided they are connected as sufficiently immediate and substantial reinforcers. Thus Tausky and Parke's (1976) review of job enrichment programs concludes that, although they are usually grounded in need theory assumptions, in practice the ones that work best are the ones that have used reinforcement principles and increased accountability, thus linking an individual's performance more directly to reinforcement contingencies such as job security and pay. And Fein (1976), who argues that the normal incentive scheme actually operates to give workers an incentive *not* to seek self-fulfillment in work and *not* to see their self-interests served by helping to increase productivity, also argues that where workers' income can be significantly affected by productivity, they become very outspokenly involved in work process suggestions and improvement. He argues further that a major reason why significant income incentives are not usually tied to productivity is precisely that managers find it more convenient for workers to be mute.

Other reinforcement theorists, particularly those emphasizing expectancy theory (Lawler 1973) and equity theory (Adams 1965) approaches to motivation and rewards, have stressed how hard it is to satisfy employee group fairness concerns and to change old patterns of expectations. At lower, middle, and upper levels, organizational participants are likely to show a great deal more reluctance and unpreparedness for extensive changes in organizational motivational schemes than anticipated in the optimistic projection of compatibility. At lower levels there is the danger of raising expectation levels unrealistically and dangerously beyond what organizations are prepared to deliver; employees are likely to remain skeptical and think it too risky to give up their previous expectations and limited commitments. At middle levels, managers may feel extremely threatened by new styles because their status and roles are seemingly undercut. At higher levels all-out change along the lines projected by Naisbitt and company, particularly *if* the changes should lead to significant increases in worker psychic and material "ownership," could be the most threatening of all, because such changes could ultimately question and lessen the size of the gaps in status, power, and economic rewards that the system of organization-employee relationships currently allow. Organizational elites may well feel more comfortable continuing to deal with a more contentious, less committed work force that fights for hourly wages instead of for proportional shares of profit, and that can be treated as expendable when market conditions suggest a contracted work force. And they may well consider the attractiveness of resorting to other options for increasing their productivity and profits, including the passage of more favorable restriction on trade policies and the sophisticated technical control mechanisms mentioned earlier for Hackman and Oldham's Route 2 (Piori and Sabel 1984).

Cautions from Occupational Sociology

Sociologists of occupations will protest that optimistic projections for a people-oriented design of work and organization based on a new "compatibility" are based on erroneously extending certain favorable developments in some sectors of the labor force to all workers, and that this kind of interpretation serves to mask trends that in reality are often negative for most workers. They will point to evidence of a long history of countertrends in deprofessionalization and deskilling of work, and they expect those trends to continue because they are rooted in the basic dynamics of the American economic system. Instead of seeing everywhere in the information society the creation of good jobs that provide fulfillment as well as livelihood, these analysts see the widespread proliferation of "McJobs" that provide very little of either (Bluestone and Harrison

(1982). Zimbalist (1979) and Shaiken (1985) have documented how the usual story is for computers, which have the capacity to create more participation by workers, to be used instead to restructure work (in the office, in the super-market, in the warehouse, and on the shop floor) in order to establish tighter control by management. Shaiken's vision also seeks to increase efficiency by tapping rather than destroying human creativity. But to illustrate how different his vision is in substance and in perceived difficulty of realization compared with that of Naisbitt and Aburdene, Shaiken believes this vision to be realizable only if (*a*) return on investment would be subordinate to human concerns in those cases where a conflict is perceived between productivity and more satis-fying work; and (*b*) unions become enlightened and actively involved in in-fluencing technological and organizational development along, with their tradi-tional concerns. Other sociologists of work, particularly Edwards (1984), would parallel Naisbitt and Aburdene's emphasis on the new "economic impetus" to the realization of people needs in the workplace by acknowledging that the "logic of accumulation" with its emphasis on reducing unit costs and increas-ing profits will cause some organizations to be tempted by the potential benefits of more committed, higher-producing workers and to experiment with self-management models of organization. But they would also predict that the risks of giving up more traditional control (direct, technical, or bureaucratic) would be undertaken only where absolutely necessary and even here with every effort to "get by" with minimums and gestures rather than changes of real substance. Most "work humanization movement" efforts are interpreted in this light. For instance, as Shaiken (1985) and others have pointed out, increased managerial control and productivity are more likely to result from establishing flexible job roles with a variety of tasks than are increases in worker satisfaction and pay.

So far, more substantial, permanent, and vertically extensive democratiza-tion experiments are found only in atypical situations of worker ownership (Plywood Cooperatives in the United States, Mondragon Cooperative in Spain) or idiosyncratic owner value commitment (IGP) (Whyte and Blasi 1982). And when self-management, commitment-based, motivational schemes are used for "appropriate" groups within an organization, there is a concern that stratifica-tion gaps between groups of workers might be increased. Thus a recent study that integrated theoretical approaches from organizational, occupational, and stratification sociology found some empirical support for the idea that organic models of organization disproportionately benefit managerial/professional levels and in some instances adversely affect lower-level participants (Rudzinski 1985).

Cautions from Research about Workers' New Values

A final important criticism of the projection for extensive change based on the new compatibility between people needs and organization needs is that it in-cludes a selective misreading of Yankelovitch's findings about workers' "new" attitudes. Despite the fact that these attitudes now show greater readiness for commitments beyond the more individualistic, narcissistic self-indulgence of ten years ago, despite the fact that Yankelovitch interprets the ideas of "new breed" young workers as reasonably realistic and not purist in what they are willing to accept as supportive of their self-fulfillment needs, despite the fact that the young workers do want to be self-fulfilled in work, there remains a great deal of vagueness and all-inclusiveness in what they want. There is ambivalence about priorities in their "wanting it all." Projections like those of Naisbitt and Aburdene seem to ignore that most "new breed" people want self-fulfillment in *many* areas, want a lot of experiences other than that of work, and juggle a lot of priorities at once. In the multiple-option society, part of their sense of self-fulfillment lies precisely in their putting together their personalized package of priorities. Again, the Naisbitt and Aburdene book shows an awareness of these issues, but these are not integrated into the main point of their view, which clearly is based on a model of fulfillment through motivated work. In fact, the personalized package of priorities being put together by many of today's workers, while including work as important, simply does not support the kind of entrepreneurial dedication or quest for excellence that Naisbitt and Aburdene seem to assume, and that would be necessary to push American companies suddenly to new levels of success through new levels of worker motivation and commitment. Yankelovitch is right in saying that the new values are incompatible with traditional hierarchic forms of organization. But these values are multiple, and there may not be any one alternative form of organization that will be compatible with more than a small portion of these new breed workers. And there remains for most an ambivalence about competition and economic productivity. Note that a recent preliminary Carnegie Foundation report was critical of the American university education system precisely because students come out of it with very low levels of initiative, challenge, and independence—levels that are considered insufficient for today's economic and organizational activity.

A recent review of organizational models, particularly models that emphasize participation, opportunity, and equality, concluded that there is a growing appreciation for a more pluralistic conception of the forms of freedom and the principles of justice. "A pluralistic approach, which seeks to articulate systematic interrelationships among a variety of alternative organizational forms and which is not premised on a principled hostility to all aspects of bureaucracy and market exchange, can perhaps provide the basis for a quite far-reaching realization of democratic and equalitarian ideals" (Sirianni 1984). While also criticizing the model of "holistic productive integrity" for having inadequate notions of equality and democracy, this review is most critical of the model's tendency to have an inadequate notion of individuality and an overly restrictive conception of the variety and flexiblity of mechanisms through which people might arrange their "fluid and flexible life course" and work commitments, including partial and unequal organizational commitments, whether in terms of dedication, time, or learning of skills. One is left then with a need to be cautious about the potential for the new emphasis on flexibility and self-management under the aura of a strong organizational culture to serve as a new form of control—one that may soon be added as an important "fourth" to Edwards's (1984) threefold typology. In Anthony's terms (1977) the values of fulfillment through work or even management's efforts to use them as a way of increasing its area of influence are not necessarily bad in themselves; but such an ideology can become dangerous when it is fostered and applied in such a way that it is *always* subordinated to managerial purposes.

Conclusions and Strategies

In this chapter's discussion of the supposed new compatibility between people needs and organization needs and its implications for bringing about a new form of organization, I presented a number of cautions critical of such optimistic projections. These cautions were drawn intentionally from perspectives that themselves share a positive bias toward such outcomes on the ideal level. Given such cautions, I suggest four conclusions that can be drawn about this compatibility and projected organizational change:

1. Considerable changes in the design of work and organizations will in fact occur along the lines of such compatibility, and the possibility for this adds enthusiasm, challenge, and hopeful optimism to the work experience and aspirations of workers at all levels

2. Conditions for this new compatibility and related organizational change will not be found in all work settings, probably not in more than one-third

3. Where such conditions do exist and where such changes are attempted, they must be carried out carefully and thoroughly with a sense of the systemic linkages among the various initiatives

4. Such changes will be accompanied by a great deal of uncertainty, anxiety, and conflict among organizational units, occupational groups, and competing individuals, all with heightened sensitivity to relative advantage and disadvantage during transition periods

The first conclusion is that, despite the cautions expressed, there will be considerable change along the lines of such compatibility and such redesigned organization. Despite Hackman and Oldham's conclusion in 1980 that we were not about to adopt "Route One" priorities in our organizations, they do mention six conditions that might get us to change direction. We might become more receptive to what they referred to as Route One priorities if (1) organized labor gets behind Route One priorities; (2) enough managers in major corporations decide that work redesign pays off in coin they value; (3) government decides to require or encourage organizations to improve quality of work life; (4) the cultural climate changes to support the idea that work experiences should be more fulfilling and growth enhancing; (5) the national economy collapses or enters a period of significant crisis; or (6) in the event of economic crisis, Route One sympathizers are ready with an attractive vision and road map. Conditions two, four, five (at least in terms of a heightened sense of foreign and internal competition), and six are all more in evidence now than in 1980. There certainly is something of substance behind the changes being described and advocated in the optimistic recent best-sellers, and there is something of a groundswell indicated by the audience hunger (much of which is within management itself). There are stronger forces (both economic and value) at work now than ever before to allow and pressure for new opportunities for change and greater diversity than exist at present in organizational design, work processes, and motivational schemes. Even if all the desired changes do not occur, commitment can occur more easily when there is some hope and optimism rather than just cynicism. Even if the optimism is excessive, there may be enough basis to hope for progressive improvements to sustain a sense of meaningfulness and to justify workers' efforts and cooperation. This process will definitely increase some people's fulfillment of those top-ten needs of variety, challenge, interest, and choice, which many workers want. And in these settings there will be a resulting gain in productivity because of the infusion of higher levels of entrepreneurial initiative and commitment.

The second conclusion is that the conditions for this new compatibility and related organizational change will not be found in all work settings, probably not in more than one-third. Most organizations will continue to organize and motivate their workers primarily in bureaucratic or Route Two fashion. However, many of these organizations may make selective use of certain "people-oriented" techniques (including flextime, quality circles, and maybe even some forms of job security and employee stock ownership). But these would be meant not so much to create the full personal growth, commitment, and self-management heralded by the new compatibility enthusiasts, but rather to overcome the negatives of costly turnover and hostile resistance and to create an atmosphere of cooperation and fairness. It is important to have more discussion of the potential gains (to organizations and workers alike) from such less extreme but more realistic (and for some more desirable) motivational levels and worker-organization relationships.

As to the third conclusion, even where the conditions for this new compatibility and related organizational change are in fact realized and acknowledged, to the point of top mangement's supporting policy directives to establish the appropriate organizational structure and culture, the actual redesign of the organization will not be easy. It must be carried out very carefully and thoroughly, with sensitivity to the systemic interrelationships between the various change initiatives, and with vigilance against numerous tendencies to backslide toward compromises that might very well undercut the essence of the projected changes. One of the biggest drawbacks to optimistic exhortative books such as Naisbitt and Aburdene's is that they present multiple individual initiatives for change without paying much attention to the priorities among such initiatives or how they might link together. This allows very diverse audiences to respond positively when reading the book to selected initiatives while ignoring others. Implementing the ideas of the book, however, requires each audience not only to integrate those initiatives that it found promising, but also to decide if and to what extent its own preferred initiatives can be integrated with different initiatives that other audiences find favorable.

As for the fourth conclusion, the considerable uncertainty as to where and how such changes can or should be instituted (conclusions two and three) means that they will be accompanied by anxiety and conflict among organizational units, occupational groups, and competing individuals. Although the hoped-for goal is harmonious enthusiasm where everyone gains (or at least where most people win most of the time), basic changes in organization-employee relationships will make everyone very sensitive to relative advantages and disadvantages, particularly during transition periods. Win/lose expectations built up under the old order will not be readily surrendered. When change occurs, it is time for each group to advance its agenda and to be suspicious of advances by other agendas.

What these conclusions emphasize are mixed conditions that managers have long lived with, even as they have searched for quick and easy solutions: risk, conflict, opportunity, challenge. The future of organizations will not make standard a model based on a 180-degree flip-flop of current organization-employee relationships. That would be too easy and too simplistic. The multiple-option society is arriving for organizations just as it is for individuals. Each organization will have to carve out its own best model, based on its own values and contingencies. With sensitivity, knowledge, and skill, its management will have to convince its employees, as groups and as individuals, that this model makes sense for them in terms of their own values and contingencies. And different groups of employees will have to decide how best to respond. In many cases compatibility of values and contingencies will be the basis for commitment, which can then be the basis for productivity and quality and satisfaction. In many cases productivity, quality, and even satisfaction (one hopes) will be based on something else, because the compatibility between people needs and organization needs simply isn't sufficient or isn't of the type to generate enough commitment to serve as the new primary basis for motivation and control.

Given these cautions and conclusions, what *strategies* are available to organizations for shaping their future? Some (very few) organizations will choose a strategy of attempting to implement an organic form throughout all units for all levels and members. A second strategy (to be chosen by a more significant but still minority group of organizations) will be to implement the organic form for those units, levels, and individuals for whom it is most necessary and appropriate, while preserving traditional mechanistic forms of control and motivation (possibly with some superficial "humanistic" modifications for all others). A third strategy (probably the most common) will be to maintain a basically mechanistic form throughout the entire organization, but with humanistic modifications added with decreasing emphasis as one moves from upper to lower levels. A fourth strategy (one that would have a quite serious and possibly disruptive effect on organizations, workers, and society) might be to implement the organic form for the entire organization, *but* to define the organization in much narrower terms and to externalize all units that do not "need" to have their motivation and productivity based on commitment and organic model work processes. Such externalization has begun to occur in a variety of ways: hiring ever larger proportions of part-time workers with minimal employee security, rights, and benefits; leasing workers "as needed" from agencies instead of hiring them as employees; subcontracting certain production or maintenance activities to small, competitive, low-profile organizations instead of synthesizing them within the organization; and shifting routine production activities to a unit or subsidiary located in a foreign country where contingencies more readily support traditional mechanistic forms of control at wage-rate savings that more than compensate for the transportation costs.

This chapter and the above strategies are based on the importance of managerial reform as the key ingredient to improving productivity, quality, and economic health. It is important at least to acknowledge in closing that other strategies that attempt to strengthen advantage through technological advance, restrictive trade practices, political influence, and other methods of influencing the external environment are also being practiced (Adams 1986). To the extent that they are successful they probably undercut the economic necessity support for compatibility between people needs and organization needs and so make even less likely the widespread adoption of organic forms of organization based on mutual commitment. Such a type of organization will certainly be present and will provide excitement and hope beyond its numerical extensiveness. However, it will be only one option in a multiple-option environment.

13

Human Resource Planning for the Future

Denise M. Rousseau

> We defy augury . . . If it be now, 'tis not to come; if it be not to come,
> it will be now; if it be not now, yet it will come: the readiness is all.
> —Shakespeare, *Hamlet* V, ii, 232

This chapter is about generating choices or options for managing human resource–related problems in organizations of the future. Options derive from linking human resource planning with strategic planning. Human resource management (HRM) encompasses a variety of techniques, programs, and information sources used to attract, maintain, develop, and allocate people to organizational roles. Formerly referred to as personnel management, HRM has been so designated to convey the increasing emphasis on people and their skills as resources critical to the effectiveness of the organization. Strategic human resource management links the functions of HRM to strategic planning and by doing so shapes the organizations of the future.

Consider a firm faced with strategic human resource problems. Its product engineers have developed an innovative calibration device built using microscopic components. As providers of innovative ideas, these engineers are recognized as vital to the success of the firm and are developed and paid accordingly. By contrast, the firm's production employees have been viewed as relatively expendable, and they face a greater risk of layoff in slow periods and receive little training or incentive pay. Turnover among production employees has been high. Especially likely to leave are highly skilled machinists who find better opportunities in other companies. The firm makes little attempt to retain skilled machinists or to develop new ones. Once the calibration device has been designed, the firm finds it has few machinists with sufficient skill in the production department who can produce the parts to the firm's strict specifications. Under competitive pressure to produce the new product, the firm tries to contract out the machining of parts, only to find that no potential subcontractor

I wish to thank Larry Cummings for his helpful comments.

has the necessary skills. The result is many months of delay while the current group of machinists is trained. A competitive advantage is lost.

The opposite approach characterizes successful firms such as Hewlett Packard, where skill development is emphasized across all functional areas. Slow economic periods are likely to be handled by temporary, across-the-board cutbacks in hours (for example, shortening the workweek to four days rather than five). Such cutbacks maintain the work force's skill level. A firm emphasizing innovation as a competitive edge must be prepared to move on new ideas, which requires a state of *readiness* among all areas interdependent in the process of implementing the innovation. Readiness is the traditional criterion used to evaluate military units during peacetime. Strategic HRM seeks to create a constant state of readiness to implement the organization's strategic plan. It also can provide the necessary infrastructure (talent, interpersonal skills, and organizational norms) for generating and implementing innovations.

Readiness is achieved when the HRM functions are aligned or developed along with the strategic plan. Such a state is most likely when human resource planning has occurred in the process of strategy formulation (see table 13–1). Strategic planning involves specifying what the organization is about (its philosophy), environmental scanning (for changes, opportunities, and threats), assessment of strengths and weaknesses of both the firm and its competitors, future analysis and forecasting, and a statement of goals and objectives (usually to be achieved in a five- or ten-year period). The product of this process is the formulation of a strategy, the identification of a position in the environment advantageous to the firm (for instance, increased service orientation in the case of ROLM, a telecommunications firm now an IBM subsidiary, or specialty steel manufacturing in the case of Worthington Industries).

HRM strategy formulating can involve specification of desired changes in structure, cultural norms, and member values if relevant to the success of the overall organization strategy. An illustration of the connection between strategy and HRM can be seen in the ROLM Corporation, a telecommunications firm acquired by IBM in 1984. Even before its acquisition by a strong, service-oriented firm, ROLM executives had recognized a need for a change from an equipment sales focus to a customer service orientation. To make this change, assessments of corporate culture were conducted during executive development programs at Northwestern University's Kellogg Graduate School of Management (several programs each year for a rotating group of ROLM managers), coupled with training in problem-solving skills to generate more innovative approaches to marketing services. One approach to change has been to incorporate service-oriented IBM employees into the firm. But innovation is difficult to acquire through new members alone. Fundamental and lasting organizational change often requires development of new skills and motives among current employees.

The strategic role of HRM derives from its impact on three basic problems faced by all organizations to some degree: efficiency (input/output ratios),

Table 13–1
Steps in Strategic Human Resource Planning

1. *Statement of philosophy:* What is the characteristic relationship of the firm to its employees (policy, culture, history)? Identifying the philosophy can involve a review of company history, organizational surveys, and change efforts.

2. *Current staffing status:* What are the present skills available, performance adequacies and deficiencies, selection needs, and retention problems? This description should include general problem-solving and interpersonal competencies in addition to specific technical needs.

3. *Identification of (present) business needs:* What are the current human resource demands? Using as a starting point the lowest level at which the business plan has been or can be segmented (for example, the division), consider the mission, strategy, and human resource needs of each unit. What skills are currently in demand? What are the usual sources of supply for required skills (internal/external)? Are they adequate? Can skills be developed in current employees? Can skill use be improved?

4. *Forecasting future needs:* What skills will be needed in the future? (Refer to organization's strategic plan for business projections.) Combine information from step 3 (present business needs) and the strategic plan to create inventory human resource needs. Translate needs into skill statement. Do a futures analysis on these skills? Will the traditional sources be adequate for future needs? Should basic source be changed? Can the organization develop what it now buys? Can it buy what it now develops?

5. *External constraints:* What environmental changes might affect our implementation of a strategic human resource plan? Consider present and anticipated government regulations as well as changing work force values and demographic trends.

6. *Goals:* What goals must be achieved to meet future staffing needs. Specify development and acquisition/recruitment targets.

7. *Strategy formulation:* How can human resource goals be met? Consider alternative scenarios, costs/benefits, and suitability to anticipated future environment(s).

Note: This planning program assumes that the organization has a strategic (business) plan.

maintenance of stable operations and work flows, and adaptation (to changing environments and in response to opportunities). Future changes will affect all three problem areas. In all problem areas there exist some traditional issues as well as new, emergent ones: the traditional personnel focus on staff selection, training, and staff development, and emerging demands for a restructuring of employer/employee relations, and enhancement of innovative activities in organizations.

Traditional Problems

The traditional HRM areas of selection, training, and development will encounter new challenges, specifically,

1. Acquisition and effective use of employees given changing occupational structures

2. Training and development of employees in skill areas made scarce by competition or organization-specific needs, coupled with ongoing education of employees to facilitate organization adaptability

3. Implementation of new technology

Acquisition and Use: The Challenge of Changing Occupational Structures

Recent labor force projections vary in the assumptions they make about the rate of future technological innovation and its impact on the demand for and availability of skilled workers in various occupational categories. Managers might profitably consider two forecasts used by the Office of Technology Assessment (1985). Postulating a very conservative rate of technological change, especially of capital-intensive innovations, the Bureau of Labor Statistics (Silvestri, Lukasiewicz, and Einstein 1984) expects employment in managerial, technical and professional, and clerical occupations to increase by about 28 percent in 1995, with 75 percent of the growth in new jobs concentrated in service-producing industries. In contrast, a study prepared for the National Science Foundation by Leontief and Duchin (1984) forecasts a very different situation, depending upon the set of assumptions employed. Assuming a faster rate of technological progress than the BLS study and more rapid adoption of new technologies, including more powerful software, Leontief and Duchin predict that intensive use of automation will make possible significant economies in labor over the next twenty years—and fewer jobs in many occupational categories. Categories affected under their scenario include *increases* in professionals, *decreases* in managers, and *decreases* in clericals. These trends are predicted to grow even stronger as the years go by. Increases in professional jobs are postulated mainly because of the demand for computer specialists and engineers. In the future, according to both forecasts, recruitment will focus increasingly on professionals, a group of people traditionally mobile. One implication is that compensation packages will increasingly reflect external market factors. Another is that employment negotiations will increasingly address work conditions, responsibilities, and development of opportunities for highly educated and intrinsically motivated professionals. Yet another concern is the changing employment relations between firms and professionals such as an ever increasing number of freelancers, as will be discussed later.

Training and Development

How will the work force accommodate to changing technology and demands for new skills? The answer depends largely on the adequacy of training programs. New technologies and resultant training needs seem to operate in cycles

(Flynn 1985). When new technology is introduced, extensive training is provided; current employees are upgraded because neither the internal nor the external labor market has the necessary expertise. Once the technology is widely adopted, to the point that equipment is standardized, employers lose employees to other firms. Company-specific skills become general ones. Training shifts out of the workplace and into the schools. Employers cease to provide general training. Increased demand makes it feasible for public and private schools to standardize and formalize training. Finally, when the industry, and perhaps the technology itself, declines, demand for skills contracts and training focuses on replacement needs for the organization and on the retraining of displaced workers. Currently, computer technology is in many cases in the penultimate phase of this cycle, with formalized training available in schools. Office automation and word-processing technologies are in the early phases. Training budgets need to reflect this technology phasing.

How much can an organization afford to invest in firm-specific training? If the budget is limited, can work be so specialized as to reduce training needs? What can be done to retain the employees whose market value has been increased by training? Firms are especially vulnerable to the loss of qualified people as the technology they are newly trained in moves from being the domain of only a few innovators into the industry's mainstream. Firms that innovate early (the "innovators" and "early adopters" of Rogers and Shoemaker 1971) must train and pay substantial salaries to the few people available externally with the right skills. The cost of a competitive technological edge is often investment in training that enhances employee value externally. Technologically innovative firms must manage turnover carefully, offering incentives (pay, status, discretionary funds) to more competent employees to encourage and retain them.

At the heart of the training issue is the choice among various HRM strategies. Miles and Snow (1980) distinguish two alternative models for acquiring skilled employees. "Make"-oriented organizations have the greatest influx of people to the organization in entry-level positions. Heavy investments are made in developing employee skills, many of which are specific to the organization's way of doing business (as in the case of EDS, IBM, Hewlett Packard). People in make-oriented organizations often earn below market wage early in their careers but expect stable, continued employment. The organization gets firm-specific skills, assimilation to its culture, and long-term loyalty. In contrast, a "buy"-oriented firm pays competitive wages to acquire people with specific technical skills (as in the case of many high-tech firms). These skills are expected to translate quickly into results that meet specific goals and targets. Buy-oriented firms have higher turnover, and spend little on development and relatively more in wages.

The readiness of the firm's skill base to meet with demand is a function of how suited its HRM strategies are to its strategic plan. This readiness can take the form of accurately forecasted skill requirements that are met through selection or by development. Firms can choose to make, to buy, or to do both. Many essentially make-oriented firms have subunits with "buy" strategies. Hybrids are possible and necessary in a highly diversified segment marketplace (for example, consumer goods).

Regardless of the strategy used to acquire needed skills, firms will continue to face problems in using available skills. In a recent critique of North American management practices, O'Brien (1986) argued that efforts at improving the quality of work and work life overlook a major determinant of employee motivation, performance, and turnover: skill use. Skill use, the extent to which the job demands exceed, match, or fail to tap an employee's current capabilities, is a major determinant of an employee's motivation and williness to stay with an organization. Employees whose jobs demand *at least* as much skill as they possess tend to be more effective than people whose jobs underuse their skills. They are also less subject to performance decrements plaguing industries where jobs are designed to demand little of the people who do them. A sizable literature on vocation of choice seeks to help match people to jobs so that skills *equal or exceed* job requirements. This is consistent with a point Jerry Hage makes in the opening chapter: American workers are often asked to do less than are those of other countries, and far less than these (often highly educated) people are capable of.

Increased technological complexity, coupled with labor-saving technologies, suggests that future employees will do work that is broader in scope than that at present. Computer-aided design specialists can work on many more projects than did their precomputerization counterparts. Greater training and expertise mean that a person can work on numerous and more complex problems. Specific technical advances will mean that skilled employees will be called upon to use more discretion, judgment, and problem solving—especially in firms whose innovativeness is their market advantage. The increased demand for use of general skills (management, conceptualization, problem solving) is evident in the decline of the first-line supervisor function, the position devoted to directing hands-on work (Kerr, Hill, and Broedling 1986). Highly skilled employees contribute more to their *own* management and thus need general skills as well as technical skills. The implications for training are clear: technical training needs to be accompanied by development of self-management capabilities, including planning and problem solving. But following training, attention must be paid to full use of acquired skills.

Implementation of New Technology

In the future we anticipate rapid introduction of new technologies. When new work systems are introduced, how should we go about institutionalizing the new technology? One important issue is investments in training and formalization of procedures (for example, manuals). Full implementation of a new technology involves the introduction of technologies in three forms: (1) the skills and knowledge possessed by people or embedded in the equipment they use, (2) the actions people employ in doing work and the cycles of activities that get the job done, and (3) the performance programs and procedures that are developed to standardize and make routine the way the work gets done (Rousseau and Cooke 1984). Adoption of a new technology or way of doing work typically begins with the introduction of new equipment or people with skills different from those currently in use. But there is no implementation until activities occur. Stumbling blocks to making use of the new equipment or skills come from incompatibility with other work systems and from resistance to change out of fear and anxiety over its implications. Problems with implementing personal computer–based systems (involving keyboards) are often linked to culture and past practices, and might be expressed in the axiom "Real men don't type" (Rousseau 1987a).

Once the skills are put to use, the equipment is operating, and processing has begun, the question is, can we establish procedures to facilitate predictable and consistent work flows? The purpose of establishing work procedures and performance programs (from menus to canned computer programs) is to ensure steady and predictable operation of the technology and its transferability from one user to another, increasing the flexibility with which people and their skills can be used. However, with the establishment of routines or performance programs, especially written ones, can come limitations on what people are able and are perhaps willing to do on the job. Organizations in which technology or market demands change rapidly find more costs than benefits in formalization. Because of this, firms such Worthington Industries have avoided written performance programs to encourage innovation in the customization of their products. Retention of skilled employees, thus, becomes important when formalization is low since they are less easily replaced. A critical issue for the HRM system is whether lack of formalization leads to flexibility or ambiguity. Here, the infrastructure becomes critical. Organizations whose norms support risk taking and experimentation and in which people are sufficiently skilled to create their own performance programs and routines will perform better with little formalization than will their more risk-averse, less training-oriented counterparts.

A special training need is created by the aging work force. Declining birthrates mean a shift in the age distribution of the work force. Although labor force participation of men over fifty-five is declining (in contrast to that of women), anticipated declines in pension fund support can alter that in the future. Senior HRM executives generally laud older workers for their experience, work habits and attitudes, but fault them for lack of aggressiveness, flexibility, and adaptability to technology. Though a plurality of executives believe older workers would benefit from skill training, new firms target them for such training (*Training*, "Rating Older Workers" 1987).

Moreover, those firms best able to train (large companies) are likely to have mandatory retirement policies. In a recent study commissioned by the American Association of Retired Persons, only 10 percent of smaller firms (with fewer than one hundred employees) had mandatory retirement in contrast to 43 percent of firms with one thousand–plus employees. Training specialists have long been concerned that older people might respond differently to training techniques than younger people (Wexley and Latham 1980). Development of training technologies for older workers is imperative.

Emerging Problems for Human Resource Managers

Although traditional HRM problems will have new twists in the future, increasingly managers must face demands for changes in areas traditionally not a part of the HRM function. Though many such problems exist, two major ones are addressed in detail here because of the increasing rate of demand for changes in these areas: the need to create and maintain structures that encourage and support innovation throughout the organization (not just in research and development units or marketing departments), and demands and opportunities for new patterns of employee/employer relations.

Managing an Internal Environment for Innovation

Other chapters in this book argue for the critical role innovation plays in creating a competitive advantage. A primary function of HRM is to create and maintain structures (arrangements among people) that work to the organization's strategic advantage. HRM's role in managing innovation involves three major areas: rewards, access and resources. It is a truism that behavior is a function of least effort: what is made easy to do is what is likely to happen. Rewards, resources, and access are the key to making innovation happen.

Encouraging Innovation. Reward systems promote innovation when promotion, pay, and development opportunities are linked to working on new areas or problems—from generating new business to exploring a different approach to old problems. Unless innovative behaviors are assessed in performance reviews and problem-solving efforts credited, these behaviors may be few and far between. Moreover, innovation does not occur without some risk. Thus, to encourage innovation the firm must support risk taking to the point of not punishing failures, even where taking risk incurs costs (time, money). In many circumstances, it might be more important to appraise *efforts* than results. At Ore-Ida, for instance, all idea champions get a certificate, regardless of the outcome of their efforts ("Ore-Ida's Crop of Home Grown Entrepreneurs" 1984). Problem solving and risk taking belong in the formal job description of many employees.

Innovations do not occur in a closed system. They are the product of novel combinations of ideas, insights, and technologies from different disciplines or from application of basic research to practical problems. The first chapter of this book makes the case for competitive advantages in cooperation between businesses and government. The innovative technologies resulting from these efforts parallel the innovation resulting from broad-scale cooperation *within* firms. The basis of these creative combinations is access: points of contact between employees of diverse backgrounds (in the office as well as socially). Access is facilitated by the presence of boundary spanners who import to the organization ideas from the outside (through external contacts with universities, industry and professional associations, and other sources of technical and market information) and by the movement of people through the organization (through promotion, lateral movement, and turnover). Contacts supporting innovation can sometimes be fueled by turnover. The influx of ideas from outside the firm is a positive by-product of attrition and replacement. Turnover rates of as much as 15 percent or more a year can be desirable.

Innovation needs resources of time, energy, money, equipment, and materials. In the short run, it costs more to adapt than to perpetuate the status quo. Yet if innovation is sought, it has to be supported with resources. Pinchot (1984), in his book on intrapreneuring, talks about the importance of slack resources (those not currently used in direct labor or for overhead) to promote new ideas and change. The most critical resource is discretionary time. IBM, Control Data, and Dupont expect employees to devote as much as 15 percent or more of their time to discretionary activities: planning, problem solving, and creating. Time is provided and effort is rewarded. Seed money for experiments and special projects can both facilitate innovation and act as a reward for it. Slack resources, in terms of people available to work on special projects and ad hoc task forces, are also important. When human resources are managed by emphasizing head counts (keeping labor costs down), slack human resources are often unavailable. Slack resources provide opportunities for flexibility, exploration, and problem solving. Time and people must be made available, use of time and people in innovative ways must be rewarded.

These general factors that foster innovation in organizations also foster effective HRM systems. When the HRM staff (training and development, planning, or information systems personnel) have no budget of their own and must seek approval for general expenditures, their capacities to assist others in development will be limited. As human resource problems become critical contingencies in strategic planning, innovation within the HRM system becomes a critical mechanism for adaptation.

HRM for Innovation: Some Prescriptions. Issues of reward, access, and resources cut across the major functional concerns of HRM staff. Prescriptions can be made for a number of changes to promote innovation through the HRM function.

Training. Emphasize interdisciplinary competencies in both selection and training. A broad background can be as important as, or more so than, in-depth specialized knowledge in generating new ideas, products, and so forth. In employee development and promotion, do not sacrifice general skills (interpersonal, problem solving) for specific technical ones. The tendency to choose first-level managers because of their technical competence (for example, engineering managers) often leads to a situation in which managers have few skills beyond the purely technical and possess a tendency to value and develop technical skills in others at the expense of broader competencies. Managers must be rewarded for developing subordinates. Training others should be a part of each employee's job, regardless of rank, since broader competence fuels innovation and facilitates communication across specialties. If there is one type of skill we might most effectively cultivate, it is that of the boundary spanner— the person who can interact with people from other areas (administrative and functional) and who is multilingual with respect to the jargon and concepts of several specialties (science/engineering, marketing/promotion). Lateral transfers and job rotation can serve as effective means of developing interdisciplinary expertise.

Interactions. Structures are needed to create points of contact between employees to facilitate communication and exchange. Cross-department committees and informal social gatherings contribute to idea exchange. Office design is also important. The open office has not produced the effects expected: communication increased but so did tension and the desire for privacy. Yet people still need ready access to others with relevant expertise, especially in high-tech or other innovation-oriented firms. Attention to which units and departments share a floor can facilitate necessary contacts. Innovators need to be kept in touch with each other, geographically and socially. Their activities should not be splintered. Though innovation seems to benefit from social interaction, privacy is also important for uninterrupted thought, reflection, and discussions. Private offices can be important to creating innovation opportunities, in part by helping to protect discretionary time.

Incentives. Document, publicize, and reward individuals who interact well with people from other departments or functional areas. Boundary spanning should be a part of many job descriptions and an item on the performance review. Acknowledge people for developing others (subordinates and peers) through feedback and the opportunity to continue to develop themselves. Praise, promote, and compensate successful innovators, but do not punish for experiments and responsible ventures that fail. Reward efforts as well as outcomes. Accept the fact that many innovations have a long lead time. Success cannot always be determined within the typical time frame of the performance review cycle.

Constructive Turnover and Selection. View turnover as a source of new ideas and competencies. Optimum turnover rates vary from firm to firm and can be much higher in some (such as in organizations seeking to change rapidly). Hire for diversity as well as fit. Studies of group problem solving support the value of heterogeneity in enhancing the quality of solutions (Shaw 1976).

Resource Allocation. Maintain flexible manpower allocations. Head counts are not in themselves meaningful indicators of the effectiveness of employee use. Distribute seed money to stimulate experimentation. Allocation of such money can be made contingent on an employee's past success as an innovator. Institute discretionary time in job duties, and reward people for using it for innovation, planning, and development. Protect discretionary time from competing job demands. Demand it by appraising problem solving and innovative efforts. Give frequent feedback on use of discretionary time, since such efforts may be long in producing an observable outcome. Reward effort.

Changing Patterns of Employee/Employer Relations

Market and technology are not the only forces of change affecting organizations. HRM managers also face social and legal changes, operating upon the values and life-styles of the work force, as well as on the relations existing between employees and their organizations. An increasingly older and often more professional work force with greater female participation could be the basis for new patterns of employee/employer relations. Legal limitations to such employer practices as at-will employment (Levin 1983) and mandatory retirement (*U.S. News and World Report*, "Up and Out" 1985) are affecting how firms meet their staffing needs. HRM systems have the need for and the capacity to generate alternative forms of employment and recruitment.

To be employed by a particular organization means that some arrangements exist between employee and employer, specifying that certain actions will be taken in exchange for some specified return. Specified actions on the part of the employee include performance of specific duties and possibly the attainment of some result(s), such as sales or production quotas. These actions might be prescribed for certain conditions (in the office or at home) and subject to some restrictions (for instance, certain documents or tools might not be removed from the workplace). Specified actions on the part of the organization include allocation of compensation, training and development of employee skills, and resource support. This arrangement might be of indefinite duration or of a specified time period, or it might involve a guarantee of long-term tenure. Where, when and even how work is done can be specified as part of such an arrangment. These arrangements are essentially *contracts* in which a mutual set of expectations exist regarding the obligations and responsibilities of the parties involved (MacNeil 1985).

Organizations of the future will face an ever increasing variety of contractual arrangements in employment. We will consider here two attributes of employment contracts that are likely to change in the future: (1) inclusion, and (2) psychological implicitness.

Degrees of Inclusion. Inclusion refers to the extent to which the employee works full-time or part-time, temporarily or long term, has employee status or is an independent contractor, works in a facility along with other employees (office, plant) or at home. Essentially, inclusion is the degree to which an individual is physically and psychologically integrated into the organization. All social roles involve some degree of what Allport (1933) termed partial inclusion, since most people perform multiple roles (spouse, parent, employee, club member). Inclusion affects, among other things, investment of time and energy, willingness to make long-term commitments to the role, and competition of one role with others. Cost economics are a primary determinant of the nature of employee inclusion.

Full-Time/Part-Time. Conversion of employee status from full-time to part-time is linked to the differential costs and benefits associated with these two employee groups (Nollen and Martin 1978). Although some workers prefer and seek opportunities for part-time employment, the number of involuntary part-time or temporary workers has been slowly and steadily increasing (Office of Technology Assessment 1985, 17). Technological changes, in particular office automation, have allowed organizations to adjust their labor costs to a fluctuating workload, to reduce some overhead costs, and to eliminate secondary labor costs such as benefits packages. Part-time employment, defined here as permanent employment of thirty-five hours a week or less, has the advantage of opening up employment opportunities for parents of young children, retired people, and individuals seeking to supplement their income from full-time work or self-employment. In the future, an aging population with shrinking retirement benefits can provide a stable part-time work force.

When part-time status is the result of cutbacks, the impact of this conversion of employment status depends on how the transition is handled and on the organization's HRM history. When workweek hours are reduced to save labor costs and employees are affected across the board, as in the case of Hewlett-Packard, employees might perceive the change as having little effect on status (since all employees have the same hours); at the same time the company signals commitment to its members. When only a few employees experience the change, it is long term, and reductions in force have occurred in the past, the conversion to part-time status can be associated with reduced motivation and increased turnover. When part-time status is viewed as permanent or as a demotion, the negative effects of reduced inclusion result (Rotchford and Roberts 1982). To date, social scientists do not know how many hours are sufficient to provide employees with a sense of inclusion and involvement, and to allow the firm's culture and norms to affect employees. Is there an optimal number of work hours that promote a sense of involvement? How can part-time status be enhanced in the eyes of employees and co-workers? If labor-saving technology means a reduced workweek (for example, thirty hours), will problems of inclusion and involvement escalate? In the future, answers to these questions will be sought.

We do know that when part-time work arrangements are used as a reduction in force, employees are likely to experience stress. This impact, however, contrasts with the potentially greater cost associated with layoff. When an employee is laid off, economic and emotional costs ensue for that individual. Moreover, those not laid off, the "survivors," are also affected. Brockner et al. (in press) suggest that employees not laid off come to perceive management and their co-workers in a much more negative way. The long-term consequence of layoffs for employee motivation and commitment can be great. The management of the termination ("the joining-up" process in reverse) is increasingly critical. Work force expectations and entitlements, coupled with the continuing erosion of at-will employment practices, mean that the process of terminating employees *begins* with company hiring practices. Employee expectations regarding long-term or full employment (or their opposites) are created with commitments expressed or understood at hire (Rousseau 1987b). To preserve flexibility in employment arrangements it can be important to describe realistically for new hires the ways in which the organization might contend with fluctuations in the economy or demands. Through such specification of the employment arrangement or contract, the firm can reduce the likelihood that contracts of full or long-term employment will be implied by recruiters or assumed by employees. However, at present social scientists do not know how employees will respond to the *absence* of such commitments by their employers.

Temporary Employment. The rise of labor-contracting firms for nurses, accountants, and other professionals signals the increasing demand for temporary employees. The advantages of temporary employment to the organization include lower secondary labor costs, reduced long-term commitment to labor overhead, and the opportunities of hiring people with suitable skills to fill a specific need. Temporaries are valuable, short-term remedies. The company assumes no responsibilities for training and development beyond limited on-the-job training and is less vulnerable to government regulations such as EEO requirements. Organizations also make fewer commitments to companies likely to be enforceable as implied contracts.

Some temporary employees have the status of *independent contractors* to whom the organization's only obligation is compensation upon fulfillment of the contract. With the use of independent contractors increasing, government scrutiny of the practice is leading to changes in tax policies such that if an independent contractor only contracts with one firm during the tax year that individual may have been treated as an employee and can require the employer to pay taxes such as unemployment and social security (Office of Technology Assessment 1985).

Independent contractors are the classic example of a "buy" strategy of employment (Miles and Snow 1980). From the individual's perspective advantages include self-employment and associated tax advantages, opportunity to compete in the external labor market or in many organizations, and negotiation of an individual contract with each employer. From the organization's point of view, independent contractors require only short-term commitments, provide potentially vast resources of readily available skills and training, and allow rapid response to changing environmental demands (when required skills are available externally and not internally). Professionals, an occupational group attracted to the independent contractor arrangement, are predicted to expand their numbers by as much as 21.5 percent by the year 2000 (Leontief and Duchin 1984), providing organizations with a highly diverse pool of talent from which to buy needed skills and expertise.

Increased regulation of employment as well as increased economic fluctuations in specific industries can create greater reliance on temporary employees. Motivational strategies for temporary employees are likely to be primarily monetary. Future use of temporaries and independent contractors depends upon the stability of the organization's business environment and on regulatory pressures. Undoutedly, the independent contractor segment is growing and will continue to do so for some time, particularly in the form of the spin-off contractors—former employees who become self-employed, often as competition with a former employer. Dental hygienists who invest money in a van and portable equipment (made possible through miniaturization) can build a business making house calls to clean teeth, take X rays, and give fluoride treatments, all in competition with the dentists who used to employ them. Independents signal a shifting pattern of employment and control.

Home-based Workers. A growing proportion of employees now work exclusively at home. Traditionally, much of the labor force has had the primary place of work in the residence (farmers, shopkeepers, weavers; Dicksen 1974). Some will engage in home-based work through self-employment, but there is considerable potential for organizations to employ people to work at home in areas ranging from clothing manufacture to home-based office work. Despite concern by the AFL-CIO and others that home-based work can be used in the future to exploit the unskilled, women, children, and immigrants, special-interest groups such as women with young children and the handicapped continue to find home-based employment an often necessary means of support. Currently, it is believed that more than 10 million Americans earn part of their income by working at home (Breathnach 1984). This home-based work is more than the overflow of work brought home to be done outside of work hours:

it reflects the use of freelancers (independent contractors), as well as a trend toward geographic decentralization of work-related activities made possible by advances in telecommunications and computers.

Computer design firms often use home-based work as a means of encouraging innovations. Conscious of the importance of settings conducive to thinking and reflection and of the need to protect creative time, designers, programmers, and other staff often have the option of working at home two days a week (or more) and coming to the office for the remainder. Computers and telecommunication systems make this possible; a management accustomed to giving employees autonomy can make it successful.

About 15.8 percent of American households had a computer in 1985, a figure expected to increase to 32.9 percent by 1990. In perhaps an over-enthusiastic view, Toffler (Breathnach 1984) predicts that there could be as many as 15 million home-based white collar workers by 1990, based on the assumption that 15 million of today's jobs could be transferred from the office to the home. Innovations in telecommunications and computer systems certainly make possible the decentralization of work. Questions remain, however, regarding the advantages and disadvantages of home-based work.

On the pro side, the average American now travels more than nine miles in each direction, often a one- to two-hour commute (Motor Vehicle Manufacturers Association 1981). The expense and stress of commuting is avoided by home-based work. From the employer's perspective, home-based workers typically cost less to employ. Lower income is typical of home work generally, often because it is shifted to part-time status or is compensated by piece rates without fringe benefits. To human resource planners, the advantages of home work include (1) the relatively untapped resource of skilled people who are homebound (parents of young children, retired people, even employees on sick leave), (2) reduced overhead costs, (3) greater flexibility in use of workers to match fluctuations in demand for the firm's goods or services. From the employee's perspective, employment opportunities might be opened up where for one reason or another the worker finds it less desirable to work away from home. A multinational software company based in Britain, with subsidiary offices in Denmark, Holland, and the United States, is deliberately structured so that nearly all of its workers are based at home. These are computer professionals, and in Europe 96 percent of them are women with small children and 95 percent work entirely at home (Fisher 1984). Electronic commuting is made possible by an efficient and cost-effective telephone system. Given the increasing quality and diversity of telecommunications in the United States, such systems are particularly feasible here. The spread of electronic mail, computer conferencing, and PBX, reduces the need for face-to-face supervision and coordination with co-workers.

The disadvantages of home-based employment center around the loss of social contact at the workplace and its informational benefits to both the employee and management. There are economies of scale in the centralized workplace, in equipment acquisition, and access to central files and reference materials that are not available in home-based work. Also, the supporting superstructure of the employee/employer relationship is weakened by geographic decentralization of work. Levels of commitment and willingness to take on exceptional levels of responsibility are likely to be lower in home-based workers, who are less exposed to organizational leadership and cultural influences. Since home-based employment often involves employees who once worked in a centralized workplace for the employing organization, such individuals might rely on established social relations and previously assimilated norms and corporate culture in interacting with other organization members. Such employees probably pose fewer problems for their supervisors, since a degree of inclusion in the organization exists for them despite the home-based nature of their work. Yet home-based workers often report that co-workers resent them if they do not have the same privileges (Pratt 1984).

When the home-based worker is employed by the organization without first having worked in a centralized setting, that individual is often minimally socialized into the organization's culture, with limited possibilities for training, development, and promotion. It is likely that these home-based employees have a single-purpose function, corresponding to the relatively small investment made in their training and development by the organization.

From the home workers' perspective, the savings associated with not going in to work (commuting, clothing) might be outweighed by the increased telephone costs (often borne by the employee) and a reduced wage. Even when home workers ostensibly earn the same wage as their office counterparts, gross wages are typically lower for the home worker. One reason is that home-based workers only count actual working minutes and many home-based workers do not bill their employers for time spent in correcting mistakes or where actual time worked exceeded the estimated time of the project (Christensen 1985). Further, home workers with small children often report significant physical and mental strains from trying to be both parent and employee simultaneously (Christensen 1985).

Home-based work frees the employer from certain overhead costs and the employee from a rigid schedule and physical presence in a centralized work place. It requires a human resource management strategy based on tapping existing skills in a labor pool (a "buy" strategy), since elaborate training is not compatible with home-based work—though some training can be undertaken, perhaps even delivered at home. Its future expansion is linked to advances in telecommunication and computer systems that are extremely likely, and to the development of alternative means of coordinating work and supervising interdependent people who do not have direct, face-to-face contact—social innovations that might lag behind the technological change that makes home-based work feasible. Quality control and employee reliability (in performance and attendance) are two objectives that historically led to the establishment of centralized factories for production (Dickson 1974). Home-based work counters the centralization long characteristic of industrialized work. It will require a structuring and allocation of work that facilitates quality control and reliability in a decentralized work system.

Employers have available three strategies for managing a geographically decentralized work system:

1. To allocate tasks to home-based workers that are especially well suited to the level of skill or training the worker possesses. More so for this group of employees than for most others, it is necessary to match skills and tasks carefully since any deficiencies are difficult to compensate for through supervision or training. Implementation of this strategy can mean either (*a*) simplifying the work assigned to home-based workers to reduce task difficulty and need for quality control, or (*b*) the opposite alternative of assigning work to individuals whose professional training and past experience makes them well suited to completing complex assignments independently of others.

2. To institute a management information system to monitor performance, gauge quality, and facilitate coordination and scheduling, relying on a computer-based data gathering and control system. This system should give ongoing, real-time feedback to both employee and employer. It is imperative to avoid having to redo the home workers' work at the office or plant because of poor quality control.

3. To establish lateral relations between home-based workers and a supervisor, or a team of home-based and office-based employees, either of which would involve some face-to-face interactions to plan, monitor, and allocate work. Any system used is likely to rely heavily on goal-setting techniques, such as management by objectives, or use of piece rating with production standards, enabling home-based workers to know what is expected of them in the absence of ongoing supervision.

Clearly, telecommunicating is not that simple. It yields an employee-organization relationship often at odds with traditional organizational structure and culture. How should supervisors manage people not on site? Can people be made to feel part of a team through the phone system? Federal Reserve Bank management has found telecommunicating not conducive to economic research: necessary policy debates that spur research do not occur (*Wall Street Journal*, "When Employees Work at Home" 1987). The in-office interactive contributions of experienced employees are often lost. Often, it is these discretionary and unpredictable interactions that make the greatest contribution to problem solving and innovation.

Home-based work produces control problems in contingent work and contribution constraints in nonroutine kinds of work. Structural innovations as well as cultural changes seem needed to address these problems.

A New Form of Labor/Management Agreement: The Psychological Contract. At the heart of the relations between employers and employees is a business agreement for the supply of tangible products or specified work in exchange for a certain price, rate, or commission—in other words, a contract. Written contracts, such as union agreements, are explicit, specifying terms as well as the actions that can and cannot be taken by the parties involved. As explicit contracts such as labor/management agreements have a more or less straightforward standing in the courts and in the interpretations made of them by the contract parties. Written agreements are subject to interpretation, which need not be shared by the employees and employers, and of course people's minds can change. Either the union or the management might wish to renegotiate soon after an agreement has been reached. But more often than not the written agreement structures labor/management relations for that contract period.

Changing Prerogatives of Management. With the decline in the proportion of unionized workers in the United States, fewer employees work under explicit contracts. In the absence of specified terms of employment, recent court cases have raised questions about employer obligations to employees regarding due process in dismissals, regulation of off-the-job activities, and protection from work hazards, as well as about employee responsibilities in complying with organizational demands to violate the law and protecting employer interests even in the period *after* termination of employment (Hunt 1984).

From management's perspective the legal status of the employment relationship is changing. Though once employment was almost universally at the will of the employer, the organization can no longer regulate all the conditions of employment. The principle of at-will termination traditionally held sway in U.S. courts (Levin 1983). Recently, courts have been deciding in favor of the employee in cases where the firing would contravene public policy: employee whistle-blowing (for instance, *Harless v. First National*), exercising freedom of speech by public criticism of the organization (for example, *Holodnak v. Avco*), refusal by an employee suspected of taking kickbacks to undergo a lie detector test (for example, *Perks v. Firestone*, cases cited by Levin 1983). Limitations on the restrictions organizations can impose on the life-style or private lives of employees, such as dating employees of a rival firm, are emerging in the judicial system. The issue of employee and employer relations and rights is expanding beyond matters of law breaking or of public policy into new forms of contractual arrangements (*Newsweek*, "You Can't Fire Me" 1982).

The Psychological Contract. In the absence of explicit contracts, it is the practices and policies of organizations in the hiring, retention, and termination of employees which form the basis of the employee/employer relationship. The expectations that organization members form based on company practices, policies, and actions constitute the basis of a psychological contract. A psychological contract is an unwritten set of expectations that organization members have about what the organization requires in terms of member effort and behavior and how the organization will respond to their contributions to it (Rousseau 1987b). Such contracts derived through a pattern of interaction (a relationship) can have legal standing (MacNeil 1985). Features of a psychological contract include expectations that an exchange of valued goods and services will occur between parties, and a mutuality such that the exchange obligates each party to the other for future exchanges. A management by objectives program for shaping performance can be the basis for a contract. A history of plant closing at other company locations can form the basis for a contract of diminished expectations of return and perhaps for contribution as well. Contracts by definition are understandings or agreements between parties that some specified actions will (or will not) be taken in exchange for some appropriate response. Unless a contract is in writing (and sometimes of course even when it is), this "understanding" need not be mutual. Parties need only believe that others share the same perspective regarding the agreement's terms and conditions. What is key to a psychological contract is the belief on the part of one party that the other owes (and is likely to supply) something for contributions made. Such contracts are intraindividual, with each employee potentially having a unique set of terms in his or her psychological contract.

Though any set of expectations an employee develops based on the first job interview through long years on the job might be the basis of a psychological contract, all expectations are not contractual, from a legal perspective. From what a fellow worker has said, an engineer might expect that the company doesn't lay off people when its workload is reduced. Such a belief is not necessarily a reasonable expectation. The existence of other employer-related conditions contribute to mutuality of the expectations and therefore to the existence of a contract, including (though not limited to):

Commitments: At hire or at some later point in the employment process, were explicit promises or guarantees made (for example, "You'll have a job here as long as you keep increasing your sales volume by 10 percent annually")?

History: What practices and policies have traditionally affected employee status, compensation, career paths? (Has management *traditionally* paid tuition for advanced degrees?)

Written policies: Do personnel manuals, job descriptions, or related documents specify typical or expected patterns of advancement, development opportunities, or other personnel actions?

Organization reputation/image: Does the firm advertise or project to the public an image as a specific type of employer? (The U.S. Army advertises its training opportunities. IBM might be viewed as a stable, long-term employer by the general public.)

Commitments, history, and written policies are all relatively explicit means of shaping expectations. The more explicit the basis of the expectation, the more enforceable it is when legal recourse is sought. The practice of paying commission on a sale can be construed as a contractual arrangement. An NCR salesman was judged to have the right to a jury trial on the company's motives for firing him near the completion of a large sale (Levin 1983). Similarly, the forced early retirement of competent employees to avoid paying pension benefits or the failure to honor recruitment promises are potential bases for suits because of the violation of covenants of good faith and fairness. Additionally, attributes that operate to form psychological contracts include the issue of timing (*ex ante* or *ex post*), where promises can be made before or after an employee's contribution is made. *Ex ante* promises can be powerful motivators. Is there a long-term or consistent basis to the expectations (history) such that expectations of rewards for contributions and of the obligations owed to the organization remain stable over time (for instance, no major changes in organizational leadership or business strategy) over a period of decades? To the extent that any or all of these conditions exist, a psychological contract can be said to exist from the employee's perspective regarding relations with his or her employer.

Distinct types of psychological contracts are likely to emerge for organizations in which innovation is an important criterion of job performance. From the employer's side of the contract, the arrangement is likely to involve providing a context and rewards for idea generating, experimentation, and risk taking. For the employee, the exchange involves patentable ideas—new products and processes—the ownership of which typically is held by the firm. Many organizations, including universities, require employees to sign a contract agreeing that innovations produced during their term of employment become the organization's property. Under such conditions sharing of profits from innovations and/or giving credit or authorship (if not ownership) are likely to emerge as incentives in innovative firms. As an illustration, a software product can be owned by the firm that publishes it while its authors are acknowledged in the product itself, thus giving them professional recognition.

Given the specialized knowledge developed from membership in an innovative organization, employees can also experience both psychological and explicit contracts that restrict the information they can take with them upon leaving the organization's employ and even restrict the activities they can perform for other firms competing in the former organization's market. In a recent case, a McDonald's market researcher left to join the marketing staff of a rival fast food company, and McDonald's sued on the grounds that the information used in the new job was proprietary since the skills needed would have been acquired through participation in McDonald's distinctive market research department (*Forbes*, "McLitigation" 1983). With increasing pressure for competition and innovation, the terms of the psychological contract for employees in innovative firms are likely to be explicitly addressed at the time of hire.

Regardless of the content of the psychological contracts employees formulate, failure to meet expectations (grandiose or modest) reduces employee trust of the organization. When trust declines, there is a great tendency to increase formalization and rules (Kochan and Barocci 1985), thereby limiting the organization's capacity for adaptation and change. One challenge organizations will surely face in the future is the creation and articulation of contracts both explicit and implied that effectively structure their relations with employees. Though one might expect that organizations will seek to avoid extensive commitments to employees to retain their flexibility, a more likely outcome is increased "contract consciousness" where greater effort is made to manage commitments and understandings between employees and employer. Commitments in some form will always be fundamental to relationships (employment or otherwise). A key part of a firm, strategic human resource plan is specifying the employment relationship(s) best suited to achieving the plan's goals.

Conclusion

The issues raised here are generic to all organizations. Doubtless, concerns over labor costs, maintaining a stable base of employees, and technological adaptability are part of virtually all organizations' futures. Strategic thinking means to consider an array of alternative futures (scenarios) that might confront organizations. Of course, we are forecasting with great uncertainty by doing so. But if we are thinking in terms of the next decade or two, it is likely that the dominant types of organizations and employee/employer relations in the future exist today in some form.

Just as there is a lag between the development and mass distribution of new technology (a fifty-five-year lag for televisions and a fifteen-year lag for xerographic machines; Will 1969), there is a lag between the development of new forms of social organizations and their broad-scale diffusion. Consider the five-day workweek as an example of a social innovation. The first five-day workweek was initiated in the United States in 1908. By 1929, only about 5 percent of the American work force worked this schedule (and the National Industrial Conference Board expressed doubt that it would ever catch on). Yet since World War II, it has been the norm. What seems like a minor experiment (for example, computerized personnel assessment and development, or an entire department working at home) actually is the source of innovations that we need to manage the future.

This chapter has addressed the critical problems for future organizations that HRM must solve. As table 13–2 summarizes, the traditional role of HRM of solving the problems of labor economics, operations management, and adaptation to change persists, but new issues in recruitment, use, readiness, and employment relations have arisen.

Table 13–2
Strategic Issues for HRM

Focus (Problem)	Future HRM Issues
Cost economics (input/output)	*Recruitment:* To "make" or "buy" employees *Replacement:* When it is cheaper to retrain than to dismiss? *Regulation:* How legally vulnerable are current and/or future HRM practices?
Capacity to maintain operations (maintenance)	*Work force characteristics:* Trends in age, skills, motives *Skill use:* Will underuse promote dissatisfaction and loss of skilled people? Are people being overdeveloped?
Capacity to change (adaptation)	*Readiness:* Does the infrastructure support innovation, risk taking, experimentation? Can managers manage new employees and relations? *Competition:* Firm's standing in external labor market *Employment relations:* Are social pressures and technological capabilities changing the traditional conditions of employment? Are employee roles and membership status likely to change? *Attrition:* Is there enough to inject new ideas? Is the labor pool stable enough to rely upon? *Contracts and culture:* Articulated enough to motivate? Flexible enough to change?

Consistent with problem-solving processes one maxim applies: *No problem's solutions fail to give rise to other problems.* We now face issues of innovation and change—into the future, maintenance and stability will again become concerns. Regardless, the HRM system functions as a source of solutions to critical problems.

Strategic planning increasingly requires links with HRM planning to realize the opportunities that HRM systems provide for creating and sustaining innovation and environmental adaptation in organizations. Unless HRM systems play a part in strategy formulation they will become constraints rather than opportunities. The linkage of strategic and human resource planning is fundamental to readiness.

Epilogue: Strategic Research Areas

Jerald Hage

Perhaps the most obvious point in a work like this is that there are not necessarily any conclusions about which everyone would agree. And this is as it should be. The fun of an enterprise like this is that we have tried to let a hundred flowers bloom at the same time that we encouraged integration. Consensus and integration are not the same thing. The former means everyone agrees, which is not true in this effort, whereas the latter means that the various contributions touch each other and illuminate similar areas of interest. There are alternative perspectives and viewpoints, as well as some of the surprising convergences that emerged after the conference which had not been anticipated.

What does appear to be a fitting conclusion to a book on the futures of organizations is the suggestion of what some strategic areas might be for managers to experiment in and for researchers—whether industrial psychologists, organizational sociologists, or management specialists—to collect data about. The rate of change may be so great that the managers in the real world cannot afford to wait for academic knowledge to develop. This is another way of saying to them, where do we go from here? My response is to suggest that there are some strategic arenas in which experimentation by managers may prove useful. Likewise, there are some lessons for academic researchers as well. As managers attempt to grapple with all the environmental changes occurring and described in this book, academics should and will take advantage of this experimentation to learn and to codify the lessons. In this epilogue, it seems worthwhile to indicate what some of the arenas of greatest payoff might be.

An epilogue can also conclude usefully by discussing some topics that were not even consideresd. Again, this reflects only my biases and perhaps they were areas worth ignoring, but I am struck at how some themes did not surface in any of the presentations. Nevertheless, these themes seem to be relevant and perhaps especially to academic researchers who, besides codifying what managers do well, also need to be concerned about what managers *fail* to do. The real world, one hopes, can sometimes learn from the Socratic questions posed in this book, and ignored opportunities would appear to be one fruitful area.

One area worthy of considerable experimentation by managers is the movement toward greater product differentiation along the lines suggested in several chapters. Rather than respond to market changes, why not anticipate them? For example, one such area is that of developing more and more products for smaller and smaller markets that are defined on the basis of demographic and value changes. Among other things this might mean a slow but steady movement toward greater product complexity and greater product customization. The idea that the manager should be proactive rather than reactive is consistent with this. But it would also allow for the development of an overall strategy and its gradual implementation across time. With this kind of market strategy, it should be easier to develop the economies of scale across the diversity, to create the more flexible structures, and to develop the more appropriate cultures that have been at the heart of the book's discussion.

When I propose that companies experiment, I mean that they should experiment with one product line or group and not with the entire company, depending upon the size of the organization. This experimentation would provide insights as to the speed with which a company can move into the future and the kinds of errors that are likely.

The themes of adaptiveness and flexibility have occurred over and over again, but in each instance they have been discussed relative to a particular part of the organizational system, whether the structure, the management, the nonmanagement, the production system, and so on. Another strategic area for research is determining how much each of these parts have to be changed before there can be any real flexibility or adaptiveness. If, for example, General Motors decides to become a large, high-tech company—in part because it perceives that customers want higher-quality cars produced with many more different kinds of attributes and in different size production runs—then perhaps it needs to alter managerial roles, nonmanagerial roles, structure, and motivational principles, as well as production lines. Thus, another arena for management is the need to experiment on many organizational fronts simultaneously.

This implies a strategic area of research for academics: what are all the reasons why organizations faced with environmental changes fail to respond to them? Part of the answer may be that they respond but only partially; they change the roles of the managers, for instance, but not the basis on which they are motivated. If the United States is to meet the challenges of competitiveness outlined in chapter 1, then organizational researchers have to understand why many organizations are not responding. In many instances, the chapters in this book have suggested what could be done, but this does not mean it will be done. And here a disciplinary approach may be fatal for the future of the United States, at least relative to the problem of creating academic knowledge about competitiveness. Just as managers think only about some parts of the organizational system and its larger environment, industrial psychologists, organizational sociologists, and management faculty tend to divide the organization and its environment into various segments that correspond to their interests and theoretical models. This compartmentalization may be part of the reason why managers change only part of the system. If we are in a postindustrial age that requires new institutions, then there is a special need for interdisciplinary research that combines micro and macro levels of analysis. In postindustrial society the issue is to develop new institutions with new roles and maybe even new principles of motivation—although this idea appears to be less clear, given the contributions to this book.

Another kind of experiment that managers may find useful is the attempt to increase steadily the sophistication of their organizational knowledge base, now using knowledge in the broad sense of including machines, models, methods, and skills. The steady and incremental increase in the knowledge base of the organization would then to some extent parallel what is occurring in the larger society, allowing for the differences between industrial sectors. Traditionally, organizational experts have argued that management attempts to protect its technological core. Here the idea is that management should attempt to add to its technological core and that this is best done by increasing its sophistication, whether this is located primarily in machines or methods or models or skills or, more likely, in the combination of these elements. Nor should one ignore adding to management knowledge in this process, as Carroll and others have suggested.

The various contributors to this book have made clear that there is considerable experimentation occurring with networks, an idea that has emerged in many ways in this book. But the many ways in which networks and interdependencies have been discussed mean that academic researchers need to have a very clear research agenda regarding the causes of these many different forms and also their consequences. Presumably some kinds of networks work best in certain situations. Furthermore, networks and participation in decision making may appear to be alike, but in many instances there may be some fundamental differences. For example, matrices within an organization, whether those described by Galbraith and Kazanjian or by Smith, do not appear to be the same as those in joint ventures or strategic alliances or venture capital. In the latter instances, there is an absence of hierarchy.

Another kind of experimentation that is going on, but can also be deliberately facilitated by managers concerned about moving faster into the future, is the replacement of structure by process and culture. Several contributors have suggested that knowledge bases will increase, jobs will be enlarged, and the differences between occupations and departments will decline. This can be planned and in specific directions, depending upon the strategic plan of the organization. But if structure is eliminated, it must be replaced with some other mechanism for assuring a coordinated effort toward organizational goals.

Training, teams, and cultures consistent with the objectives of the organization are what managers can stress. The chapters by Schneider and Rentsch and by Rousseau indicate how managers can proceed.

The gradual elimination of structure becomes especially interesting and vital at the top of the organizational pyramid, especially in large organizations. The creation of multiple profit centers and the downsizing of headquarters are experiments taking place today. The question remains, though, of how to decouple these many centers—that is, how to give them enough autonomy and at the same time obtain meaningful integration. Matrix structures are one possibility but not the only one. Here is another area for cautious experimentation by managers who are concerned about being proactive.

All of this calls attention to one of the areas not discussed in this book: the relationship between the overall structure or design of a firm (especially a large one), and the specific components called jobs or roles. One implication appears in some of the chapters, that as structures become flatter, the specific components become larger as part of the necessary adjustment. This requires research, especially in relation to the various kinds of networks that have been discussed. In general, there is an absence of macro/micro research in the social sciences, particularly on organizations. But if there is some sense that an organization is a system, the various parts of it all have to be in sync.

The role of training and retraining has been emphasized in many of the contributions, and this is one way of increasing the knowledge base. But what is missing is any discussion or speculation about the mobilization of human capital. This appears to be a serious omission and suggests something about the way in which we think about the problem.

Consistent with this concern about the knowledge base of the organization is the suggestion that management adopt an experimental mode. This increases the likelihood of learning and contributing to the technological core of the business and especially to the expertise of the management, which is a key component of the knowledge base of the organization. Small, incremental improvements in the knowledge base each year can produce enormous changes in the effectiveness and efficiency of the firm.

Experimentation with the knowledge base and with product differentiation obviously should be coordinated because they are two sides of the same coin, the technical-market context of the organization. But this idea deals with only some of the changes occurring in the larger environment. One major absence in this book about anticipating the future is any consideration of the relationship between firms and government. Nevertheless, one sees many cooperative relationships developing. In Europe and Asia one finds that the state and business leaders in many ways coordinate the economy much as managers in a large corporation do. Although the United States has its own traditions, it is hard to imagine that firms can effectively plan their futures and their strategies without more input from government. Likewise, because of the ability of government policies to disrupt strategic plans, businesses increasingly need to contribute input to government policies. This can occur through networks as it does in many parts of the world. Perhaps the most critical interface between government and business is the production of knowledge, precisely because this is becoming so expensive—even too expensive for the U.S. federal government—and because it is occurring at such a fast pace.

An important area for academic researchers is that of the relative importance of training for maintaining motivation, or perhaps some contingency theory that would suggest which kinds of rewards—money, education, praise, and the like—are most important for what kinds of people. Similarly, the contributors to this book indicate that we want to know more about the conflict between individual and organizational needs, and whether this is increasing, decreasing, or, more likely, both, depending upon the context and management responses to it.

With the possible exception of the discussion of motivation, much of this book can be described with the single observation that as the changes described in chapter 1 occur, managers need to create far more complex strategies, structures, and roles. Furthermore, there is not a single panacea but instead a variety of scenarios. As a consequence, experimentation within the framework of broad long-term plans becomes essential for survival. But the fruits of this experimentation will be realized only as more and more members of the organization are actively involved in the problem solving needed for this.

Bibliography

Adams, J.S. "Inequity in Social Exchange." In *Advances in Experimental Social Psychology*, vol. 2, edited by L. Berkowitz. New York: Academic Press, 1965.

Adams, W., ed. *The Structure of Industry*. 7th ed. New York: Macmillan, 1986.

AFL-CIO Committee on the Evolution of Work. *The Changing Situation of Workers and their Unions*. Washington, D.C.: AFL-CIO publication no. 165, 1985.

Aiken, M., and Jerald Hage. "Organizational Interdependence and Intra-Organizational Properties." *American Sociological Review* (Dec. 1968):912–31.

Aldrich, Howard. *Organizations and Environments*. Englewood Cliffs, N.J.: Prentice-Hall, 1979.

Allen, Stephen A. "Organizational Choices and General Management Influence Networks in Divisionalized Companies." *Academy of Management Journal* (Sept. 1978): 341–65.

Allport, F.H. *Institutional Behavior*. Chapel Hill: Univ. of North Carolina Press, 1933.

Anderson, C.R. *Management: Skills, Functions and Organization Performance*. Dubuque, Iowa: William C. Brown, 1984.

Anthony, P.D. *The Ideology of Work*. London: Tavistock Publications, 1977.

Argote, L., and P.S. Goodman. *Investigating the Implementation of Robotics*. Pittsburgh: The Robotics Institute, Carnegie-Mellon University, 1984.

Argyris, C. "Some Problems in Conceptualizing Climate: A Case Study of a Bank." *Administrative Science Quarterly* 2 (1957):501–20.

———. *Integrating the Individual in the Organization*. New York: Wiley, 1965.

Armour, Henry Ogden, and David J. Teece. "Organizational Structure and Economic Performance: A Test of the Multidivisional Hypothesis." *Bell Journal of Economics* 9 (Spring 1978):106–22.

Arnowitz, S. "The Myth of Full Employment." *The Nation*, Feb. 8, 1986, 135–38.

Aronson, E. *The Social Animal*. 4th ed. New York: Freeman, 1984.

Ayres, R.U. *The Man-Machine Interface*. Pittsburgh: The Robotics Institute, Carnegie-Mellon University, 1984.

Ayres, R.U., and S.M. Miller. "Robotic Realities: Near-Term Prospects and Problems." *Annals of the American Academy of Political and Social Science* 470 (Nov. 1983):28–55.

Bandura, A. *Social Learning Theory*. Englewood Cliffs, N.J.: Prentice-Hall, 1977.

Barnard, C.I. *The Functions of the Executive*. Cambridge: Harvard Univ. Press, 1938.

Bartlett, Chris A. "MNCs: Get off the Reorganization Merry-Go-Round." *Harvard Business Review* (Mar.–Apr. 1983):138–47.

Bass, B.M. *Stogdill's Handbook of Leadership*. New York: Free Press, 1981.

Bateman, T.S., and D.W. Organ. "Job Satisfaction and the Good Soldier: The Relationship Between Affect and Employee 'Citizenship.' " *Academy of Management Journal* 26 (1983):887–95.

Beer, M. *Organizational Change and Development: A Systems Review*. Santa Monica, Calif.: Goodyear Publishing, 1980.

Bell, D. *The Coming of the Post-Industrial Society*. New York: Basic Books, 1973.

Bennis, W.G. *Changing Organizations*. New York: McGraw-Hill, 1966.

———. "Organizations of the Future." *Personnel Administration* 6:5 (1967):6–19.

Berney, E.J. "Management Team Decision-Making in Acquisitions: An Intergroup Perspective." Ph.D. diss., University of Maryland, 1985.

Best, F. "Changing Sex Roles and Worklife Flexibility." *Psychology of Women Quarterly* 6 (1981):55–78.

Blackburn, R.S. "Dimensions of Structure: A Review and Reappraisal." *Academy of Management Review* 7:1 (1982):59–66.

Blau, Peter. *The Organization of Academic Work*. New York: Wiley-Interscience, 1973.

Blauner, Robert. *Alienation and Freedom: The Factory Worker and His Industry*. Chicago: Univ. of Chicago Press, 1964.

Bluestone, B., and B. Harrison. *The Deindustrialization of America*. New York: Basic Books, 1982.

Boehm, V.R. "What Do Managers Really Do?" Paper presented at the annual meeting of the AACSB Graduate Admission Council, Toronto, June 1981.

Bolman, L.G., and T.E. Deal. *Modern Approaches to Understanding and Managing Organizations*. San Francisco: Jossey-Bass, 1984.

Bowen, D.E., and B. Schneider. "Toward Understanding Boundary Roles in Service Organizations: Some Research Findings and Future Directions." In *The Service Encounter*, edited by J.A. Czepiel, M.R. Solomon, and C. Suprenant. Lexington, Mass.: Lexington Books, 1985.

Boyatzis, R.R. *The Competent Manager: A Model for Effective Performance*. New York: John Wiley and Sons, 1982.

Breatnach, S.B. "Trends: Mothers and Others of Invention," *Washington Post*, July 16, 1984.

Brockhaus, R.H. "I-E Locus of Control Scores as Predictors of Entrepreneurial Intentions." *Proceedings, New Orleans Academy of Management*, Aug. 1975:433–35.

———. "Risk Taking Propensity of Entrepreneurs." *Academy of Management Journal* 23(3):509–20. (Sept. 1980).

Brockhaus, R.H., and W.R. Nold. "An Exploration of Factors Affecting the Entrepreneurial Decision: Personal Characteristics vs. Environmental Calculations." *Academy of Management Proceedings*, Aug. 1979:364–68.

Brockner, J., L. Greenberg, A. Brockner, J. Bortz, J. Davy, and C. Carter. "Layoffs, Equity Theory and Work Performance: Further Evidence of the Impact of Survivor Guilt." *Academy of Management Journal* 29 (1986):373–84.

Buono, Anthony, James Bowditch, and John Lewis III. "When Cultures Collide: The Anatomy of a Merger." *Human Relations* 38:5 (1985):477–500.

Bureau of National Affairs. *Personnel Activities, Budgets, and Staffs, 1979–1980.* Washington, D.C.: BNA, June 5, 1980, bulletin no. 1578.

Burns, T., and G.M. Stalker. *The Management of Innovation.* London: Travistock Publications, 1961.

Business Week. "Ore-Ida's Crop of Home Grown Entrepreneurs." June 11, 1984.

Campbell, D.P., and J.C. Hansen. *Manual For the SVIB-SCII.* Stanford, Calif.: Stanford Univ. Press, 1981.

Campbell, J.P., M.D. Dunnette, E.E. Lawler, and K.E. Weick, Jr. *Mangerial Behavior, Performance, and Effectiveness.* New York: McGraw-Hill, 1970.

Carnoy, M., and D. Shearer. "Democratizing the Workplace." In *Work in Modern Society,* edited by L. Perman. Dubuque, Kendall/Hunt, 1986.

Carroll, S.J., and D.A. Gillen. "The Classical Management Functions: Are They Really Outdated?" *Proceedings, Academy of Management* (1984):132–36.

———. "How Useful Are the Classical Management Functions in Describing Managerial Work?" *Academy of Management Review* 12 (1987):38–51.

Carroll, S.J., and R.S. Schuler. "Professional HRM: Changing Functions and Problems." In *Human Resource Management in the 1980s,* edited by S.J. Carroll and R.S. Schuler. Washington, D.C.: Bureau of National Affairs, 1983.

Carroll, S.J., and W.H. Taylor. "A Study of the Validity of a Self-Observational Method of Work Sampling." *Personnel Psychology* 21 (1973):359–64.

Chandler, Alfred. *Strategy and Structure: Chapters in the History of the American Industry.* Cambridge: MIT Press, 1962.

———. *The Visible Hand.* Cambridge: Harvard Univ. Press, 1977.

Child, J., H.D. Ganter, and A. Kieser. "Technological Innovation and Organizational Conservatism." In *New Technology as Organizational Innovation,* edited by J.M. Pennings and A. Buitendam. Cambridge, Mass.: Ballinger, 1987.

Christensen, K.E. *Impacts of Home-based Work on Women and Their Families.* New York University, Contractor Report prepared for the Office of Technology Assessment, 1985.

Clarke, A.C. *July 20, 2019: Life in the 21st Century.* New York: Macmillan, 1986.

Cole, R. *Japanese Blue Collar.* Berkeley: Univ. of California Press, 1971.

Collins, O.R., and D.G. Moore. *The Enterprising Man.* East Lansing: Michigan State University Press, 1964.

Collins, Paul, and Jerald Hage. "Radical Change in Production: A Longitudinal Study of Manufacturing Establishments." Forthcoming, 1987.

Collins, Paul, Jerald Hage, and Frank Hull. "A Framework for Analyzing Technical Systems in Complex Organizations." Unpublished manuscript, 1986.

Comegys, C. "Cognitive Dissonance and Entrepreneurial Behavior." *Journal of Small Business Management* 14 (Jan. 1976):1–6.

Cooper, A.C. "Incubator Organizations and Other Influences on Entrepreneurship." In *Entrepreneurship and Enterprise Development: A World Wide Perspective* (Proceedings of Project ISEEP). Milwaukee: Center for Venture Management, 1975.

Crosby, P. *Quality Is Free: The Art of Making Quality Certain.* New York: McGraw-Hill, 1979.

Crozier, Michael. *The Bureaucratic Phenomenon.* London: Tavistock, 1964.

Czepiel, J.A., M.R. Solomon, and C. Suprenant. *The Service Encounter.* Lexington, Mass.: Lexington Books, 1985.

Daft, Richard. *Organization Theory and Design.* St. Paul, Minn.: West, 1983.

Damanpour, F., and W.M. Evan. "Organizational Innovation and Performance: The Problem of 'Organizational Lag.' " *Administrative Science Quarterly* 29 (1984):392–409.

Dansereau, F., Jr., G. Graen, and W.J. Haga. "A Vertical Dyad Linkage Approach to Leadership within Formal Organizations: A Longitudinal Investigation of the Role-making Process." *Organizational Behavior and Human Performance* 13 (1975):46–78.

Davidson, William H., and Philippe Haspeslagh. "Shaping a Global Product Organization." *Harvard Business Review* (July–Aug. 1982):125–32.

Davis, S.M. *Managing Corporate Culture.* Cambridge, Mass.: Ballinger, 1984.

Deal, Terrence, and Allan Kennedy. *Corporate Cultures.* Reading, Mass.: Addison-Wesley, 1982.

DeCarlo, J.F., and P.R. Lyons. "A Comparison of Selected Personal Characteristics of Minority and Nonminority-owned Female Entrepreneurs." *Journal of Small Business Management* 17:4 (1979):22–29.

Dhir, A.K. "Office Technology Modernization—An Approach." In *Proceedings, Institute of Industrial Engineering Conference.* Atlanta, Ga.: Institute of Industrial Engineers, 1987.

Dickson, D. *The Politics of Alternative Technology.* New York: Universe Books, 1974.

Didsbury, H.F. *Creating a Global Agenda.* Bethesda, Md.: World Future Society, 1984.

Donaldson, Lex. *In Defence of Organization Theory.* Cambridge, England: Cambridge Univ. Press, 1985.

Dorfman, Nancy S. *Massachusetts' High Technology Boom in Perspective: An Investigation of Its Dimension, Causes, and of the Role of New Firms.* Cambridge: Center for Policy Alternatives at the Massachusetts Institute of Technology, 1982.

Driscoll, J.A. "How To Humanize Office Automation." *Office: Technology and People* 1 (1982):167–76.

Drucker, P. *Innovation and Entrepreneurship.* New York: Harper and Row, 1985.

Duncan, Robert B. "Characteristics of Organizational Environments and Perceived Environmental Uncertainty." *Administrative Science Quarterly* 17 (1972):313–27.

Dundas, K.N.M., and P.R. Richardson. "Implementing the Unrelated Product Strategy." *Strategy Management Journal* 3 (1982):287–301.

Dunnette, M.D. "Mish-mash, Mush, and Milestones in Organizational Psychology." In *Humanizing Organizational Behavior,* edited by H. Meltzer and F.R. Lickert. Springfield, Ill.: Charles C. Thomas, 1976.

Editors of *Fortune. Working Smarter.* New York: Viking, 1982.

Edwards, R. "Forms of Control in the Labor Process: An Historical Analysis." In *Critical Studies in Organization and Bureaucracy,* edited by F. Fischer and C. Sirianni. Philadelphia: Temple Univ. Press, 1984.

Elazar, Daniel J. *American Federalism: A View for the States.* New York: Thomas Crowell, 1972.

Emery, F. "Cities, Markets, and Civilized Work, anno 2000." *Human Relations* 38 (1985):1101–12.

Emery, F.E., and E.L. Trist. "The Causal Texture of Organizational Environments." *Human Relations* 18 (1965):21–32.

Estes, K.W. "Stimulus-Response Theory of Drive." In *Nebraska Symposium on Motivation,* edited by M.R. Jones. Lincoln: Univ. of Nebraska Press, 1958.

Etzioni, A. *A Comparative Analysis of Complex Organizations.* Rev. ed. New York: Free Press, 1975.

Fayerweather, John. "Four Winning Strategies for the International Corporation." *Journal of Business Strategy* 25:1 (1984):37–54.

Fayol, H. *General and Industrial Management.* Translated by Constance Stoors. London: Pitman, 1949.

Fein, M. "Motivation for Work." In *Handbook of Work, Organization, and Society,* edited by R. Dubin. Chicago: Rand McNally, 1976.

Festinger, L. "A Theory of Social Comparison Processes." *Human Relations* 7 (1954): 117–40.

Fielder, Fred. *A Theory of Leadership Effectiveness.* New York: McGraw-Hill, 1967.

Fischer, M.J. "Firm Turns Telecommuting into a Reality." *MIS,* November 28, 1984.

Flanagan, J.C. "The Critical Incident Technique." *Psychological Bulletin* 51 (1954):327–58.

Flynn, P. *The Impact of Technological Change of Jobs and Workers.* Waltham, Mass.: Bentley College Press, 1985.

Forbes. "McLitigation." June 6, 1983.

Forester, Tom. *The Information Technology Revolution.* Cambridge: MIT Press, 1985.

Frayne, C.A., and G.P. Latham. "The Application of Social Learning Theory to Employee Self-management of Attendance." *Journal of Applied Psychology* 72 (1987):387–92.

Freeman, Christopher. *The Industrial Economics of Innovation.* 2d ed. Cambridge: MIT Press, 1982.

French, W.L., and C.H. Bell. *Organization Development: Behavioral Science Interventions for Organization Improvement.* Englewood Cliffs, N.J.: Prentice-Hall, 1978.

Frost, P.J., L.F. Moore, M.R. Louis, C.C. Lundberg, and J. Martin, eds. *Organizational Culture.* Beverly Hills, Calif.: Sage, 1985.

Fullerton, H.N. "The 1995 Labor Force: BLS's Latest Projections." *Monthly Labor Review* (Nov. 1985):17–25.

Galbraith, Jay R. *Designing Complex Organizations.* Reading, Mass.: Addison-Wesley, 1973.

———. *Organization Design.* Reading, Mass.: Addison-Wesley, 1977.

Galbraith, Jay R., and Robert K. Kazanjian. *Strategy Implementation: Structure, Systems, and Process.* St. Paul, Minn.: West Publishing, 1986.

Galinsky, E. "Family Life and Corporate Policies." In *Stresses and Supports for Families,* edited by M. Yogman and T.B. Brazelton. Cambridge: Harvard Univ. Press. Forthcoming.

Gallie, Duncan. *In Search of the New Work Class: Automation and Social Integration within the Capitalist Enterprise.* Cambridge, England: Cambridge Univ. Press, 1978.

Gardner, J.N. *Excellence: Can We Be Equal and Excellent Too?* New York: Harper, 1961.

Garreau, Joel. *The Nine Nations of North America.* New York: Avon Books, 1981.

Gerwin, D. "Do's and Don'ts of Computerized Manufacturing." *Harvard Business Review* 60:2 (1982):107–16.

Gilder, G. *The Spirit of Enterprise.* New York: Simon and Schuster, 1984.

Gillen, D.A., and S.J. Carroll. "Relationship of Managerial Ability to Unit Effectiveness in Organic Versus Mechanistic Units." *Journal of Management Studies* 22 (1985):351–59.

Goldstein, I.L. *Training in Organizations: Needs Assessment, Development, and Evaluation.* 2d ed. (Monterey, Calif.: Brooks/Cole, 1986.

Goodman, P.S., and L.B. Kurke. "Studies of Change in Organizations: A Status Report." In *Change in Organizations: New Perspectives on Theory, Research, and Practice,* edited by P.S. Goodman and Associates. San Francisco: Jossey-Bass, 1982.

Greenhouse, S. "Reshaping Labor to Woo the Young." *New York Times,* sec. 3 (1985), pp. 1, 2, 6F.

Greer, W.R. "In Professions, Women Now the Majority." *New York Times,* sec. C (1986), p. 1.

Gregory, Kathleen L. "Native-View Paradigms: Multiple Cultures and Culture Conflicts in Organizations." *Administrative Science Quarterly* 28 (1983):359–76.

Greiner, L.E. "Evolution and Revolution as Organizations Grow." *Harvard Business Review* 50 (July–Aug. 1972):37–46.

Gruchy, Allan. *Comparative Economic Systems.* 2d ed. Boston: Houghton Mifflin, 1977.

Guiliano, V.E. "The Mechanization of Office Work." *Scientific American* 247:3 (1982):148–64.

Haas, J.A., A.M. Porat, and J.A. Vaughan. "Actual vs. Ideal Time Allocations Reported by Managers: A Study of Managerial Behavior." *Personnel Psychology* 1 (1969):2261–75.

Hackman, J.R. "Designing Work for Individuals and for Groups." In *Perspectives on Behavior in Organizations,* edited by J.R. Hackman, E. Lawler, and L. Porter. New York: McGraw-Hill, 1983.

Hackman, J.R. "The Design of Work Teams." In *Handbook of Organizational Behavior,* edited by J. Lorsch. Englewood Cliffs, N.J.: Prentice-Hall, 1987.

Hackman, J.R., and G.R. Oldham. "Development of the Job Diagnostic Survey." *Journal of Applied Psychology* 60 (1975):159–70.

———. "Motivation through Design of Work: Test of a Theory." *Organizational Behavior and Human Performance* 16 (1976):250–79.

———. *Work Redesign.* Reading, Mass.: Addison-Wesley, 1980.

Hage, Jerald. *Theories of Organizations: Form, Process, and Transformation.* New York: Wiley, 1980.

———. "Organizational Theory and the Concept of Productivity." In *Productivity Research in the Behavioral and Social Sciences,* edited by Arthur Brief. New York: Praeger, 1984.

Hage, Jerald, and Remi Clignet. "Coordination Styles and Economic Growth." *Annals of the American Academy of Political Science* 459 (Jan. 1982):77–92.

Haire, M., E.E. Ghiselli, and L.W. Porter. *Managerial Thinking: An International Study.* New York: Wiley, 1966.

Hall, F.S., and D.T. Hall. *The Two Career Couple.* Reading, Mass.: Addison-Wesley, 1979.

Hall, Richard. *Organization Structure and Process*. 4th ed. Englewood Cliffs, N.J.: Prentice-Hall, 1987.

Hambrecht, William R. "Venture Capital and the Growth of Silicon Valley." *California Management Review* 27:2 (1984):74–82.

Hambrick, D.C., and P.A. Mason. "Upper Echelons: The Organization as a Reflection of Its Top Managers." *Academy of Management Review* 9(2) (1984):193–206

Hamel, Gary, and C.K. Prahalad. "Managing Strategic Responsibility in the MNC." *Strategic Management Journal* 4 (1983):341–51.

———. "Do You Really Have a Global Strategy?" *Harvard Business Review* 63:4 (1985):139–48.

Hamilton, G.G., and M. Orru. "The Organizational Structure of East Asian Business Groups: A Comparative Analysis of Japan, South Korea, and Taiwan." *Proceedings, Pan Pacific Conference IV*, Taipei, Taiwan, (1987):124–27.

Hannon, Michael, and John Freeman. "The Population Ecology of Organizations." *American Journal of Sociology* 82 (1977):929–64.

Harris, P. "Future Work." *Personnel Journal* 77 (1985):53–58.

Hartman, H. "Managers and Entrepreneurs: A Useful Distinction?" *Administrative Science Quarterly* 3:4 (Mar. 1959):429–51.

Hawken, P., J. Ogilvy, and P. Schwartz. *Seven Tomorrows: Toward a Voluntary History*. New York: Bantam Books, 1982.

Hayes, R.H., and W.J. Abernathy. "Managing Our Way to Economic Decline." *Harvard Business Review* 58 (July–Aug. 1980):68–73.

Hayes, Robert H. and Steven C. Wheelwright. *Restoring Our Competitive Edge: Competing through Manufacturing*. New York: Wiley, 1984.

Hebb, D.O. *Organization of Behavior*. New York: Wiley, 1961.

Herbst, P.G. *Alternatives to Hierarchies*. Leiden, The Netherlands: Martinus Nijhoff, 1976.

Heron, W.T., and B.F. Skinner. "Changes in Hunger during Starvation." *The Psychological Record* 1 (1937):51–59.

Herzberg, F. "One More Time: How Do You Motivate Employees?" *Harvard Business Review* 46 (Jan.–Feb. 1968).

Heyduk, R.G., and A. Fenigstein. "Influential Works and Authors in Psychology: A Survey of Eminent Psychologists." *American Psychologist* 39 (1984):556–59.

Hickson, D.J., et al. "Operations Technology and Organization Structure: An Empirical Reappraisal." *Administrative Science Quarterly* 14 (Sept. 1969): 378–97.

Hiltz, S.R. *Online Communities: A Case Study of the Office of the Future*. Norwood, N.J.: Ablex Publishing, 1984.

Hollingsworth, J. Rogers and Leon Lindberg. *Patterns of Governance in American Industry*. Madison: Univ. of Wisconsin. Forthcoming.

Hornaday, J.A., and J. Aboud. "Characteristics of Successful Entrepreneurs." *Personnel Psychology* 24 (Summer 1971):141–53.

Hout, Thomas, Michael E. Porter, and Eileen Rudden. "How Global Companies Win Out." *Harvard Business Review* 60(5) (Sept.–Oct. 1982):98–108.

Huber, G.P. "The Nature and Design of Post-Industrial Organizations." *Management Science* 30(8) (Aug. 1984):928–51.

Hull, C.L. *Principles of Behavior*. New York: Appleton-Century-Crofts, 1943.

Hull, Frank, Koya Azumi, and Jerald Hage. "Organizing for Innovation and Productivity." *Proceedings of the National Science Foundation Conference on Industrial Policy,* May 1983.

Hull, Frank, and Jerald Hage. "Organizing for Innovation: Beyond Burns and Stalker's Organic Type." *Sociology* 16:4 (1982):564–77.

Hunt, H.A., and T.L. Hunt. *Human Resource Implications of Robotics.* Kalamazoo, Mich.: The W.E. Upjohn Institute for Employment Research, 1983.

Hunt, J.W. *The Law of the Workplace: Rights of Employees and Employers.* Washington, D.C.: Bureau of National Affairs, 1984.

Japan Economic Journal. "Computer-aided Decision Making More Popular among Managers." June 19, 1984, p. 7.

Jenkins, G.D., and N. Gupta. "Financial Incentives and Productivity Improvement." *Journal of Contemporary Business* 11:2 (1982):43–56.

Jonsson, B., et al., eds. *Ergo: Workshop on Productive Technology and Quality of Working Life.* Gothenburg, Sweden: Volvo AB, 1984.

Kanfer, F.H. "Self-management Methods." In *Helping People Change: A Textbook of Methods* (2d ed.), edited by F.H. Kanfer and A.P. Goldstein. New York: Pergamon Press, 1980.

Kantor, R.M. "Power and Entrepreneurship in Action: Corporate Middle Managers." In *Varieties of Work,* edited by P. Stewart and M. Cantor. Beverly Hills, Calif.: Sage, 1982.

———. *The Change Masters.* New York: Simon and Schuster, 1983.

Katz, D., and R.L. Kahn. *The Social Psychology of Organizations.* 2d ed. New York: Wiley-Interscience, 1978.

Kaufman, A., A. Baron, and R.E. Kopp. "Some Effects of Instructions on Human Operant Behavior." *Psychonomic Monograph Supplements* 1 (1966):243–50.

Kaufman, H. *The Forest Ranger.* Baltimore: Johns Hopkins Univ. Press, 1960.

Kepner, C.H., and B.B. Tregoe. *The New Rational Manager.* New York: McGraw-Hill, 1984.

Kerr, C. "Introduction: Industrialism with a Human Face." In *Work in America: The Decade Ahead,* edited by C. Kerr and J. Rosow. New York: Van Nostrandt, 1979.

Kerr, S., K.D. Hill, and L. Broedling. "The First-Line Supervisor: Phasing out or Here to Stay." *Academy of Management Review* 11 (1986):103–17.

Khandwalla, P.N. *The Design of Organizations.* New York: Harcourt Brace Jovanovich, 1977.

Kidder, Tracy. *The Soul of a New Machine.* New York: Avon, 1979.

Killing, J. Peter. "How to Make a Global Joint Venture Work." *Harvard Business Review* 60 (May–June 1982):120–27.

Kilmann, R.H. *Beyond the Quick Fix.* San Francisco: Jossey-Bass, 1985.

Kimberly, J.R., and R.H. Miles. *The Organizational Life Cycle.* San Francisco: Jossey-Bass, 1980.

Kochan, T.A., and T.A. Barocci. *Human Resource Management and Industrial Relations.* Boston: Little Brown, 1985.

Kohn, M.L., and C. Schooler. *Work and Personality.* Norwood, N.J.: Ablex, 1983.

Komives, J.L. *A Preliminary Study of the Personal Values of High Technical Entrepreneurship: A Symposium.* Milwaukee: Center of Venture Management, 1972.

Kopelman, R.E. *Managing Productivity in Organizations: A Practical, People-Oriented Perspective.* New York: McGraw-Hill, 1986.

Kotkin, J., and Y. Kishimoto. "Theory F." *Inc.* 8 (1986).

Kotler, Phillip, Liam Fahey, and S. Jatusripitak. *The New Competition.* Englewood Cliffs, N.J.: Prentice-Hall, 1985.

Kotter, J.P. "The Psychological Contract: Managing the Joining-up Process." *California Management Review* 15 (1973):91–99.

———. *The General Managers.* New York: The Free Press, 1982a.

———. "What Effective General Managers Really Do." *Harvard Business Review* 60 (1982b):156–67.

Krefting, L.A., and P.J. Frost. "Untangling Webs, Surfing Waves, and Wildcatting: A Multiple-Metaphor Perspective on Managing Organizational Culture." In *Organizational Culture,* edited by P.J. Frost, L.F. Moore, M.R. Louis, C.C. Lundberg, and J. Martin. Beverly Hills, Calif.: Sage, 1985.

Kutscher, R.E. Talk presented by associate commissioner of the Bureau of Labor Statistics before the Equal Employment Advisory Council, San Francisco, 1984.

Landes, David. *The Unbound Prometheus: Technological Change and Industrial Development in Western Europe from 1750 to the Present.* Cambridge, England: Cambridge Univ. Press, 1969.

Lao, R.C. "Internal-External Control and Competent and Innovative Behavior among Negro College Students." *Journal of Personality and Social Psychology* 14:3 (1970):263–70.

Latham, G.P. "Job Performance and Appraisal." In *Review of Industrial and Organizational Psychology,* edited by C. Cooper and I. Robertson. Chichester, England: Wiley, 1986.

Latham, G.P., and D.L. Dossett. "Designing Incentive Plans for Unionized Employees: A Comparison of Continuous and Variable Ratio Reinforcement Schedules." *Personnel Psychology* 31 (1986):47–61.

Latham, G.P., C.H. Fay, and L.M. Saari. "The Development of Behavioral Observation Scales for Appraising the Performance of Foremen." *Personnel Psychology* 32 (1979):299–311.

Latham, G.P., and B. Finnegan. "The Practical Significance of the Situational Interview." Paper presented at the annual meeting of the Academy of Management, New Orleans, 1987.

Latham, G.P., and E.A. Locke. "Goal Setting: A Motivational Technique That Works." *Organizational Dynamics* (Aug. 1979):68–80.

Latham, G.P., and L.M. Saari. "The Application of Social Learning Theory to Training Supervisors through Behavioral Modeling." *Journal of Applied Psychology* 64 (1979):239–46.

———. "Do People Do What They Say? Further Studies on the Situational Interview." *Journal of Applied Psychology* 69 (1984):569–73.

Latham, G.P., L.M. Saari, E.D. Pursell, and M. Campion. "The Situational Interview." *Journal of Applied Psychology* 65 (1980):422–27.

Latham, G.P., and G.A. Yukl. "A Review of Research on the Application of Goal Setting in Organizations." *Academy of Management Journal* 18 (1975):824–45.

Lawler, E. *Motivation in Work Organizations.* Monterey, Calif.: Brooks-Cole, 1973.

Lawler, E. "Creating High-Involvement Work Organizations." In *Perspectives on Behavior in Organizations,* edited by J.R. Hackman, E. Lawler, and L. Porter. New York: McGraw-Hill, 1983.

———. "The Mythology of Management Compensation." *California Management Review* 9 (1966):11–22.

———. *Pay and Organizational Effectiveness: A Psychological View.* New York: McGraw-Hill, 1971.

———. *Pay and Organization Development.* Reading, Mass.: Addison-Wesley, 1981.

———. "The Design of Effective Reward Systems." Los Angeles: Center for Effective Organizations, Univ. of Southern California, 1983. Unpublished manuscript.

———. *High Involvement Management.* San Francisco: Jossey-Bass, 1986.

Lawrence, P., and S. Davis. *Matrix.* Reading, Mass.: Addison-Wesley, 1978.

Lawrence, P.R., and J.W. Lorsch. *Organization and Environment: Managing Differentiation and Integration.* Boston: Graduate School of Business Administration, Harvard Univ., 1967.

Leonard-Barton, D., and W.A. Kraus. "Implementing New Technology." *Harvard Business Review* 63 (1985):102–10.

Leontief, W., and F. Duchin. *The Impacts of Automation on Employment, 1963–2000.* New York: New York University, Institute for Economic Analysis, 1984.

Levin, M. "Do Workers 'Own' Their Jobs?" *Fortune* (Feb. 1983):7.

Levinson, H. "A Psychologist Diagnoses Merger Failure." *Harvard Business Review* 48 (1970):139–47.

Levitt, Theodore. "The Globalization of Markets." *Harvard Business Review* 61(3) (May–June 1983):92–102.

Lewin, K., R. Lippitt, and R.K. White. "Patterns of Aggressive Behavior in Experimentally Created 'Social Climates.' " *Journal of Social Psychology* 10 (1939): 271–99.

Lewis, H., and D. Allison. *The Real World War.* New York: Coward, McCann and Geoghegan, 1982.

Liles, P.R. *New Business Ventures and the Entrepreneur.* Homewood, Ill.: Irwin, 1974.

Litwin, G.H., and R.A. Stringer. *Motivation and Organizational Climate.* Boston: Division of Research, Harvard Business School, 1968.

Locke, E. "The Myths of Behavior Mod in Organizations." *Academy of Management Review* 4 (1977):131–36.

Locke, E.A. "Toward a Theory of Task Motivation and Incentives." *Organizational Behavior and Human Performance* 3 (1968):157–89.

Locke, E.A., D.B. Feren, V.M. McCaleb, K.N. Shaw, and A.T. Denny. "The Relative Effectiveness of Four Methods of Motivating Employee Performance." In *Changes in Working Life,* edited by K. Duncan, M. Gruneberg, and D. Wallis. Chichester, England: Wiley, 1980.

Locke, E.A., and G.P. Latham. *Goal Setting: A Motivational Technique That Works.* Englewood Cliffs, N.J.: Prentice-Hall, 1984a.

———. *Goal Setting for Individuals, Groups, and Organizations.* Chicago: Science Research Associates, 1984b.

London, M., and S.A. Stumpf. *Managing Careers.* Reading, Mass.: Addison-Wesley, 1982.

Louis, M.R. "Surprise and Sense-making: What Newcomers Experience in Entering Unfamiliar Organizational Settings." *Administrative Science Quarterly* 25 (1980): 226–51.

Louis, M.R. "An Investigator's Guide to Workplace Culture." In *Organizational Culture,* edited by P.J. Frost, L.F. Moore, M.R. Louis, C.C. Lundberg, and J. Martin. Beverly Hills, Calif.: Sage, 1985.

Lynn, L. "Japanese Robotics: Challenge and—Limited—Exemplar." *Annals of the American Academy of Political and Social Science* 470 (Nov. 1983):16–27.

Macarov, D. "Changes in the World of Work: Some Implications for the Future." In *The World of Work: Careers and the Future,* edited by H.F. Didsbury, Jr. Bethesda, Md.: World Future Society, 1983.

MacNeil, I.R. "Relational Contracts: What We Do and Do Not Know." *Wisconsin Law Review* 3 (1985):483–525.

Mahoney, T.A., T.H. Jerdee, and S.J. Carroll, Jr. *Development of Managerial Performance: A Research Approach.* Cincinnati: Southwestern, 1963.

——. "The Jobs of Management." *Industrial Relations* 4 (1965):97–110.

Mahoney, T.A., and W. Weitzel. "Managerial Models of Organizational Effectiveness." *Administrative Science Quarterly* 14 (1969):357–65.

Maister, D. "Managing Service Enterprises in the Eighties." In *The Service Economy,* edited by E.E. Sheuing. New York: KCG Productions, 1982.

Majchrzak, A., and K.J. Klein. "Things Are Always More Complicated Than You Think: An Open Systems Approach to the Organizational Effects of Computer-automated Technology." *Journal of Business and Psychology* 2 (1987):27–49.

Mancuso, J.R. "The Entrepreneurs' Quiz." In *Entrepreneurship and Venture Management,* edited by C.M. Baumback and J.R. Mancuso. Englewood Cliffs, N.J.: Prentice-Hall, 1975.

March, James G., and Herbert A. Simon. *Organizations.* New York: Wiley, 1958.

Marks, M., and P. Mirvis. *Corporate Acquisition: Models of Organizational and Individual Response.* Boston: Graduate School of Management, Boston Univ., undated.

Martin, A. "Additional Aspects of Enterpreneurial History." In *Encyclopedia of Enterpreneurship.* Edited by C.A. Kent, D.L. Sexton, and K.H. Vesper. Englewood Cliffs, N.J.: Prentice-Hall, 1982.

Marx, R.D. "Relapse Prevention for Managerial Training: A Model for Maintenance of Behavioral Change." *Academy of Management Review* 7 (1982):433–41.

Maslow, A. *Motivation and Personality.* New York: Harper, 1954.

Maslow, A.H. "A Theory of Human Motivation." *Psychological Review* 50 (1943): 370–96.

McClelland, D.C. *The Achieving Society.* New York: D. Van Nostrand, 1961.

——. "Need Achievement and Entrepreneurship: A Longitudinal Study." *Journal of Personality and Social Psychology* 1:4 (1965):389–92.

McClelland, D.C., and D.G. Winter. *Motivating Economic Achievement.* New York: Free Press, 1969.

McGhee, P.E., and B.C. Crandall. "Beliefs in Internal-External Control of Reinforcement and Academic Performance." *Child Development* 39:1 (1968):91–102.

McGregor, D. *The Human Side of Enterprise.* New York: McGraw-Hill, 1960.

McMillan, C.I. *The Japanese Industrial System.* New York: Walter de Gruyter, 1985.

Miles, R., and C. Snow. *Organizational Strategy, Structure and Process.* New York: McGraw-Hill, 1978.

Miles, R., and C.C. Snow. "Designing Strategic Human Resource Systems." *Organizational Dynamics* (1980):36–52.

Mill, J.S. *Principles of Political Economy with Some of Their Applications to Social Philosophy.* London: John W. Parker, 1848.

Miller, E.J., ed. *Task and Organization*. New York: Wiley, 1976.

Miller, L.M. *American Spirit: Visions of a New Corporate Culture*. New York: Warner Books, 1984.

Miner, J. *Theories of Organizational Behavior*. Hinsdale, Ill.: Dryden, 1980.

———. *Theories of Organizational Structure and Process*. New York: The Dryden Press, 1982.

Mintzberg, H. "Structured Observations as a Method of Studying Managerial Work." *Journal of Management Studies* 7 (1970):87–104.

———. "Managerial Work: Analysis from Observation." *Management Science* 18 (1971):97–110.

———. *The Nature of Mangerial Work*. New York: Harper and Row, 1973.

———. "The Manager's Job: Folklore and Fact." *Harvard Business Review* 53 (1975):49–61.

———. *The Structuring of Organizations*. Englewood Cliffs, N.J.: Prentice-Hall, 1979.

Mintzberg, H., and J.A. Waters. "Tracking Strategy in an Entrepreneurial Firm." *Academy of Management Journal* 25:3 (1982):465–99.

Mitchell, T.R. "Organizational Behavior." In *Annual Review of Psychology* 30, edited by M.R. Rosenzweig and L. Porter. Palo Alto, Calif.: Annual Review, Inc., 1979.

———. "Motivation: New Directions for Theory, Research, and Practice." *Academy of Management Review* 7 (1982):80–88.

Moeller, A., and B. Schneider. "Climate for Services and the Bottom Line." In *Creativity in Services Marketing*, edited by C. Marshall, D. Schmalansee, and V. Venkatesan. Chicago: American Marketing Association, 1986.

Moeller, A., B. Schneider, F.D. Schoorman, and E. Berney. "Development of the Work Facilitation Diagnostic." In *Facilitating Work Effectiveness*, edited by D. Schoorman and B. Schneider. Lexington, Mass.: Lexington Books, 1988.

Moses, J., and K. Lyness. "Individual and Organizational Responses to Ambiguity." In *Facilitating Work Effectiveness*, edited by D. Schoorman and B. Schneider. Lexington, Mass.: Lexington Books, 1988.

Mowday, R.T., L.W. Porter, and R.M. Steers. *Employee-Organization Linkages: The Psychology of Commitment, Absenteeism and Turnover*. New York: Academic Press, 1982.

Nadler, D.A., J.R. Hackman, and E.E. Lawler III. *Managing Organizational Behavior*. Boston: Little, Brown, 1979.

Naisbitt, John. *Megatrends: Ten New Directions Transforming Our Lives*. New York: Warner Books, 1982.

Naisbitt, J., and P. Aburdene. *Reinventing the Corporation*. New York: Warner Books, 1985.

Napier, N.K., and G.P. Latham. "Outcome Expectancies of People Who Conduct Performance Appraisals." *Personnel Psychology*. Forthcoming.

Nath, Raghu. "Role of Culture in Cross-Cultural and Organizational Research." Paper presented at the National Meeting of the Academy of Management in San Diego, Aug. 11–14, 1985.

Nathanson, Daniel R. "The Relationship between Situational Factors, Organizational Characteristics and Firm Performance." Ph.D. diss., Wharton School, University of Pennsylvania, 1980.

National Aeronautics and Space Administration. *A Framework for Action: Improving Quality and Productivity in Government and Industry.* Report of the NASA Symposium on Quality and Productivity. Washington, D.C.: NASA, 1984.

Newsweek. "You Can't Fire Me, I'll Quit." July 12, 1982.

Nieva, V.F. "Work and Family Roles." In *Management of Work and Personal Life: Problems and Opportunities,* edited by M.D. Lee and R.N. Kanungo. New York: Praeger, 1984.

Nininger, J.R. *Managing Human Resources: A Strategic Perspective.* Ottawa: Conference Board of Canada, 1982.

Nollen, S. *New Patterns of Work.* Scarsdale, N.Y.: Work in America Institute, Work in America Institute Studies in Productivity, 1979.

———. *The Work Schedules in Practice.* New York: Van Nostrand Reinhold, Work in America Institute Series, 1982.

Nollen, S.D., and V.H. Martin. *Alternative Work Strategies, Parts 1 and 2.* New York: AMACOM, 1978.

Norman, R. *Service Management.* New York: Wiley, 1984.

O'Brien, B.E. *Psychology of Work and Unemployment.* Chichester, England: Wiley, 1986.

Office of Technology Assessment. *Computerized Manufacturing Automation: Employment, Education, and the Workplace.* Washington, D.C.: U.S. Government Printing Office, Apr. 1984.

———. *Automation of America's Offices.* Washington, D.C.: U.S. Government Printing Office, Dec. 1985.

Olds, J. "Self-Stimulation of the Brain." *Science* 127 (1958):315–23.

Olds, J., and P. Milner. "Positive Reinforcement Produced by Electrical Stimulation of Septal Area and Other Regions of a Rat's Brain." *Journal of Comparative Physiology Psychology* 47 (1954):419–27.

Olson, M.H. "Remote Office Work: Changing Work Patterns in Time and Space." *Communications of the ACM* 26 (1983):182–87.

Olson, M.H., and H.C. Lucas, Jr. "The Impact of Office Automation on the Organization: Some Implications for Research and Practice." *Communications of the ACM* 25 (1982):838–47.

O'Neill, G.K. *2081: A Hopeful View of the Human Future.* New York: Simon and Schuster, 1981.

Ouchi, W.G. *Theory Z: How American Business Can Meet the Japanese Challenge.* Reading, Mass.: Addison-Wesley, 1981.

Parkington, J.J., and B. Schneider. "Some Correlates of Experienced Job Stress: A Boundary Role Study." *Academy of Management Journal* 22 (1979):270–81.

Parsons, H.M., and G.P. Kearsley. "Robotics and Human Factors: Current Status and Future Prospects." *Human Factors* 24 (1982):535–52.

Pascale, R.T., and A.G. Athos. *The Art of Japanese Management.* New York: 1981.

Penfield, R.V. "Time Allocation Patterns and Effectiveness of Managers." *Personnel Psychology* 27 (1975):245–55.

Perrow, C. *Organizational Analysis: A Sociological View.* Monterey, Calif.: Brooks/Cole, 1970.

Perrow, Charles. "A Framework for the Comparative Analysis of Organizations." *American Sociological Review* 32 (Apr. 1967):194–209.

Personick, V.A. "A Second Look at Industry Output and Employment Trends through 1995." *Monthly Labor Review* (Nov. 1985):26–41.

Peters, T. "Role Model in Steel." *U.S. News and World Report,* Jan. 20, 1986.

Peters, T., and N. Austin. *A Passion for Excellence.* New York: Random House, 1985.

Peters, T.J., and R.H. Waterman. *In Search of Excellence.* New York: Harper and Row, 1982.

Pfeffer, J., and G.R. Salancik. *The External Control of Organizations: A Resource Dependence Perspective.* New York: Harper and Row, 1978.

Pinchot, B. *Intrapreneurship.* Chichester, England: Wiley, 1984.

Pinder, C.C. *Work Motivation.* Glenview, Ill.: Scott, Foresman, 1984.

Piori, M., and C. Sabel. *The Second Industrial Divide: Possibilities for Prosperity.* New York: Basic Books, 1984.

Porter, L.W., E.E. Lawler, and J.R. Hackman. *Behavior in Organizations.* New York: McGraw-Hill, 1975.

Porter, M.E. *Competitive Strategy: Techniques for Analyzing Industries and Competitors.* New York: Free Press, 1980.

Power, D.J. "The Impact of Information Management on the Organization: Two Scenarios." *MIS Quarterly* 7:3 (Sept. 1983):13–20.

Power, D.J., and A.R. Hevner. "Executive Workstations: Issues and Requirements." *Information and Management* 8 (Apr. 1985):213–20.

Prahalad, C.K., and Yves L. Doz. "An Approach to Strategic Control in MNCs." *Sloan Management Review* 22(4) (Summer 1981):5–13.

Pratt, J.H. "Home Teleworking: A Study of Its Pioneers." *Technological Forecasting and Social Change* 25 (1984):1–14.

Pugh, D., D.J. Hickson, and C.R. Hinings. "An Empirical Taxonomy of Structures of Work Organizations." *Administrative Science Quarterly* 14 (1969):115–26.

Reich, R.B. "The Next American Frontier." *Atlantic Monthly* (Apr. 1983):97–108.

———. *The New American Frontier.* New York: Penguin Books, 1984.

———. "Entrepreneurship Reconsidered: The Team as Hero." *Harvard Business Review* 65 (May–June 1987):77–83.

Reichers, A.E. "A Review and Reconceptualization of Organizational Commitment." *Academy of Management Review* 10 (1985):465–76.

Rentsch, J.R. "Expectations for Organizational Combinations." Master's thesis, Univ. of Maryland, 1985.

Rice, A.K. "Individual, Group and Intergroup Processes." *Human Relations* 22 (1969):565–84.

Rogers, E., and F.F. Shoemaker, F. *Communication of Innovations.* New York: Free Press, 1971.

Rogers, Everett M., and Judith K. Larsen. *Silicon Valley Fever.* New York: Basic Books, 1984.

Rosen, C., K.J. Klein, and K. Young. *Employee Ownership in America: The Equity Solution.* Lexington, Mass.: Lexington Books, 1985.

Rotchford, N.L., and K.H. Roberts. "Part-Time Workers as Missing Persons in Organizational Research." *Academy of Management Review* 7 (1982):228–34.

Rotter, J.B. "Generalized Expectancies for Internal versus External Control of Reinforcement." *Psychological Monographs: General and Applied,* whole no. 69980, no. 1, 1966.

Rousseau, D.M. "Managing the Change to the Automated Office." *Office: Technology and People,* 1988 (in press).

――――. "Implied and Psychological Contracts in Employment." Paper presented at the Academy of Management meeting, New Orleans, 1987.

Rousseau, D.M., and R.A. Cooke. "Technology and Structure: The Concrete, Abstract, and Activity Systems of Organizations." *Journal of Management* 10 (1984):345–61.

Rudzinski, K. "Occupational Class and Industrial Influences on Absenteeism." Ph.D. diss., Univ. of Maryland, 1985.

Rumelt, Richard P. *Strategy, Structure and Economic Performance.* Boston: Division of Research, Harvard Business School, 1974.

Rushing, W.A., and M.N. Zald. *Organizations and Beyond: Selected Essays of James D. Thompson.* Lexington, Mass.: D.C. Heath, 1976.

Saari, L.M., and G.P. Latham. "Employee Reactions to Continuous and Variable Ratio Reinforcement Schedules Involving a Monetary Incentive." *Journal of Applied Psychology* 67 (1982):506–8.

Sales, A., and P. Mirvis. "Acquisitions and the Collision of Cultures." In *Managing Organizational Transitions,* edited by R. Quinn and J. Kimberly. New York: Dow Jones, 1984.

Sashkin, M. "Participative Management Remains an Ethical Imperative." *Organizational Dynamics* 14 (1986):62–75.

Sauter, S.L., M. Gottlieb, K. Jones, V. Dodson, and K. Rohrer. "Job and Health Implications of VDT Use: Initial Results of the Wisconsin-NIOSH Study." *Communications of the ACM* 26:4 (1985).

Schein, Edgar. *Organizational Psychology.* 3d. ed. Englewood Cliffs, N.J.: Prentice-Hall, 1980.

Schein, Edgar H. "Coming to a New Awareness of Organizational Culture." *Sloan Management Review* 25 (1984):3–16.

――――. *Organizational Culture and Leadership.* San Francisco: Jossey-Bass, 1985.

Schmidt, F.L. "Implications of a Measurement Problem for Expectancy Theory Research." *Organizational Behavior and Human Performance* 10 (1973):243–51.

Schneider, B. "Notes on Climate and Culture." In *Creativity in Services Marketing,* edited by M. Venkatesan, D.M. Schmalensee, and C. Marshall. Chicago: American Marketing Association, 1986.

――――. "The People Make the Place." *Personnel Psychology.* 40:3 (1987):437–53.

Schneider, B., and D.E. Bowen. "New Services Design, Development, and Implementation and the Employee." In *Developing New Services,* edited by W.R. George and C.E. Marshall. Chicago: American Marketing Association, 1984.

――――. "Employee and Customer Perceptions of Service in Banks: Replication and Extension." *Journal of Applied Psychology* 70 (1985):423–33.

Schneider, B., and A. Reichers. "On the Etiology of Climates." *Personnel Psychology* 36 (1983):19–39.

Schneider, B., and N. Schmitt. *Staffing Organizations.* 2d ed. Glenview, Ill.: Scott, Foresman, 1986.

Schollhammer, H. "Internal Corporate Entrepreneurship." In *Encyclopedia of Entrepreneurship,* edited by C.A. Kent, D.L. Sexton, and K.H. Vesper. Englewood Cliffs, N.J.: Prentice-Hall, 1982.

Schon, E. "Entrepreneurs, Champions, and Technological Innovation." *Sloan Management Review* 21:2 (1980):59–76.

Schoorman, F.D., and B. Schneider, eds. *Facilitating Work Effectiveness.* Lexington, Mass.: Lexington Books, 1988.

Schumpeter, J.A. *The Theory of Economic Development.* Cambridge: Harvard Univ. Press, 1934.

——. "Economic Theory and Entrepreneurial History." In *Explorations in Enterprise,* edited by H.G. Aiken. Cambridge: Harvard Univ. Press, 1965.

Scott, B.R. *Stages of Corporate Development.* Boston: Harvard Business School, Intercollegiate Case Clearing House, 1968.

Scott, W.G., and D.K. Hart. *Organizational America.* Boston: Houghton Mifflin, 1979.

Sengoku, T. *Willing Workers: The Work Ethics in Japan, England, and the United States.* Westport, Conn.: Greenwood Press, 1985.

Sethy, S.P., N. Namiki, and C.L. Swanson. *The False Promise of the Japanese Miracle.* Boston: Pitman, 1984.

Shaiken, H. "Automation in Industry: Bleaching the Blue Collar." *IEEE Spectrum* (June 1984a):77–79.

——. *Work Transformed: Automation and Labor in the Computer Age.* Lexington, Mass.: Lexington Books, 1985.

Shapero, A. *An Action Program of Entrepreneurship.* Austin: Multi-Disciplinary Research, 1971.

——. "The Displaced, Uncomfortable Entrepreneur." *Psychology Today* (Nov. 1975):83–88, 133.

Shapero, A., and L. Sokol. "The Social Dimensions of Entrepreneurship." In *Encyclopedia of Entrepreneurship,* edited by C.A. Kent, D.L. Sexton, and K.H. Vesper. Englewood Cliffs, N.J.: Prentice-Hall, 1982.

Shaw, M.S. *Group Dynamics: The Psychology of Small Group Behavior.* New York: McGraw-Hill, 1976.

Shils, E. "Commentary on Internal Corporate Entrepreneurship." In *Encyclopedia of Entrepreneurship,* edited by C.A. Kent, D.L. Sexton, and K.H. Vesper. Englewood Cliffs, N.J.: Prentice-Hall, 1982.

Shinn, Terry. "Scientific Disciplines and Organizational Specialty: The Social and Cognitive Configuration of Laboratory Activities." *Sociology of the Sciences* 4 (1982):239–64.

Shinn, Terry, and Jerald Hage. "Post-Industrial Society and the New Work Organizations: PME de haute Technologie and Small High Technology Firms." Paper presented at the ASA conference in Washington, D.C., 1987.

Shortell, S., and A. Kaluzny. "Organization Theory and Health Care Management." In *Health Care Management,* edited by S. Shortell and A. Kaluzny. New York: Wiley Medical, 1983.

Siehl, C., and J. Martin. "Symbolism, Metaphors, and Manipulation of Meaning." In *Leaders and Managers: International Perspectives on Managerial Behavior and Leadership,* edited by J.G. Hunt, D. Hosking, and C.A. Schriesheim. New York: Pergamon, 1984.

Silvestri, G.T., J.M. Lukasiewicz, and M.E. Einstein. "Occupational Employment Projections through 1995," *Monthly Labor Review.* 106(11) (Nov. 1983):37–49.

——. *Occupational Employment Projections through 1995, Employment Projections for 1995.* Washington, D.C.: U.S. Department of Labor Statistics, bulletin 2197, Mar. 1984.

Simon, H. *Administrative Behavior.* 3rd. ed. *New York: Free Press, 1976.*

Sink, D.S., T.C. Tuttle, and S.J. DeVries. "Productivity Measurement and Evaluation: What Is Available." *National Productivity Review* 3 (1984):265–87.

Sirianni, C. "Participation, Opportunity, and Equality: Toward a Pluralist Organizational Model." In *Organization and Bureaucracy,* edited by F. Fischer and C. Sirianni. Philadelphia: Temple Univ. Press, 1984.

Skinner, B.F. *Science and Human Behavior.* New York: Macmillan, 1953.

Skrentny, Roger. "Spotlight on Silicon Valley's 'Laid Back' Style of Management." *Management Review* (Dec. 1984):10–14.

Smircich, Linda. "Concepts of Culture and Organizational Analysis." *Administrative Science Quarterly* 28 (1983):339–58.

Smith, K.G., and M. Gannon. "Organizational Growth and Variation in Environmental Uncertainty." Paper presented to the Strategic Management Society, Barcelona, Spain, 1986.

Smith, K.G., and J.K. Harrison. "In Search of Excellent Leaders." Paper presented at the fourth annual meeting of the Strategic Management Society, Philadelphia, Penn., 1984.

Smith, K.G., T.R. Mitchell, and C.E. Summer. "Top Level Management Priorities in Different Stages of the Organizational Life Cycle." *Academy of Management Journal* 28(4) (1985):799–820.

Smith, K.K. *Groups in Conflicts: Prisons in Disguise.* Dubuque, Iowa: Kendall/Hunt, 1982.

Sokol, M.B. "Innovation Utilization: The Implementation of Personal Computers in an Organization." Ph.D. diss., University of Maryland, 1986.

Solberg, J., D. Anderson, M. Barash, and R. Paul. *Factories of the Future: Defining the Target.* Report of research under National Science Foundation Grant MEA8212074. West Lafayette, Ind.: Purdue University, Computer Integrated Design Manufacturing and Automation Center, 1985.

Stevenson, H.H., and D.E. Gumpert. "The Heart of Entrepreneurship." *Harvard Business Review* 63 (Mar.–Apr. 1985).

Stewart, R. "To Understand the Manager's Job: Consider Demands, Constraints, and Choices." *Organizational Dynamics* 4 (1976):22–32.

Strauss, G. "Personnel Management: Prospects for the Eighties." In *Personnel Management,* edited by K.M. Rowland and G.R. Ferris. Boston: Allyn and Bacon, 1982.

Tarkenton, F. "How to Motivate People." *Tarkenton Productivity Update* 5:2, (1986).

Tausky, K., and E.L. Parke. "Job Enrichment, Need Theory and Reinforcement Theory." In *Handbook of Work, Organization, and Society,* edited by R. Dubin. Chicago: Rand McNally, 1976.

Taylor, F.W. *The Principles of Scientific Management.* New York: W.W. Norton, 1967.

Teece, David J. "Internal Organization and Economic Performance: An Empirical Analysis of the Profitability of Principal Firms." *Journal of Industrial Economics* 30 (Dec. 1981):173–99.

Thompson, J.D. *Organizations in Action.* New York: McGraw-Hill, 1967.

Thurow, Lester. *The Zero-Sum Solution: Building a World-Class American Economy.* New York: Simon & Schuster, 1985.

Toffler, Alvin. *The Third Wave.* New York: Bantam, 1981.

Toffler, Alvin. *Previews and Premises.* New York: Bantam Books, 1983.

Tornatzky, L.G., W.A. Hetzner, and J.D. Eveland. "Fostering the Use of Advanced Manufacturing Technology." *Technology Review* (1984).

Tosi, H.L., and S.J. Carroll. *Management: Contingencies, Structure, and Process.* Chicago: St. Clair Press, 1976.

Tosi, H.L., J.R. Rizzo, and S.J. Carroll. *Managing Organizational Behavior.* Boston: Pitman, 1986.

Tosi, Henry L., and Stephen J. Carroll. *Management.* New York: Wiley, 1983.

Training. "Rating Older Workers." Apr. p. 69.

Trist, Eric L. "Collaboration in Work Settings: A Personal Perspective." *Journal of Applied Behavioral Science* 13 (1977):268–78.

Uhlig, R.P., D.J. Farber, and J.H. Bair. *The Office of the Future: Communications and Computers.* New York: North Holland, 1979.

U.S. Bureau of the Census. *Statistical Abstract of the United States.* Washington, D.C.: U.S. Government Printing Office, 1982, 417.

——. *Statistical Abstract of the United States.* Washington, D.C.: U.S. Government Printing Office, 1983.

——. *Statistical Abstract of the United States.* Washington, D.C.: U.S. Government Printing Office, 1986.

U.S. Department of Labor. Office of the Secretary. Women's Bureau. *Child Care Centers Sponsored by Employers and Labor Unions in the United States.* Washington, D.C.: U.S. Government Printing Office, 1980.

——. *20 Facts on Women Workers.* Washington, D.C.: U.S. Government Printing Office, 1984a.

U.S. Department of Labor. Office of Information. Women's Bureau. *News.* 1984b.

U.S. News and World Report. "Up and Out." Dec. 30, 1985.

Van de Ven, Andrew, Andre Delbecq, and Richard Koenig. "Determinants of Coordination: Modes within Organizations." *American Sociological Review* 41 (Apr. 1976):322–28.

Van Maanen, J. "Breaking In: Socialization to Work." In *Handbook of Work, Organizations and Society,* edited by R. Dubin. Chicago: Rand McNally, 1976.

Vance, Rupert B. "The Regional Concept as a Tool for Social Research." In *Regionalism in America,* edited by Merrill Jensen. Madison: Univ. of Wisconsin Press, 1952.

Vroom, V.H. *Work and Motivation.* New York: Wiley, 1964.

Wahba, M.A., and L.G. Bridwell. "Maslow Reconsidered. A Review of Research on the Need Hierarchy Theory." *Proceedings of the Thirty-third Annual Meeting of the Academy of Management* (1973):514–20.

Wall Street Journal. "When Employees Work at Home, Management Problems Often Arise." Apr. 20, 1987.

——. "Dental Hygienists to Seek Practices on Their Own—Raising the Ire of Dentists." Apr. 24, 1987.

Watson, Craig. "Counter-Competition abroad to Protect Home Markets." *Harvard Business Review* 60 (Jan.–Feb. 1982): 40–45.

Weber, M. *From Max Weber: Essays in Sociology.* Translated and edited by H.H. Gerth and C. Wright Mills. New York: Oxford Univ. Press, 1946.

Weick, Karl. "Educational Organizations as Loosely Coupled Systems." *Administrative Science Quarterly* 21 (Mar. 1976):1–19.

Wexley, K., and G. Latham. *Developing and Training Human Resources in Organizations.* Glenview, Ill.: Scott, Foresman, 1982.

Whyte, W.F., and J.R. Blasi. "Worker Ownership, Participation, and Control: Toward a Theoretical Model." *Policy Science* 14 (1982):137–62.

Williamson, O. *Markets and Hierarchies*. New York: Free Press, 1975.

Woodward, J. *Industrial Organization: Theory and Practice*. London: Oxford Univ. Press, 1965.

Woodward, J. *Industrial Organization: Behavior and Control*. London: Oxford Univ. Press, 1970.

Yankelovitch, D. "Work Values and the New Breed." In *Work in America,* edited by C. Kerr and J. Rosow. New York: Van Nostrand, 1979.

———. *New Rules for Work: Searching for Self-Fulfillment in a World Turned upside Down*. New York: Random House, 1981.

———. Address at the American Sociological Association annual meeting, Washington, D.C., Aug. 1985.

Yankelovitch, D., and J. Immerwahr. *Putting the Work Ethic to Work*. Public Agenda Foundation, 1983.

Zimbalist, A. *Case Studies on the Labor Process*. New York: Monthly Review Press, 1979.

Zohar, D. "Safety Climate in Industrial Organizations: Theoretical and Applied Implications." *Journal of Applied Psychology* 65 (1980):96–102.

Index

About the Contributors

Stephen J. Carroll is affiliated with the College of Business and Management, Center for Innovation, and Center for Entrepreneurship, University of Maryland. His books, monographs, and articles have focused on managerial work, management by objectives, compensation, performance appraisal, managerial innovation, and Asian management systems.

André L. Delbecq is dean of the Leavey School of Business and Administration at Santa Clara University, Santa Clara, California. For a number of years his research and scholarship have focused on three topics: managerial decision making techniques for strategic planning; the development of new products and technologies; and organizational design for facilitating innovation. He is the author of the Nominal Group Technique and the Program Planning Model, both of which have been widely adopted for facilitating decision making and planning.

Jay R. Galbraith is currently a professor of management at the University of Southern California, Los Angeles. He is also a research scientist at USC's Center for Effective Organizations. Dr. Galbraith is the author of several major books on strategy and design.

Rosalie Hall is currently a Ph.D. candidate at the University of Maryland at College Park. Her research interests include issues in technological innovation and work motivation.

Robert Kazanjian is currently an assistant professor at the University of Michigan's Graduate School of Business Administration. He is interested in the problems of strategy and new ventures. He has consulted and done executive education work in the areas of organization and innovation.

Katherine J. Klein is an assistant professor of industrial and organizational psychology in the Psychology Department at the University of Maryland. Her research focuses on the impact of workplace innovation (particularly employee ownership, worker participation, and computerized manufacturing technology) on organizational dynamics and individual attitudes and behavior.

Gary Latham is Ford Motor Research Professor and chairman, Management and Organization Department; and adjunct professor in the Department of Psychology at the University of Washington. He is a fellow in both the American and Canadian Psychological Associations, and he is a fellow in the Academy of Management.

Joseph J. Lengermann, Ph.D., is associate professor of sociology at the University of Maryland, College Park, Maryland. Currently he is director of graduate studies in the Department of Sociology, as well as co-president of the District of Columbia Sociological Society. Recent research efforts have focused on a series of articles on work site health promotion programs in Fortune 500 and in New Jersey companies. He is also working on a book on hospital organization and performance.

Daniel J. Power is associate professor of management in the College of Business and Management at the University of Maryland, College Park, and director of the Maryland Management Support Systems Research Lab. Dr. Power has developed a number of computerized decision aids and an input keyboard for nontypists. He has also authored and coauthored twenty papers and articles and an innovative textbook.

Joan Rentsch is a Ph.D. candidate in psychology at the University of Maryland at College Park, Maryland. Her research interests include organizational climate and culture, meanings in organizations, and the use of quantitative methods in organizational behavior.

Denise M. Rousseau is an associate professor of organizational behavior at Northwestern University's J.L. Kellogg School of Management. Her research addresses changing employment relations, the emergence and violation of psychological contracts, and the impact of organizational culture on effectiveness and quality of work life.

Benjamin Schneider is professor of psychology and business management at the Univesity of Maryland, College Park, and is affiliated with the Center for Innovation. His research interests concern organizational climate and culture, specifically the creation and maintenance of service climates and cultures.

Ken G. Smith is an assistant professor in strategic management and the co-director of the Small Business Development Center with the College of Business and Management at the University of Maryland, College Park. He has published numerous articles on subjects of strategy, entrepreneurship, and stages of organizational growth and development.

Thomas Tuttle is director of the Maryland Center for Productivity and Quality of Working Life. The center is an outreach arm of the University of Maryland College of Business and Management. Dr. Tuttle consults and conducts research on strategic productivity and quality measurement and management.

Joseph Weiss is an associate professor in the Department of Management at Bentley College in Waltham, Massachusetts. He teaches international business and management and the changing environment. He is author of two books and actively consults in high-technology firms.

About the Editor

Jerald Hage is director of the Center for Innovation and a professor of sociology at the University of Maryland, College Park. For many years he has studied organizations, with a special interest in the problem of innovation. Currently he is doing a study of what factors at the plant predict survival during the period of 1903 to 1987. He is also working on the problem of interorganizational networks.